UNIONS AND
GLOBALISATION

Routledge Studies in Employment and Work Relations in Context

Edited by Tony Elger and Peter Fairbrother

The aim of the *Employment and Work Relations in Context Series* is to address questions relating to the evolving patterns and politics of work, employment, management and industrial relations. There is a concern to trace out the ways in which wider policy-making, especially by national governments and transnational corporations, impinges upon specific workplaces, occupations, labour markets, localities and regions. This invites attention to developments at an international level, marking out patterns of globalization, state policy and practices in the context of globalization and the impact of these processes on labour. A particular feature of the series is the consideration of forms of worker and citizen organization and mobilization. The studies address major analytical and policy issues through case study and comparative research.

Reshaping the North American
Automobile Industry
Restructuring, Corporatism and
Union Democracy in Mexico
John P. Tuman

Work and Employment in the High
Performance Workplace
Edited by Gregor Murray, Jacques
Belanger, Anthony Giles and
Paul-Andre Lapointe

Trade Unions and Global
Governance
The Debate on a Social Clause
Gerda van Roozendaal

Changing Prospects for Trade
Unionism
Edited by Peter Fairbrother and
Gerard Griffin

Unionization and Union Leadership
The Road Haulage Industry
Paul Smith

Restructuring the Service Industries
Management Reform and
Workplace Relations in the UK
Service Sector
Gavin Poynter

Trade Unions at the Crossroads
Peter Fairbrother

Between Market, State and Kibbutz
The Management and
Transformation of Socialist
Industry
Christopher Warhurst

Globalization and Patterns of
Labour Resistance
Edited by Jeremy Waddington

The State and "Globalization"
Comparative Studies of Labour and
Capital in National Economies
Edited by Martin Upchurch

State Regulation and the Politics of
Public Service
The Case of the Water Industry
Graham Taylor

Global Humanization
Studies in the Manufacture of
Labour
Edited by Michael Neary

Women, Work and Trade Unions
Anne Munro

The Global Economy, National
States and the Regulation of Labour
Edited by Paul Edwards and
Tony Elgar

History of Work and Labour
Relations in the Royal Dockyards
Edited by Ann Day and
Kenneth Lunn

Japanese Management Techniques
and British Workers
Andy Danford

Young People in the Workplace
Job, Union and Mobility Patterns
Christina Cregan

Globalization, Social Movements
and the New Internationalisms
Peter Waterman

Young Adult Women, Work and
Family
Living a Contradiction
Ian Procter and Maureen Padfield

The Sociology of Industrial Injury
Theo Nichols

Global Tourism and Informal
Labour Relations
The Small Scale Syndrome at work
Godfrey Baldacchino

Unions and Globalisation
Governments, Management, and the State at Work

Peter Fairbrother
Director of the Centre for Sustainable Organisations and Work,
and Professor of International Employment Relations
RMIT University

John O'Brien
University of New South Wales

Anne Junor
Deputy Director, Industrial Relations Research Centre
University of New South Wales

Michael O'Donnell
Professor of Human Resource Management
University of New South Wales

Glynne Williams
Lecturer in Employment Studies
Centre for Labour Market Studies
University of Leicester

Routledge
Taylor & Francis Group

NEW YORK AND LONDON

First published 2012
by Routledge
711 Third Avenue, New York, NY 10017

Simultaneously published in the UK
by Routledge
2 Park Square, Milton Park, Abingdon, Oxon OX14 4RN

Routledge is an imprint of the Taylor & Francis Group, an informa business

Library of Congress Cataloging-in-Publication Data

Unions and globalisation : governments, management, and the state at work / by Peter Fairbrother. [et al.].
p. cm.—(Routledge studies in employment and work relations in context; 7)
Includes bibliographical references and index.
1. Government employee unions—Australia. 2. Government employee unions—Great Britain. 3. Employee-management relations in government—Australia. 4. Employee-management relations in government—Great Britain. I. Fairbrother, Peter.
HD8005.2.A8U55 2011
331.88'1135141—dc22
2010050575

ISBN13: 978-0-415-41664-1 (hbk)
ISBN13: 978-0-203-81458-1 (ebk)

Typeset in Sabon
by Integra Software Services Pvt. Ltd, Pondicherry, India

Printed and bound in the United States of America on acid-free paper by IBT Global

Contents

List of Tables and Figures

List of Abbreviations

ABS	Australian Bureau of Statistics
ACOA	Administrative and Clerical Officers' Association
ACTU	Australian Council of Trade Unions
AGPS	Australian Government Publishing Service
AIRC	Australian Industrial Relations Commission
ANAO	Australian National Audit Office
APS	Australian Public Service
APSA	Australian Public Service Association
APSC	Australian Public Service Commission (2002–)
ASO	Administrative Service Officer
ATO	Australian Taxation Office
AWA	Australian Workplace Agreement
CCSU	Council of Civil Service Unions
CEO	Chief Executive Officer
CPSA	Civil and Public Service Association (UK)
CPSU	Community and Public Service Union (Australia)
CSIRO	Commonwealth Scientific Industrial Research Organisation
DEET	Department of Employment, Education and Training (Australia)
DoFA	Department of Finance and Administration
DEEWR	Department of Employment, Education and Workplace Relations (Australia post-2007)
DEIR	Department of Employment and Industrial Relations (Australia pre-1987)
DEWR	Department of Employment and Workplace Relations (Australia 2002–7)
DEWRSB	Department of Industrial Relations (Australia 1998–2002)
DFAT	Department of Foreign Affairs and Trade (Australia)
DIR	Department of Industrial Relations (Australia 1987–96)
DSS	Department of Social Security
DWP	Department of Work and Pensions (United Kingdom)
DWRSB	Department of Workplace Relations and Small Business (Australia 1997–98)

EEO	Equal Employment Opportunity
EL	Executive Level
EU	European Union
FDA	Association of First Division Association
FMI	Financial Management Initiative
FMIP	Financial Management Improvement Program
FSS	Forensic Science Service
FTO	Full Time Officer
HEO	Higher Executive Officer
HMSO	Her Majesty's Stationery Office
HRM	Human Resource Management
IPMS	Institute of Professionals, Managers and Specialists (IPMS)
IRSF	Inland Revenue Staff Federation NDPB
NDPB	Non-Departmental Public Bodies
NPM	New Public Management
NUCPS	National Union of Civil and Public Servants
NUCPS	National Union of Civil and Public Servants (United Kingdom)
PCS	Public and Commercial Services Union (United Kingdom)
PDP	Performance Development Plan
PI	Performance Indicator
PPS	Public Private Partnerships
PSB	Public Service Board (Australia)
PSC	Public Service Commission (Australia)
PSMPC	Public Service and Merit Protection Commission (Australia 1987–2001)
PSU	Public Service Union (Australia)
RAS	Recruitment and Assessment Services Agency
SES	Senior Executive Service
SSCFPA	Senate Standing Committee on Finance and Public Administration
TUC	Trades Union Congress
UK	United Kingdom
ULR	Union Learning Representatives
USA	United States of America

Preface

The genesis of this book can be found in a paper given by Peter Fairbrother and John O'Brien at the Work, Employment and Society Conference in Nottingham on 12 September 2001. The hour was early, the audience modest and the conferees were much more concerned with the momentous events of the day before. Both authors had been puzzled by the apparent similarities between the restructuring of British and Australian federal states and their impact on the work and industrial relations in both countries. How was it there were striking parallels between changes made by an assertive Conservative government in the United Kingdom and a mildly social democratic Labor government in Australia? Was the link globalisation? Was it the triumph of neo-liberalism in the English speaking states? Following the conference, and a period of reflection on the themes that eventually informed the book, we submitted a proposal for research funding to the Australian Research Council and received funding in 2003 for three years. This funding enabled several of the authors to work in both countries to facilitate comparative analysis and enabled a considerable proportion of the data gathering to be undertaken. The book is the principal outcome.

Peter Fairbrother came up with the notion of 'depoliticisation' that he had borrowed from Paul Burnham and others. This term had some salience in the UK, but was unknown in Australia. In fact, the most common characterisation given to the restructure of the Australian Public Service was 'politicisation'. How then could we say that there were close parallels between the changes made to the UK civil service and the Australian Public Service? The book establishes that depoliticisation and politicisation were two aspects of the one process. We argue that this concept helps to explain the apparently contradictory coupling of structural decentralisation and tight managerial control systems, characteristic of Anglophone public sector reform.

The book addresses contemporary issues, while placing them in historical context of the past thirty. The Global Financial Crisis of 2007–9 has called into question the authority of the international financial system, and challenged neo-liberal certainties about the relationship between state and market. Our longitudinal study of the restructuring of state sector internal labour markets, and of the relationships among managers, workers and state sector unions, is therefore timely.

The book aims to explore how public service agencies in the UK and Australia reorganised their organisational structures and implemented more managerial approaches consistent with different versions of the neo-liberal project of public sector reform advocated by governments in both countries. The book also examines how changes in management strategies and structures have affected public service employees and their trade union representatives. It uses examples to illustrate the argument, drawn from our data base of interviews spanning three decades in the UK and Australia. The research data base pays particular attention to the Benefits Agency (now Jobcentre Plus) in the United Kingdom and Centrelink in Australia. These large public welfare delivery agencies were key sites for the restructuring of public sector work in both countries. Because the Australian Public Service was used to a greater degree than the UK civil service as a testing ground for government-driven industrial relations reforms, the Australian material ranges more widely across other agencies in order to illustrate commonalities in management strategy and shifting bargaining arrangements during the period under review. The way these approaches have been played out in social democratic contexts (Australia: 1984–1996; UK: 1997–) and neoconservative ones (UK: 1979–1997; Australia: 1996–) points to differences in focus and emphasis as well as similarities in outcomes. The 'hybrid' aspect of these approaches informs the analysis.

Theoretically, the analysis brings together debates about state restructuring, employee response and union revitalisation or renewal. These debates tend to take place in separate domains and this book will address the complex relationship between state restructuring and industrial relations changes, and the ways they have played out in relation to the administrative services of the modern state over a quarter-century and more.

The book has four main objectives:

1. To provide a new perspective on the debates about the restructuring of the central administrative structures in two liberal democratic states under governments of contrasting political complexions.
2. To provide a longitudinal empirical basis to reflections about public service reform.
3. To bring the discussion of public sector restructuring down to the level of everyday workplace experience.
4. To lay the foundation for further debates about possible trade union responses to the restructuring of state sector work.

All authors contributed to the underlying research and to the writing of the book. We eschewed dividing the chapters amongst us. Three authors conducted field work in both countries. We were assisted in a number of other ways by our respective departments and schools, including the provision of study leave, and we are grateful for that assistance. We collectively remain responsible for our analysis and conclusions.

Acknowledgements

The authors would like to thank all the state workers who have discussed the changes that have taken place in the public services in both countries and are continuing to do so. These workers gave so much of their time and tolerance with us. They have provided much of the grist of this story. Equally important and helpful and supportive, many trade union leaders, in the workplaces and nationally from both countries gave generously of their time to help us in our researches. Many state managers, often experiencing the uncertainties of state policy, shared with us their experiences. In some cases trade union leaders and their management counterparts provided us with documents and records that have enriched and informed the account.

We have all worked on questions relating to the public services for many years. In that time we have incurred debts to researchers and academic colleagues. First and foremost we thank Glynne Williams for much of the recent data collection in the United Kingdom. Michael O'Donnell interviewed extensively in Centrelink and other data collection in Australia was done by the three Australian-based authors. Thanks also to Mark Gepp and Robyn Blackwell from the CPSU and Sue Vardon formerly of Centrelink in Australia; Mark Serwotka form the PCS; and Steve Davies (Cardiff University), Bob Carter (University of Leicester), Bob Fryer (University of Southampton), Gavin Poynter (University of East London), Paul Smith (Keele University), Howard Stephenson (University of Leicester) and David Winchester (University of Warwick) from the United Kingdom. A considerable amount of the material and arguments presented in this book were 'rehearsed' at various conferences in Australia, Canada and the United Kingdom. John O'Brien, Michael O'Donnell and Anne Junor are most appreciative of assistance provided by Maeve Houlihan (University College Dublin), Sharon Bolton (Strathclyde University), Linda Dickens (Warwick University) and Lorenzo Bodogna. Each in their own way helped shape the book, but probably not in ways that they would recognise or indeed agree with. Nonetheless, the book would be less relevant had they not had their say in its gestation and development

We particularly thank Jason Alferink, who created a very useful database for us; Kate Murphy for research assistance and Amanda Baird from the

University New South Wales for assistance with the bibliography and formatting. John O'Brien and Anne Junor were assisted by periods of study leave granted by the University of New South Wales as was Michael O'Donnell from the Australian National University. John O'Brien is most appreciative of the two study leave periods at Cardiff University and at the University of Sydney and for the scholarly hospitality of the Australian National University. Anne Junor is also grateful for time at spent at Cardiff and the ANU. John O'Brien and Anne Junor are particularly grateful to Jan Clark for her friendship and hospitality. Much of the research was funded by the Australian Research Council Discovery Grant DP0344391.

1   State Restructuring in Two States

This book is a study of the modern liberal democratic state. The focus is on the Australian federal state and the unitary state of the United Kingdom (although also a partially devolved state). These two states, bound together by a colonial past, a financially-linked present and a shared political practice, often look to each other for examplars as well as for contrasts. Although governments in each country did not explicitly model these developments on each other, they occasionally cross-referenced to the other country. Over the last three decades, these two states reshaped and refocused their core administrative sectors. More notably, these changes to the administrative functions of the state have impacted upon workplace relations, labour organisation and state management. Public service roles have been redefined and reorganised, and in both countries there has been a process of institutional fragmentation and the promotion of individuated state labour markets. State sector employees and trade unions experienced and responded to structural changes in each state.

Both states followed different paths to similar destinations, adapting neo-liberal reform programmes, legitimated by invocations of the imperatives of globalisation. From the early 1980s, the administrative apparatus of the United Kingdom, the civil service, was restructured, initially by Conservative governments with the broad contours of this process continued by Labour governments. In Australia, public sector 'reform' was promoted initially by Labor governments and intensified by conservative Coalitions. In each state, governments of both political complexions sought to create managerial state structures, predicated on either the incorporation or marginalisation of organised state labour. Conservative governments actively sidelined public sector unions. In Australia, Labor governments initially incorporated unions into the restructuring processes; in the United Kingdom, as part of a so-called 'New' Labour approach to governance. In the case of the state sector, the government moved from attempts at partnership with civil and public service unions to efforts to marginalise them. In both states, trade unions developed into active opponents of managerial policies.

Our purpose is to outline and evaluate these processes, in particular examining the intersection between managerial initiatives and the ways in which public sector union leaders and activists in each country addressed the changed work and employment situations of their members. These responses were coloured by unions' shifting capacities for action in restructured state formations, labour relations systems and labour markets. In particular, we seek to clarify the implications for unions of the apparent similarities between the restructuring approaches of the United Kingdom and Australian governments, and their impact on labour relations in both countries. There is, however, a puzzle in these processes. In each country, the election of assertive conservative governments and mildly social democratic governments were the reverse reflections of each other. The question is whether the parallels in process and outcome can be explained by business cycle phases, the overarching imperatives of globalisation, or the ideological triumph of neo-liberalism in these two English-speaking states? By focusing on the complex history and developing relationships between state managerialism and state trade unionism, we address key aspects of the research question, and in particular the pervasiveness of neo-liberal ideas in this process.

In the context of neo-liberal reform of the state, governments attempted to secure reform either through accommodations with or marginalisation of, state-based trade unions. In turn state sector trade unions, in articulating the interests of state workers, attempted to utilise their capacities to address such policies. Yet throughout this period of state reform, unions faced severe challenges, suggesting that they no longer had their former salience (Fairbrother and Yates, 2003). It has also been suggested that state sector unions may have been in a position to take the opportunities signified by state restructuring to more than just 'make do' and reposition themselves to question the detail and direction of these changes (Fairbrother, 1994; Danford *et al.*, 2003). So the central question that we seek to address is, to what extent were state sector unions able to mitigate the effects of 'reform' or even influence its direction?

The focus of public service reform and the reconstitution of managerial structures present a challenge to employees and their unions. Civil and public service unions in both countries developed in the context of standardised employment and industrial arrangements, largely characterised by national level pay bargaining in the United Kingdom, and service-wide arrangements in Australia, mediated by compulsory conciliation and arbitration. Unions had to adapt to a fragmentation of both organisational and industrial relations structures.

In terms of the political climate for unionism, the restructuring of civil service work in the United Kingdom took place amidst a comprehensive assault on trade union power by Conservative governments in the 1980s. Public service reforms were a reflection of a wider exclusion of unions and a radical recasting of labour market regulation. In Australia, however, the first phase of comprehensive public service reform occurred within a context of limited experiments in industrial democracy and subsequently the managed decentralisation of the industrial relations system; predicated on unions co-operating with work reorganisation in exchange for wage increases. Thus, on the surface, the system in Australia was apparently more benign for unions, whereas in the United Kingdom unions were effectively marginalised. Nonetheless, and perhaps paradoxically, such developments presented both opportunities and pitfalls for the wider union movement's participation in economic and industrial relations restructuring.

From the second half of the 1990s, there was a reversal of the political climate in each country. Based on the institutional and industrial frameworks already laid down, what were the continuities and discontinuities between the major political parties in the United Kingdom under the Conservatives and most recently New Labour (from 1997–2009)? Did the Labor governments in the 1980s and 1990s in Australia commence the trends that escalated under the neo-conservative Liberal-National coalitions of the 1990s and 2000s, and to what extent has the re-elected Labor government of the late 2000s met the aspirations of those public sector workers who helped elect it on the promise of restored workplace rights?

These paradoxical trajectories focus the book. They serve to shape and refine the core questions that are addressed. Our aim is to explain how similar outcomes were apparent in each country, despite the distinctiveness of each state. First, however, we provide an overview of the argument that informs the book.

THE ARGUMENT

Whilst accepting the instability of capital accumulation since the 1970s, as evidenced in the financial crises of 1987, 1997 and 2007, our starting point is the neo-liberal offensive it helped generate. Neo-liberalism is an ideology where the core components comprise: (a) a rejection of the mixed economy and the promotion of capitalism (business, trade and competition); (b) the institutional encouragement of a marketised and international set of economic and financial relations; and (b) the reshaping of state policies and practices towards this end (Daniels and McIlroy, 2009: 4; see also Tickell and Peck, 2003). Central to this agenda is the restructuring and reorganisation of the state apparatus, not only to reflect a market and trade based economy, but also to become the model for recasting employment and industrial relations in an individualised and restricted way.

This agenda gave rise to the reshaping of public sector organisations based on market models, reinforced by attempts to enhance labour market flexibility by de-collectivising industrial relations systems. There was a restructuring of public sector organisations into agencies or cost centres, coordinated through new mechanisms of managerial control. Yet this process was not achieved in either country according to top-down blueprints: its implementation was varied and incompletely accomplished. The picture that emerges is complex and contradictory. On one side, governments are defining and embracing a neo-liberal agenda, with implications for managers, management and managerialism (McIlroy, 2009a and 2009b). The other side of this process is worker organisation and action. The means of resistance and compliance was largely via workers' collective efforts, through union-based negotiation, to influence the direction of change, as well as more *ad hoc* forms of resistance to its impacts (cf. Daniels and McIlroy, 2009). Unions in turn recast themselves, developing new ways of supporting workplace activity.

During the 1980s and 1990s, each state articulated distinct approaches in terms of policy formulation and institutional reform of their public services; they each promoted a managerial reform of their public and civil services. In pursuit of a neo-liberal agenda, social democratic governments in both Australia (1983–96; 2007–9) and the United Kingdom (1997–2009) formulated approaches that promoted an internationalisation of the domestic economy and reconfigured the domestic state apparatus, accompanied by partnership arrangements with trade unions; more thoroughgoing in Australia than the United Kingdom. Mirroring this policy approach, Conservative governments in the United Kingdom (1979–97) and Australia (1996–7) sought to marginalise trade unions as a condition for achieving this neo-liberal agenda. The two states developed these policies in line with the political configurations that distinguish both of them as liberal democratic states. Industrial relations in Australia are defined in part by the juridical-based approach that continued to prevail both as a goal of the policy process and as a mechanism for reform. In the United Kingdom, the state-specific bargaining arrangements are located within a more voluntaristic tradition and this has had the consequence that governments were better positioned in the attempt, more top-down and less constrained processes of institutional reform.

It is important, however, not to overstate the specificity of particular arrangements. Rather, it is necessary to locate the ways in which governments in distinct contexts may pursue the same broad objectives. During the 1970s, liberal democratic states, particularly in the Anglo-US orbit, faced problems relating to public expenditure and in these circumstances, governments of different persuasions began to consider neo-liberal policies. While the governments were different, the overall concerns appeared to be the same: namely how to recast the central administrative arrangements in each country to achieve a closer alignment between service provision and the national economies to achieve increased financial savings and enhance productivity. No longer were governments seeking to make judgements on services primarily on the basis of collective value.

Within the rhetorical framework of 'modernisation' and 'reform' and the increasingly perceived demands of 'globalisation', governments of various persuasions sought to redraw the boundaries of the state, via privatisation, contracting-out and outsourcing and as well as recasting managerial hierarchies, under the rubric of 'New Public Management' (NPM). Operational relations were redefined with the emergence of a more explicit managerial stratum and a more 'managed' workforce. This pattern of reorganisation played out differently in each country, depending on both the government in office and the overall structure of the state. Nonetheless, in each case, the aim was to secure more 'accountable' and thus more flexible state workforces.

Paradoxically, part of the explanation for the apparent similarity of outcome between the two states, is found in the different relationships that governments promoted with trade unions. These 'reforms' were predicated on two contrary processes impacting upon unions. On the one hand, the Australian model was predicated initially on incorporation, with unions conceived as (unequal) partners in the processes of restructuring. One outcome was the promotion of more vibrant forms of workplace representation in some of the major departments, such as social security and taxation (on the taxation unions, see Mathews, 1989), although these experiments were aberrant and short-lived. On the other hand, the United Kingdom model was predicated on the marginalisation of unions. In Australia, the period after 1996 was characterised by a more systematic marginalising approach by government.

Whilst this account gives weight to the importance of institutional arrangements in different societies and traditions (Hall and Soskice, 2001), by the end of the period under consideration, institutional and political differences appeared to be less important than a convergence towards union marginalisation. On the one hand, while Australia and the United Kingdom were both liberal market economies (where economic actors are coordinated via market institutions), institutional differences and historical practices weighed heavily on the detail of the relations between the state as employer in each country. On the question of state restructuring, and the relationship between state managers and unions, there was distinctiveness, particularly during the 1980s. On the other hand, over time, approaches coalesced around a common concern, irrespective of government in office, to restrict and focus the relationship between state managers, public employees and trade unions. In yet another twist it was precisely these marginalising tendencies that would appear to have provided the impetus for union renewal and revitalisation.

Unions in the state sector were transformed over the last thirty years. Up until the 1970s, these types of unions were centrally organised, accommodative and relatively quiescent. In the period that followed, these unions not only faced a process of restructuring, with its increased emphasis on managerial prerogative and discretion, they also sought to re-lay the foundations for collective organisation and operation. Such moves were contested and were often implemented in *ad hoc* ways; nonetheless, they were part of a process of union renewal, whereby these unions addressed their forms of organisation and attempted to promote and extend their capacities as collective bodies (Lévesque and Murray, 2002; see also Simms and Wills, 2004). However, while analyses are clear that unions organise and operate in relation to state policy and practice, class relations and labour markets

(Kelly, 1998; Hyman, 2001), the processes, tension and contradictions involved in renewal are less so.

While these processes were at play in both states for much of the last thirty years, the latest financial crisis raises a conundrum about the future. Whilst it is likely that the major neo-liberal governments – the United States and the United Kingdom – and governments embracing neo-liberal economics – China and India – will rebuild financial arrangements and market practices, and attempt to rebuild threatened production and trade relations, the challenge for workers and their unions remains. In both Australia and the United Kingdom, these developments throw the relations of government with their core administrative services into sharp relief.

Clearly, the global financial crisis raises difficult and puzzling questions for public service workers, their unions and governments. Both governments have displayed a willingness to advocate direct forms of state intervention, more evident in the United Kingdom than in Australia, especially with a return to more active forms of financial regulation and control. However, it is likely that in both states the public and civil services will become both part of the means to implement interventionist policies but also an object for achieving financial stringency. It remains to be seen whether this recent bout of state intervention is merely temporary until the next crisis or a prelude to more sustained measures over time. More specifically, it is not clear what all this means for state workers and their unions, especially where they are the focus of restrictive wages policies. It is nonetheless, possible that these events could presage a process of union renewal as unions seek to address the specificities of the challenges heralded by this global financial upheaval.

APPROACH

In constructing this analysis, we take a longitudinal approach to the restructuring of public sector work from the late 1970s, when the legitimacy of both the post-war market/welfare state compromise and the twentieth century bureaucratic state came under challenge. Concentrating our focus on the civil and public service in each country, we explore ways in which a succession of structural changes to the state resulted in a recasting of relationships among state managers, public employees and state trade unions. The focus is comparative: to identify the processes at work in two historically-related states, the United Kingdom and Australia. The purpose is to identify how similar outcomes emerged in each country, despite the distinctive trajectories of change, in both form and process.

To provide the comparative foundation for the study, a matched study, we examine two major welfare to work ('workfare') institutions, Centrelink (Australia) and its predecessors and Jobcentre Plus (United Kingdom) and its predecessors. These two state sponsored bodies provide welfare and other services that constitute basic economic and social conditions. Whilst there is variation in provision of these services between the two countries, there is also sufficient commonality to justify a close examination of the way that management and workers have contributed to the shaping of these institutions over the last thirty years. Nonetheless, we also look further afield and refer to other institutional arrangements that make up each state, to throw light on the core focus of the study.

Whilst this comprehensive longitudinal database informs the analysis for each country, we have been rather sparing in our use of case study evidence, selecting just sufficient to carry forward the argument, and returning to the same agencies (such as Centrelink and Jobcentre Plus and their antecedents) at different periods in successive chapters. Whilst also relying on wider evidence, we draw quite heavily on these matched agencies: each represented about 20 per cent of their respective countries' civil service workforces, and contained a wider than average grade distribution of employees. We have restricted the analysis to the core public service, and to the unions covering administrative officers – the Public and Commercial Services Union (PCS) in the United Kingdom and the Community and Public Sector Union (CPSU) in Australia.

The data are drawn from research over a thirty-year period. This material includes interviews with civil and public service managers including departmental heads, senior executives, middle managers and team leaders, as well as with administrative officers and front-line staff. It also includes interviews with national union leaders in each country, as well as regional and local union leaders and activists. Whilst only sixty interviewees are cited directly in the text, more than 120 in-depth interviews have been conducted in each country, and these have a background influence on the narrative. At different times over the last thirty years, all of us have been involved in briefing sessions and educational activity with civil and public service managers, employees and trade unionists. These experiences also inform our analysis. Similarly, our analysis was shaped by in-depth coding of archival sources. The Centrelink internal minutes are a case in point, although they are only cited directly several times. We also draw upon secondary literature on changes in public management, neo-liberalism, globalisation and trade union renewal and revitalisation, as well as on previous published and unpublished work by the five authors.

STRUCTURE

The organisation of the chapters is primarily thematic, being chronological only to the extent that the chapters are designed to contrast the approaches of successive governments in the two countries to specific issues. The book is structured into three broad parts: the neo-liberal agenda and government approaches to state reform of the public sector (Chapter 2); an historical overview of the pathways to state restructuring and union engagement (Chapters 3 and 4); and shifting relations between states and unions throughout the period (Chapters 5 to 7). In line with the comparative focus, each of Chapters 5 to 7 carries both United Kingdom and Australian material, although the material is not always treated in parallel fashion, either in content or in depth of coverage, mainly because of the differences in structure and level of industrial relations frameworks in the two countries. The final chapter, Chapter 8, provides a summary analysis of the argument, completing the analysis and speculating about the future. In the rest of this chapter, we outline how the book's successive chapters open up these themes.

Neo-liberalism, Globalisation and Depoliticisation

In the context of an increasing internationalisation of economic relations and contested national politics, successive governments in liberal democracies, particularly in the Anglo-American world, restructured and reorganised the core administrative structures of the modern state. The relationships between state and economy were reconfigured, via such programmes as privatisation, contracting out services, and the introduction of state-based market proxies. These developments impacted upon the forms of governance that characterised these countries. Central to these processes is the political advocacy of neo-liberal ideologies and associated practices. One outcome is a reformulation of the relationship between state and market and the character of economic intervention.

An analysis of the lively debate about the impact of neo-liberal agendas on national institutions is thus the focus of Chapter 2. On the one hand, there were those who regarded these developments as inevitable: in the words of President Clinton, not 'policy' but rather 'an inevitable condition of our time' (Clinton, 2003). This literature, however, overlooks the fact that change occurred through the constitution and reconstitution of state administrations through waves of change, slowly emerging from a bureaucratic set of arrangements, to (in the case of New Public Management), a set of more managerial forms of organisation.

From a hierarchical and multi-layered set of structures, the administrative state was, from the late 1970s, gradually transformed through developments that in Anglo-US countries were characterised as 'New Public Management' (Hood, 1991). Despite recent debates over the coherence of this concept the term 'NPM' refers to a well-recognised set of changes to the state sector, carried out most radically in New Zealand, followed by Australia and the United Kingdom, with a lesser impact in Canada and the United States (Aucoin, 1995; Boston *et al.*, 1996; Halligan, 2003; Kelsey 1996; Pollitt and Bouckaert, 2004; Zifcak, 1994). NPM reforms included the restructuring of boundaries between state and markets through competition, outsourcing, or structural fragmentation and the devolution of responsibility based on market-simulating relationships among 'delivery' and 'client' agencies or cost centres. New systems of managerial co-ordination were then required, based on the management of performance 'contracts'. Chapter 2 contains a comparative analysis of these institutional changes and their outcomes in the United Kingdom and Australia (on this type of comparative analysis, see Barton and Turnbull, 2002: 2–5).

The study is not of the manner in which the forces of globalisation shaped outcomes at a national or sectoral level; rather, it analyses the ways in which governments' pursuit of policies furthering these changes, was affected by contests between state managerial agents and organised labour. We argue that discourses of globalisation are understood best as attempts by various governments to cast public sector efficiencies and as a necessary and non-discretionary response to inexorable external forces: a process that has been dubbed 'depoliticisation' (Burnham, 2001; 2006a). Other depoliticisation strategies included the displacement of discretionary policy by automatic rules such as inflation targets, and the arms'-length separation of 'client' and 'delivery' agencies and cost centres, coordinated through contractual relationships and performance regimes.

Depoliticisation is 'the process of placing at one remove the political character of decision-making' (Burnham, 2001: 128). The concept points to both an 'indirect governing relationship' (Flinders and Buller, 2006a: 296) and a distanced one (Flinders and Buller, 2006a: 526–7). This process has been embraced by successive governments in both countries, irrespective of political complexion, although the emphasis in practice may vary. It is a process whereby the responsibility for operational and technical matters appears to lie with managers rather than government ministers. Nonetheless, governments ensured that they retained control over these core activities, through centralised financial control. This mix of policy and practice provided the opportunity for a reconstitution of the state in each country as a 'managerial' state, with implications for workers and their unions.

This analysis has been subject to critique. One argument is that the modernised state has become more centralised, rather than depoliticised (Carter, 2006: 144–7). This type of analysis misses the point of the depoliticisation process, where the emphasis is on a complex set of material and ideological concerns. The argument of Chapter 2 is that depoliticisation of the administrative state did not involve the relinquishing of central control, but rather a reconstitution of the architecture of control. The task facing analysts is to disaggregate this architecture of control, over time, to specify the relations of control between management and employees, and the implications of union representation and action. Similarly, public service employees and their unions addressed these restructuring processes, both by encouraging local action and by increasing centralised co-ordination of that activity.

Our argument is that central to a depoliticisation strategy is New Public Management. Whilst this suggestion will be contested, with some arguing that it overstates historical practice, our argument is that a more nuanced analysis should be developed (Pollitt and Bouckaert, 2004: 194; Lindblom, 1979). There have been sustained attempts to elaborate a nationally distinctive New Public Management model in the main Anglo-American countries – the United Kingdom, Australia, Canada, New Zealand and the United States. We suggest that with the promotion of NPM there has been a change in both the architectural structure of Anglophone states and in the governance mechanisms through which NPM states operate. Our claim is that these strategies have resulted in the promotion of performance management with implications for the organisation and operation of work and employment in the state sector.

Our claim is that to understand the history and texture of these developments, attention should be give to the inter-relationship between state management, state workers and their trade unions. Public sector managers and state workers operate in an evolving liberal democratic state. The state sector has been reorganised and now operates differently from the past. Central to these developments, the state labour process was shaped in terms of a reconstituted and recomposed state manager-state worker relationship. These relationships are part of a process of depoliticisation, underpinned by a neo-liberal approach to governance and economic relations. Faced with these changes, unions have sought to both shape the forms of managerialism that have emerged, as well as to defend and advance the interests of their members. In the process, unions were caught on the cusp of an ongoing tension between central and participative forms of union organisation and operation. The analysis focuses on the ways that these processes worked out in practice in both Australia and the United Kingdom.

Paths to State Restructuring and Union Engagement

Both the British and Australian states are long-standing liberal democracies, whose administrative arrangements until the 1970s were characterised by 'bureaucratic' relations, indicated by formal hierarchy, multi-tiered employment relations and rule-bound and process-oriented behaviour (on Australia see Caiden, 1967 and on United Kingdom, see Dunleavy, 1989). In both societies, the administrative services were characterised as providing professional, trained and independent support to successive governments (Caiden, 1967: 27–43). The close historical relationship between them derived from the colonial past, but Australia differed from the United Kingdom in the role of the state in nation-building (Caiden, 1967: 28–9). From the 1970s, and particularly the 1980s, governments in both countries embraced projects of state 'reform' and 'modernisation', mobilising 'political and popular discontent with "bureaucracy"' (Pollitt, 1993: 37). In pursing these reforms, the United Kingdom and Australian states maintained a close relationship, involving degrees of knowledge transfer over restructuring between senior administrators and government officers in the two countries, despite party-political differences (Rhodes, 2005; Zifcak, 1994).

The institutional comparison between the two countries is via the interplay of depoliticisation and politicisation. Key aspects of change in each state are presented: workforce recomposition based on the creation of a new class of managers; the structural fragmentation of the state apparatus; and the use of managerial control systems to recentralise the operational activity of the state (Chapter 3). The chapter begins by comparing the size and composition, including gender composition and distribution across grades, of each country's core public sector workforce in 1976 and 2009. Each of the administrative arrangements were recast to align more closely with neo-liberal economic policy agendas. Structural change required new forms of active 'management' (rather than passive 'administration') (Pollitt, 1993: 1–10). Over the period, from the 1980s onwards, successive governments utilised different rationales to commit themselves to interventionist programmes of public service reform. The outcome in both countries was an institutionally reorganised and recomposed set of core administrative structures. There was the trend in both countries towards centralised control of the civil and public services, via devolved forms of accountability and operation.

To cast light on how unions had to adapt in order to meet these changes, Chapter 4 traces the history of public service unions in each nation. In both countries, civil and public service unions were first founded in the late nineteenth century (for Australia, see Caiden, 1967: 251–74, Simms 1987; and for the United Kingdom, see Bain, 1970: 21–39). Initially, civil service unions were relatively quiescent organisations, often designated and operating as staff associations. They mirrored many of the features of civil and public service employment in each country, with an emphasis on consultation and 'responsibility', rather than adversarial actions. These unions often represented staff from particular grades and sections of the service, initially resulting in numerous organisations, distinguished in some cases by gender. Over time, these various associations and unions in each country merged to produce the CPSU in Australia and the PCS in the United Kingdom: respectively the major civil/public service unions in each state. One important difference between the two countries was that unions in Australia were recognised by the conciliation and arbitration institution known after 1988 as the Australian Industrial Relations Commission. This conferred a quasi-judicial status upon unions that was absent in Britain. Nevertheless, this difference meant that the institutional form of change and the themes addressed by each union movement were articulated in different ways. While state sector unions may have had limited impact on the overall shape of the restructured state, certainly by their survival, resistance, and their commitment to pose alternative strategies to civil and public service organisation and provision, they altered the course of labour market and industrial change. In the process, in some cases, they moderated aspects of the implementation or operation of management systems. Moreover, their policies and their actions also suggest different possible futures.

Shifting Frontiers of Control and Representation within the Managerial State

Having located the processes of change historically, the ways that these developments emerged are presented. Chapter 5 sets the scene for an empirical investigation in Chapters 6 and 7, of aspects of the role that state sector unions were able to play in shaping or contesting managerial changes. Managerialism refers to the 'regimes of power' that emerged with new organisational forms, 'structured through the domination of decision-making, agenda setting and normative power' (Clarke and Newman, 1997: 82). Top tiers of the new public service hierarchies, supported by governments, promoted a process of control and organisation, driving ongoing change in the organisation and operation of the labour process, and reconfiguring the relations among the different layers of the new hierarchies based on individual performance contracts. What distinguished such developments as 'managerialism' was the creation of power relations around executive control, quality measurement, assessment of performance against targets, and complex forms of personnel management, including team working. (Clarke and Newman, 1997; Pollitt and Bouckaert, 2004: 193).

The marketisation and managerialisation of state administrations led to a reconfiguration of class relations within the state, with implications for labour representation and collective state worker activity. The primary focus for this was the restructuring of the labour process with the explicit definition of a 'frontier of control' between a 'new' stratum of managers and a more 'proletarianised' workforce. Outsourcing, or the threat of it, had an indirect effect similar to that of increased direct managerial control, in that employees disciplined themselves in order to remain competitive. Managerialism, however, carried internal contradictions. As will become evident as the analysis is developed, the 'loose-tight' control techniques of NPM involved attempts to gain high commitment whilst pursuing cost-minimisation objectives. Strong accountability and performance regimes, coupled with work intensification, tended to generate concerted resistance that provided a basis for workplace union mobilisation. Episodes of governmental repression of workplace union activity, such as occurred in Australia between 2005 and 2007, provided a basis for union members' participation in wider community mobilisations in support of workplace rights.

The underlying tendencies identified in Chapter 5 emerged in piecemeal fashion, mediated or moderated by the conditions under which managerialism was introduced in different agencies. Chapter 6 thus explores the processes by which new settlements were achieved between state managers and employees and public sector unions. Despite the quite different pathways dictated by each state's distinctive industrial relations arrangements and their employees and their organisations, the United Kingdom and Australia adopted similar processes for the determination of pay and conditions: fragmented negotiation within centrally determined parameters. Managing their multiple roles as employer, source of labour market regulation policy, and financial regulator, governments were able to impose constraints that, when unevenly contested at local level, resulted in greater dispersion of pay and conditions. Nevertheless, where workplace union density and activism were significant, and effectively backed by central union resources, governments could not ignore collective voice, as expressed by unions. The chapter considers different phases of the 'reform' era, of union efforts to avoid the twin risks of marginalisation and incorporation, as they sought to influence the reshaping of managerial structures and work processes. Its case study vignettes include examples of Australian experiments in industrial democracy and decentralised bargaining arrangements in Australia, and an instance of the breakdown of partnership arrangements in the United Kingdom. Both the PCS and the CPSU have used central co-ordination in order to prevent being marginalised by the sheer workload of fragmented negotiation, or by a repressive organising and bargaining environment. Nonetheless, the success of both unions rested on active workplace memberships, with locally based forms of representation. Over the twenty-year period, each union had laid the foundation for an active and participative workplace membership. The outcome was a form of campaigning unionism, more so in the United Kingdom than Australia.

Finally, Chapter 7 analyses specific examples of both unions' effectiveness in maintaining collectivity: they resisted efforts to individualise the employment relationship through performance-related pay and associated remuneration schemes. Whilst, the two principal unions in the two countries faced the challenge of managerial promotion of individuated forms of employment, the unions developed strategies at an immediate workplace level as well as policies in relation to the structure and organisation of civil and public service workers. In Australia between 1997 and 2007, there was the added encumbrance of individual contracts and concerted efforts by the then government to marginalise and restrict union organisation and activity. Although there is an unevenness in these trajectories, it is nonetheless the case that the unions in each country have not only responded to the structural and polemical challenges that they faced, from governments and by managers, these unions have also experimented with different forms of organisation and collective operation. The outcome in each country is a union form of organisation in the core administrative areas that continues to influence and challenge government agendas.

Assessment

The final chapter, Chapter 8, draws these themes together with an assessment of the past and potential role of public sector unions in the reformed state. The restructuring of the state administrative sector in both countries over the past three decades took place within two civil and public services that had long been organised in centralised and hierarchical ways. In the context of increasing difficulties with private capital accumulation, growing trade union militancy in the state sector and a shift in government ideology, governments began to impose more stringent financial regimes on state services and to re-structure work processes. These change trajectories in both countries were, however different, involving nationally specific approaches to the perceived problem of labour inclusion or exclusion. Nonetheless, the overall outcome is two managerial states developing in parallel ways as modern capitalist states.

Equally, state employees and trade unions in each sector met these developments in complex ways. Building on past relations within each state, as bureaucratised and hierarchical administrative structures, state workers built up prominent national unions. Given the different political trajectories in each country, the trade unions did not pursue identical strategies, but tailored them to the circumstances that they confronted. These union memberships also made choices as they went along, in terms of the tensions between participation and centralisation. The outcome in both cases was more active and mobilised forms of unionism. They followed different paths, one emphasising participation and mobilisation (United Kingdom), albeit encouraged and coordinated by the centre, and the other affirming forms of more centralised forms of organisation and operation in order to counter the operational decentralisation of industrial relations, within tight guidelines specified by government (Australia). Nonetheless, they both ended up as cohesive campaigning unions, capable of playing an active part in the further process of state restructuring.

'THE NEXT STEPS'

Thus, the central argument of this book is that the restructuring of the state and its impact on the work of public employees led to the emergence of more active and potentially more mobilised campaigning unions. Governments have increasingly adopted neo-liberal agendas, with stark implications for the core administrative functions in each state. Central to these agenda have been sustained attempts to either marginalise or secure union compliance with these programmes of change. To begin the analysis, Chapter 2 will analyse the impact of the restructuring of state administrative arrangements and its implications for state-employee and union relations.

2 A Conceptual Analysis: Changing State Management and Trade Unions

Central to the recently evolving liberal democratic state is a reconstitution of relations between state managements and trade unions. The commentary on these developments has been extensive. Thus, this chapter has two purposes. First, it overviews the extensive debates on how best to conceptualise the public service reforms that have been salient in many nation-states over the last three decades (e.g. Pollitt and Bouckaert, 2004). These reforms are reflective of the complexity and diversity of the changes that have been in process. The second purpose is to draw out the implications of state restructuring for state sector employees and their unions. State bodies have been reconstituted, specifically with the recomposition of administrative grades into separate strata of state managers and state sector workers. Such developments have implications for the capacity of state sector workers to shape the implementation of change via their unions.

The rationalisation for the restructuring of public sector institutions and workforces is usually presented in terms of the 'modernisation' or 'reform' of state apparatuses, designed to reposition national economies more effectively in an increasingly globalised world (Rhodes, 2005). Restructuring processes, from the late 1970s to the 2000s, took place in the context of an increasing internationalisation of economic relations and contested national politics. Resulting reconfigurations of capitalist states involved major adaptations of the historical forms of the relationship between state and economy (privatisation, contracting out services, and constructing market proxies within the state apparatus). They also involved the establishment of forms of governance to underpin the reformulated market-state relationship (devolution and decentralisation of forms of governance, partnership arrangements between the public and private sectors, and increasing alignment with international policies and agencies) (Jessop, 2002: 454). The wider political shifts accompanying these changes included political advocacy of neo-liberal ideologies and associated practices, and changes in the character of economic intervention.

The forms of state restructuring have not been uniform. Governments have followed different courses to similar destinations. This suggests the continuing relevance of national contexts and arrangements in relation to state policy formulation and implementation (e.g. Swank, 2002;

Fourcade-Gourinchas and Babb, 2002; Iversen, 2005). Pollitt and Bouckaert (2004), for example, differentiate 'core NPM' states from various continental European models, including a 'neo-Weberian' group that has continued to emphasise distinctiveness, professionalism, democratic representation, and consultation (see also Pollitt, 2007: 20–1). While path dependency theory may explain differences in institutional formations, it is less useful as an explanation for commonalities in ideas or ideologies in different state settings. Thus, in considering these themes, it is necessary to take into account the ways that political configurations (constituencies and related coalitions of interest) shape the way in which different governments address specific goals (Boix, 1998). One tradition of writing emphasises the 'power-resource' model, whereby welfare state development is partly shaped by unions (and public sector employees generally), and supportive political parties. Such accounts, however, are challenged by theories that locate the elaboration of state politics in terms of social and economic structures, electoral politics, and citizen demands (Iversen, 2005; see also Esping-Andersen, 1990). Within our two 'core NPM' states, we trace similarities and differences between state organisational forms and regulatory approaches under social democratic and liberal-conservative governments, exploring whether they have offered different scope for agency by state sector workers and their unions.

Our argument is that there is a commonality of approach by governments. Processes of depoliticisation have been implemented, creating opaqueness in political decision making on economic management, the organisation and provision of services, and relationships between state and market. The focus here is on the way these approaches impact on the provision of state services, and the place of labour in this reconfiguration. Of course, there are a number of aspects to such developments. A unifying feature of the reform period has been the recomposition of core administrative structures and workforces, involving an attempt to maintain the distinctive features of central public administration while embracing selected areas of private sector employment practice. The operational devolution of management has been linked to an increased use of short-term contract employment (Hood, 1991). Human resource management practices have placed an emphasis on individual performance regimes, with accountability mechanisms based on performance contracts. These reforms have been premised on two assumptions: that the re-construction of 'administrative' grades as 'managerial' levels is a condition for an 'effective and efficient' public service, and that the means of doing this is to reconstitute bureaucratised state functions into marketised or monetarised ones (Hoggett, 1994).

In reforming the state apparatus along more managerial lines, governments have either attempted accommodation with state-based trade unions, or fostered their marginalisation (Fairbrother and Rainnie, 2006). In turn, state-based trade unions have articulated the interests of their members in ways that were not always straightforward. More specifically, we will be testing the argument that state sector unions may be able to take the opportunities provided by state restructuring in order to reposition themselves and to question the detail and direction of the changes (Fairbrother, 1994; Danford *et al.*, 2003; Carter, 2006).

In this chapter, the aim is to explore theoretically the complex relationships that may evolve among public employees, organised labour and the 'new' managerial stratum within the state sector. The chapter begins by identifying the common underlying pressure facing the governments of all capitalist nation-states: the need to shore up their own legitimacy as economic managers by maintaining the value of their currencies in international financial markets. We briefly canvass the debate over convergence and divergence of responses to these pressures. In Anglo-American states, albeit with somewhat different emphases when led by liberal-conservative or social democratic parties, there has been a tendency to place key aspects of economic management outside the arena of political debate: a process of depoliticisation (Burnham, 2006a; Flinders and Buller, 2006a and 2006b). The appearance of small government has been created through an organisationally scaled-back public sector, and through reliance on technocratic rules such as non-discretionary interest rate targeting. The result has been a path-dependent reliance on indirect forms of central control and horizontal co-ordination. Despite significant institutional and political differences, the Anglo-American states all embraced neo-liberal ideologies to frame their reform programs (on framing, see Schön and Fein, 1994; Fischer, 2003). Thus common economic and political pressures drove apparently divergent forms of 'New Public Management', as state organisations were restructured and their governance mechanisms redesigned.

The first section of the chapter addresses the issue of path-dependent differences between the UK and Australia. In the second section, we outline the neo-liberal approaches through which state restructuring, in both countries, was legitimated. The third section outlines a theory of depoliticisation – the distancing of regulatory activity (and operational approaches) from political debate and ministerial discretion. In the fourth section we outline the phases of the NPM experiment, focusing on managerialism as the element most closely linked to our theme – the recomposition of state sector workforces. The fifth section brings the analysis back to a discussion of the impact of state restructuring on public sector workers and overview the separate and distinct literature on state sector trade union responses. We then draw the threads of the analysis together in the sixth section and propose an analytic framework that guides and informs our understanding of state restructuring and the place and part of labour in this process. A brief conclusion completes the chapter.

PATH-DEPENDENT CONVERGENCE?

In the twenty years since the emergence of the term 'New Public Management' (Hood, 1991) there has been considerable international divergence from the local forms identified by the early NPM writers. Some sceptics question the actual existence of NPM (e.g. Hughes, 2008), or less radically, question whether a single common term can be applied to diverse institutional reforms. Amongst those who accept a degree of convergence, some see the variety of reforms as involving a common response to fundamental pressures on the capitalist state; others rely on neo-institutional explanations based on cultural imitation and diffusion, rejecting what they see as a functionalist view that agencies were responding rationally to environmental pressures (Powell and DiMaggio, 1991; Scott, 2001). Similar public management approaches are variously explained in terms of coercive pressure from powerful institutions (World Bank, ratings agencies, etc.) normative pressure (from professional bodies and networks) or mimetic pressure (the scripts and fads emanating from consultants). We do not see any incompatibility between explanations based on underlying structural pressures and explanations based on the agency of institutional actors: rather, they belong to different levels of analysis. To accept that managers faced structural constraints is not to fall into economic determinism, and thus institutional responses have had an element of contingency.

On the one hand, Christensen and Lægreid (2006) are surely correct in arguing that ideas promoted by dominant global agencies are liable to mutate as they are adopted, with the result that similar labels may refer to divergent practices in different country contexts (cited in Pollitt, 2007: 12). On the other hand, once adopted, practices begin to have a structural impact, shaping options for future action. Thus, NPM is not a static phenomenon, but one that has taken different forms over time. Although periodisation is difficult, some commentators document a first, decentralising wave of NPM, followed by a 'second wave' of vertical regulation and horizontal co-ordination (see for example the contributors to Christensen and Lægrid, 2006). Other commentators argue that differences over time have involved no more than a shift of emphasis, with decentralising and centralising tendencies present from the beginning (see for example Halligan, 2006 on Australia).

In later chapters we will compare the restructuring trajectories of comparable public sector agencies over three decades in the UK and Australia, mapping the path-dependent emergence of new forms of public sector governance and their legitimating discourses, and charting convergence or divergence within the 'core NPM' fold. The almost mirror-image patterns of political parties in power in the two countries since the 1970s provides a quasi-experimental research design (Table 2.1) for comparing reforms under Conservative and Labo(u)r party governments.

As political rhetoric, NPM was characterised by the contradictions and overlaps that are to be expected within any discourse designed to accommodate and neutralise opposition (Fairclough, 1992; 2000). When translated into practice, policies tend to exhibit a certain incoherence, resulting from the perseverance of established organisational norms and routines (Cooper *et al.*, 2002). NPM exhibited gaps between rhetoric and reality, resulting

Table 2.1 Political Parties in Control of Government, UK and Australia, 1975–2010

United Kingdom	Australia
1979–1991 Conservative (Thatcher)	1975–1983 Liberal/National (Fraser)
1991–1997 Conservative (Major)	1983–1991 Labor (Hawke)
1997–2007 New Labour (Blair)	1991–1996 Labor (Keating)
2007–2009 New Labour (Brown)	1996–2007 Liberal/National (Howard)
2010– Conservative/Liberal Democratic (Cameron)	2007– Labor (Rudd/Gillard)

Note: The New Labour period ran from 1997 to 2010.

from the messy and indeterminate play of organisational micro-politics. Thus, as Ackroyd and others (2004: 1–10) argue, its adoption has been a 'contested and uneven process' and it has emerged as 'varied and incoherent'. In examining and explaining these internal tensions, our first step is to examine the dominant neo-liberal ideology that over the past twenty years, has contributed to the legitimation of NPM reforms.

Neo-liberal Projects

In the Anglo-American bloc during the 1980s and 1990s, governments of different political hues embraced neo-liberal reform projects. Neo-liberalism has been defined as a political project to 'visualise a free-market utopia', involving the 'downsizing of nation-states [that] enlarges the space for private accumulation, individual liberties and market forces' (Tickell and Peck, 2003: 163). Governments became the facilitators of markets, while applying quasi-market procedures to their own managerial agents and public sector labour generally.

Neo-liberalism as a political project originated in the classic liberal period. The concept was elaborated in eighteenth- and nineteenth-century debates about political economy, involving such thinkers as David Ricardo, Adam Smith, Thomas Malthus, John Stuart Mill and Karl Marx. The classic liberal ideas were founded on an 'objective' or 'perfectionist' theory of human well-being. Markets were seen to foster specific qualities in humans, which are constitutive of the good life, such as industriousness, benevolence, and self-reliance. Thus, Smith had a 'positive' conception of freedom as enhancing an individual's sense of self-determination, integrity and responsibility. These ideas were formulated into arguments about the market, laissez-faire economic policies, and the minimalist state. For example, even when fostering vulgar egoism, the market's consequence was argued to be the elevation of society's cultural and material well-being (George, 1999).

Such notions were supplanted in the early twentieth century by ideas associated with social liberalism, social democracy and communism. The state was seen as a beneficent player, regulating of markets, and promoting equality and egalitarianism. Like liberal ideas, these themes were also based on conceptions of human potential and need. However, in the mid-to late twentieth century a neo-liberal revival linked core ideas about freedom, and particularly economic freedom, to market relations. In Europe this movement was led by the Austrian School – Friedrich von Hayek (e.g. 1944), Ludwig Elder von Mises (e.g. 1962) and in the USA by the Chicago School – Gary Becker (e.g. 1992); James Buchanan (e.g. 1958); Milton and Rose Friedman (e.g. 1977; 1982).

A key aspect of neo-liberalism, as an economic and political project, is its celebration of the beneficial aspects of competition (Fourcade-Gourinchas and Babb, 2002; Jessop, 2002; Larner, 2005). Equally important is its advocacy of social individualism (rather than collective forms of organisation) and its promotion of choice. Neo-liberalism argues that social democratic, welfarist and communist state projects neither realise the freedoms associated with choice and individualism nor provide the grounds for market prosperity. Thus, while there is a long history of argument about liberalism, the distinctiveness of its most recent neo-liberal version is that it has critically been an argument about a particular version of freedom.

Neo-liberalism is founded on a 'subjective' concept of well-being, and a 'negative' conception of freedom, the latter defined as freedom from external supervision. The celebration of markets is based, not so much on their efficiency, as on their capacity to maximise freedom of choice. What people do with this freedom is not for politicians or economists to decide. In complex and contradictory ways, these ideas have been elaborated in state policies. Importantly, they present choice and social individualism as synonymous with freedom.

The 'New Right' or neo-liberal view of society as a state of 'unfreedom' and negation of the individual thus relies on neo-classical economic theory. This theory became a core part of the critique and dismantling of the welfare state and social democratic politics. One particular focus was on the role and place of trade unions in contemporary society; they were seen as part of a profile of coercion centred on the citizen and the state. These ideas were taken up by the Republican Party in the US under Ronald Reagan and the Conservative Party in the UK under Margaret Thatcher. They were popularised by think tanks such as the Institute for Economic Affairs (UK) (Stone and Denham, 2004), the Heritage Society and the National Centre for Public Policy Research in the USA (Stefancic and Delgado, 1996), and the Centre for Independent Studies, the Institute of Public Affairs, and the H.R. Nicholls Society and the Business Council (of Australia) (Sawer, 1982; HR Nicholls Society, 1985; Murray, 2006; Smith and Marden, 2009).

Despite the rhetoric of freedom and limited government, the 'New Right' also supported the strengthening of the coercive arms of the state (i.e. army and police), particularly after 2001. Tickell and Peck characterise this phase of neo-liberalism as its state-centred phase (2003: 169). Whilst agreeing that the appeal of neo-liberalism lies in its universal and ahistorical claims, they argue that in practice, it has been elaborated differently in different states or state clusters. They identify three phases of such elaboration – proto neo-liberalism (pre-1980); state 'roll-back' neo-liberalism (roughly from 1980 to the early 1990s) and 'roll-out' neo-liberalism (roughly from the early 1990s onward), associated with discourses of globalisation (Tickell and Peck, 2003: 169). While the detail of the periodisation may be questioned, it is clear that neo-liberalism has developed and evolved along the broad trajectory suggested by Tickell and Peck (2003).

Policies associated with neo-liberalism have been based on a positive view of globalisation, on a belief that social benefits will flow from a borderless world where trade and market relations thrive (Ohmae 1990; Osborne and Gaebler, 1992; Cerny, 1997). The liberalisation of trade, of financial markets and foreign capital flows, based on a unified and competitive exchange rate, has required nation-states to reform taxation and reduce public spending or switch it to marketable areas such as health; to privatise production and secure property rights; to increase labour market flexibility, and to minimise the social safety net (Tickell and Peck, 2003: 166–7). The neo-liberal project, however, is neither seamless nor undifferentiated (Hall, 2003; Larner, 2005). Rather it is a mosaic of approaches, defined by a range of policy formulations grounded in specific constitutional and governing arrangements.

The outcome has been a variety of forms of neo-liberalism that developed over time and were shaped by different political configurations. Rather than being a 'hybrid' form, neo-liberalism, is a cluster of practices, reflecting an increasing subordination of social democratic ideals (Hall, 2003; Peck, 2004: 395, 403). Its core elements are economic deregulation, the displacement of traditional state forms, and the re-regulation of economic organisation, underpinned by the negative view of freedom described above – one that sees state control and economic intervention simply as constraining (Rainnie and Fairbrother, 2006). Yet the embrace of neo-liberalism has not been without dissension. An example is the emergence, in both the USA and Australia, of a neo-conservative strand within its ideology and in tension with it (for some of the diverse ingredients of such thought, see Kristol, 1995 and Scruton, 2002). One strand of neo-conservatism has been concerned that excessive individual freedoms and rights may erode social institutions and values, leading to a questioning of the moral relativism implicit in liberalism. Strands of thought within neo-liberalism have opposed practices ranging from stem cell research to affirmative action for minority groups, and increasingly supported values ranging from creationist education to aggressive and unilateralist foreign policy. It may be that we have witnessed the fragmentation of the dominant neo-liberal agenda. A further split is between neo-liberalism and traditional conservative thought in the UK centring on approaches to social intervention and welfare, separating 'one-nation' Toryism from the neo-liberal emphasis on choice and competition (see Quinton, 1978).

Nonetheless, central to the neo-liberal agenda has been a concern with the role of state. Neo-liberal think tanks and politicians in the US and the UK have maintained a sustained attack on welfare state institutions. Rather than rolling back the state, however, the effect has been to extend the scope of state action. For example, the privatisation of institutions was accomplished through active state intervention based on competition policies. Similarly, international trade re-regulation has further extended the scope of state intervention, creating the foundation for a global economy. An example was the US government's opposition in 2005, on behalf of Boeing, to European Union (EU) support for Airbus as an unfair trade practice. By 2009, the rapid internationalisation of the 2007–8 US financial crisis had demonstrated the limitations of the laissez-faire doctrine that minimalist state intervention allows the market's hidden hand to transmute individual self-interest into social well-being. The role of the state in economic management had become overt again, with a return in countries such as the USA, UK and Australia to explicit fiscal stimulus measures. The contradictions of the expanding but self-effacing operations of the neo-liberal state are usefully captured in the concept of depoliticisation, to which we now turn.

Depoliticisation

The argument of the book rests substantially on an analysis of 'depoliticisation'. This term had some salience in the United Kingdom, but is relatively unknown in Australia, especially in the areas of labour studies, industrial relations and state restructuring. The process has been analysed in recent years in the United Kingdom, through the writings of Peter Burnham (1999a, 1999b, 2001, 2006a, 2006b), among others. In the words of Burnham, depoliticisation involves 'the process of placing at one remove the political character of decision-making' (2001: 128; see also 2006b: 12). He emphasises two aspects. First, it is a process associated with 'appearance' rather than reality. It is a political measure, a form of 'ideological mobilisation' (2006b: 13). Market relations are promoted under the guise of 'inclusiveness, democratisation and empowerment' (2006b: 13). The second point is that this form of ideological mobilisation has implications for the state apparatus. He argues that:

> We are witnessing the creation of 'managerial states' as part of the process of depoliticising labour management relations in the public sector, as responsibility for the operational activity of state bodies shifts from central government and is placed in the hands of managers who represent a more distant and disembodied form of regulation via financial control and restriction.
>
> (2006b: 22)

Thus, there is the development of the appearance of technocratic decision making, coupled in reality with managerial discretion and decision.

In an elaborating these arguments, Hay (2007) suggests that the process of depoliticisation has allowed elected representatives to avoid having to accept responsibility for policies for which previously they had been directly accountable (2007). For Hay, depoliticisation also obscures the normalisation of neo-liberal approaches to the management of public services. He believes that the outcome of this process is that neo-liberal solutions to the problems of public sector management are increasingly proposed as the only solutions available to governments and that:

> neo-liberalism's normalisation has been achieved through a process of rationalication which is itself powerfully depolitizing.
>
> (Hay, 2007: 99)

Thus, Hay believes that since the 1990s, 'a process of institutionalisation, normalisation and depoliticisation' (what he calls 'normalized neo-liberalism') rendered the adoption of neo-liberal policies non-negotiable. (2007: 98). Thus neo-liberalism became hegemonic: the unchallengeable idea underpinning governance.

In a similar vein, Flinders and Buller (2006a: 296) emphasised the 'indirect governing relationship' created through

> [t]he range of tools, mechanisms and institutions through which politicians can attempt to move to an indirect relationship and/or seek to persuade the demos that they can no longer be reasonably held responsible for a certain issue, policy field or specific decision [sic].
>
> (Flinders and Buller, 2006a: 295–6)

Thus the concept embodies both a practical process of distancing relationships, as well as its outcome – 'appearance' of such distancing (Buller and Flinders, 2005: 526–7). It is about the material 'process of devolving decisions' (Buller and Flinders, 2005: 527) and the way this process is perceived and presented (see also Van Gramberg, 2002).

The processes of depoliticisation are complex. In reference to state policy and practice there are three levels to consider (Flinders and Buller, 2006b). First, governments formulated a macro-level commitment to such strategies, as we will argue is the case for both the United Kingdom and Australia. Second, within the state apparatus, and related bodies, there was a meso-level choice of distancing tactics and legitimating discourses. Finally, there was the micro-level level practice of day-to-day implementation.

Central government commitment to a depoliticisation agenda was of course profoundly political, both as an approach to statecraft and as an exercise of power. Flinders and Buller (2006b) define the political strategy as 'arena-shifting', whilst Burnham (2006b) uses the term 'displacement'. Governments evaded any appearance of neutrality, and minimised fears about 'state overload', even whilst acting to help maintain the flow of global capital through the regulatory creation and maintenance of 'deregulated' markets, which created the appearance of small government. At the macro-level, the displacement was rhetorical: globalisation was portrayed as an intransitive force, beyond the power of human intervention. At the meso-level, central government maintained a loose-tight 'steering' control over implementation activities. Delegation might be contractual or simply based on the required internalisation of values. At the micro-level, the displacement involved a shifting of responsibility for unpopular policies from politicians to front-line service-deliverers, whether located in public or in privatised agencies. These workers, in confronting consumer-citizens, were bound, nevertheless, through the accountability mechanisms of the contractual state, to a non-discretionary implementation of unpopular policies. Thus, the displacement of discretion occurred at every level, from the international application of IMF (International Monetary Fund) 'structural adjustment' conditionality requirements, through to the administration of benefit eligibility rules by local welfare agency staff.

Depoliticisation as a political response to global forces is best illustrated by the Thatcherite mantra of TINA ('there is no alternative'). Burnham argues that in the United Kingdom, particularly in the first period of government, New Labour followed the path of successive Conservative governments in presenting its domestic policies as being necessary to the maintenance of the value of sterling in international financial markets. This stance deflected a local backlash against unpopular measures 'requiring' resolute, non-discretionary commitment in order to secure national growth goals. Burnham argues that by combining the language of necessity with a new 'language of inclusiveness, democratisation and empowerment' the Blair government created a powerful form of 'ideological mobilisation' (Burnham, 2001: 128–9).

At the tactical level, depoliticisation involved the establishment of new organisational forms based on the now-familiar separation of the functions of policy 'steering' and implementation through 'rowing' (Osborne and Gaebler, 1992). Organisational structures were established at varying degrees of separation ('autonomisation') from overt political control, ranging from non-ministerial departments to independent statutory bodies and foundations (Flinders and Buller, 2006b: 57; see also Christensen and Lægreid, 2006). In addition to such organisational depoliticisation, governments also bound themselves to automatic rules: steering, as it were, with 'hands tied'. Among the decision-making processes placed outside ministerial discretion and thus largely outside public policy debate, perhaps the best known was the linking of monetary policy to inflation targets; and its management by technical experts.

Such formal, structural distancing was possible only after tight control mechanisms had been established. Thus at the micro-political level, depoliticisation involved the use of indirect operational controls. It was here that the managerial techniques of NPM were called into play. Whatever the chosen combination of arm's length organisational forms, the governance mechanisms of centralised regulation have characteristically involved accountability, surveillance and performance management techniques. Contractual and quasi-contractual arrangements were used, both within public sector organisations, and across a new public sector characterised by 'a permeable set of relations, where there is a mix of responsibility between public sector enterprises and the private sector for the provision of public sector functions' (Fairbrother, 1998: 1).

Depoliticisation has had both critics and defenders. Perhaps the most passionate critic is Rancière, who argues that:

> historical faith has changed camps ... Proclaiming themselves to be simply administrating the local consequences of global historical necessity, our governments take great care to banish the democratic supplement. Through the invention of supra-State institutions which are not States, which are not accountable to any people, they ... depoliticize political matters; reserve them for places that are non-places, places that do not leave any space for the democratic invention of polemic. So the State and their experts can quietly agree among themselves.
>
> (Rancière, 2006: 81–2)

At this supra-national level, defenders of depoliticisation include Moravcsik (2002), who argues that the EU derives its legitimacy, not from participatory or deliberative democracy, but from its very insulation from majoritarian voting systems and from its reliance on technocratic expertise. Thus Hay (2007: 91–93) contrasts academic critique of depoliticisation as inimical to collective deliberation and decision-making with the practitioner view that depoliticisation, by handing policy over to neutral 'experts', serves to protect 'the people' from the politicking of powerful interest groups.

At the national level, similar affirmations of the need to protect policy-makers from short-term political pressures, and the same mystification of technical expertise, have been used to justify the depoliticisation of monetary policy. Central bank operational independence is a condition for membership of the European Monetary Union. In both the United Kingdom and Australia, it is also coupled with the rule-based depoliticisation strategy of whereby interest rate policy is governed by inflation targets. In the UK the process began in 1992, when the Conservative government of John Major required the Bank of England to undertake quarterly monitoring of the containment of interest rates within a target range of 1–4 per cent, and in 1995, price stability was legislatively enshrined as the overriding objective of monetary policy. The incoming Blair government continued this approach, formally reinforcing the operational independence of the Bank of England (Burnham, 2006b: 21).

In Australia, similarly, from 1993, Reserve Bank interest rate policy was shaped by the delegated responsibility of meeting an inflation target of

2–3 per cent over the business cycle. Bernie Fraser, the Bank's outgoing Governor, affirmed the need for a board that was:

> an independent, expert body not bound up in the electoral cycle would do a better job than politicians in conducting monetary policy ... Monetary policy is, in a number of respects, more 'technical' and less 'political' than fiscal policy.
>
> (Fraser, 1996: 15)

Nevertheless, he warned, however, against replacing the 'short-termism' of politics by the 'short-termism' of financial markets (Fraser, 1996: 19). The Howard government confirmed Reserve Bank independence and inflationary targeting, citing the goals of full employment and welfare protection among its legitimations. In its first month of office in December 2007, the Rudd Labor government signed a formal agreement on Reserve Bank independence and inflation stabilisation. Whilst instituting regular Bank-Treasury policy discussions, the new government also made the dismissal of the the Bank Governor and Deputy Governor possible only with bicameral parliamentary approval (Reserve Bank of Australia, 2009). Within a year, however, the 2008–9 financial crisis revived the role of discretionary fiscal policy.

From the late 1970s, depoliticisation in the United Kingdom and Australia also involved labour market re-regulation through ongoing legislative intervention, designed to weaken state industrial relations machinery and to enable the disempowering of collectively organised workers. These measures were backed by the restructuring of welfare benefit entitlements in a way that was designed to expand the supply of workers competing for jobs in the low-paid sector. The new approach to welfare was based on a rugged doctrine of self-help. Accompanying Margaret Thatcher's 'there is no alternative' was her equally famous 'there is no such thing as society':

> I think we've been through a period where too many people have been given to understand that if they have a problem, it's the government's job to cope with it ... They're casting their problem on society. And, you know, there is no such thing as society. There are individual men and women, and there are families ... It's our duty to look after ourselves and then, also to look after our neighbour. People have got the entitlements too much in mind, without the obligations. There's no such thing as entitlement, unless someone has first met an obligation.
>
> (Thatcher, 1987)

This was a vision in which individuals were to be shaken free from the supposed cocoon of welfare supports to compete as atomised individuals in a flexible labour market. The main protection from unemployment was the market-clearing wage and unemployment was to be tolerated to the extent that it curtailed inflation. Work was the source of opportunity for the socially excluded. In a community defined as free of outmoded class conflict, individuals were presented as competing in globally-exposed labour markets, where social protection depended on contributing to 'national development' by accepting real wage-cutting and work intensification (Burnham, 2001: 137). New Labour, too, according to Watson and Hay (2003), offered voters in the 1997 and 2001 elections a 'new deal' based on an industrial relations policy that was little more than a restatement of its labour market policy:

> [The] world is changing. ... Companies need both the capability and the flexibility to succeed in this new world. ... We must avoid rigidity in labour market regulation and promote the flexibility we require.
>
> (Labour Party, 1996, cited in Watson and Hay, 2003: 300)

Thus depoliticisation, in the case of employment relations policy and practice, involved promulgation of a sense that working class claims were untenable in the face of the inevitable global forces modelled by expert econometricians.

In Australia since 1904 the industrial relations landscape had already been characterised by the arms' length role of a commission for arbitrating and conciliating industrial relations – Higgins' (1915) 'new province for law and order'. Federal public servants were, initially, however, outside its scope. Between 1983 and 2008, a series of government-union 'Accords' and successive five waves of legislation have reflected the attempt by both Labor and Coalition governments to find an electorally-acceptable means of generating wage restraint and labour market flexibility. The Labor government-union Accords of 1983–95, whilst apparently a politicisation of industrial relations, had the effect, first of removing bargaining from the workplace, and then of subsequently decentralising it, fragmenting the combined bargaining power of unions through local productivity bargaining requirements. Post-1996 conservative neo-liberal governments engaged in radical decollectivisation measures. The Committee of Experts of the International Labour Organisation annually criticised the Howard Government's Workplace Relation Act 1996 and its 2005 'Work Choices' amendments, for giving primacy to individual agreement-making, and for limiting freedom of association and the right to organise and bargain collectively (Romeyn, 2007). Relegation of the employment relationship to the arena of individual contract, under minimalist state supervision, was an attempt to depoliticise industrial and work relations. The overtly political path to this end created an electoral backlash, and the Rudd Labor government's Fair Work Act 2009 offered a cautious attempt to reconcile collectivism and flexibility. As we shall see, it was during the two decades of labour market and employment relations reform in the 1980s and 1990s that public sector workers were brought into the mainstream industrial relations system, while at the same time, the Commonwealth government used its employer status to model its reforms to this system.

Depoliticisation has been a bipartisan strategy. Indeed some argue that in the United Kingdom at least, it has been Labour governments especially that have invoked discourses of globalisation and technical efficiency. Burnham (2001) sees such discourses as largely a domestic electoral strategy, designed to create distance between New and Old Labour, and to dampen societal expectations. Watson and Hay (2003: 290–5) argue that the globalisation invoked by the Blair government was designed for internal political consumption and assembled from three contradictory texts. First, there was the 'business school' orthodoxy that in a borderless world, the national post-war compromise between the welfare state and the self-regulating market (Polanyi, 1944) had been swept away. Second was the thesis of the state's 'structural dependence' on capital: the view that, to safeguard jobs, Labour governments in particular must accommodate business demands for tax cuts, labour market flexibility and fiscal austerity. Third was the need for 'counter-inflationary credibility', based on an exaggerated fear of capital flight, to be allayed only by locking stabilisation policies into legislation. Watson and Hay (2003: 295–6) thus define depoliticisation, in the first place, as the imposition of self-fulfilling limits on the scope of future political decision making, and in the second place, as the path-dependent entrenchment of policies that began as contingent:

> That the contingent politics of labour market and welfare reform has seemingly been rendered necessary is a triumph, not of the non-negotiable character of globalisation, but of political rhetoric and electoral expediency over economic reality.
>
> (Watson and Hay, 2003: 301)

Both the creation and operation of markets required increasing regulation. Under privatisation, direct provision was displaced by contract management. With the shift from welfare to workfare, beneficiaries became 'cases', whose 'management' became more interventionist. Application of proliferating rules required discretion but public servants became ever more tightly managed workers. In this process, public sector workers lived the contradiction between the reality of their work processes and the rhetoric of small government. Public service work was diminished in status and legitimacy but not in volume. Later chapters provide an assessment of the capacity of public sector unions to contribute to some new form of settlement, redefining both labour relations and the work of public service. Our next task, however, is to apply the concept of depoliticisation to an understanding of the array of practices characterised as aspects of new public management or modernisation.

New Public Management and Modernisation

The embrace of NPM by successive governments is central to a depoliticisation strategy. However, some argue that to interpret these developments as a strategy overstates historical practice. Pollitt and Bouckaert (2004: 194) explain the public services reform agenda as a process of 'muddling through' rather than an exercise in the articulation and implementation of a conscious strategy. While acknowledging that the problems of fiscal restraint and legitimacy are real, they argue that governments have dealt with them in partial and *ad hoc* ways, including those governments that have argued for forms of NPM. Following Lindblom (1979) who argued for a public policy analysis emphasising incrementalism rather than wholesale transformation, these authors stress the extent to which the state has been structured around 'small steps', *ad hoc* analyses, and partial and initially accommodative approaches (Pollitt and Bouckaert, 2004: 194). With reference to the United Kingdom, they apply the analysis to demonstrating the initially unintended scale of the Conservatives' privatisation programme, resulting from internal political debates about civil service reorganisation, and 'failures' of previous reform policies (p. 195). From such beginnings, NPM has come to characterise the emerging neo-liberal state.

Our argument is that NPM is central to the depoliticisation process. The NPM approach has been embraced most comprehensively in those countries marked by relatively comprehensive, well-organised and competent administrative arrangements (Wright, 1997: 9–10). Most accounts of public service reform in the main Anglo-American countries – the United Kingdom, Australia, Canada, New Zealand and the US – have been based on attempts to elaborate a nationally distinctive New Public Management model. There have been many attempts to classify its defining features, which have varied with time, place and political orientation of the government in power. Despite the NPM sceptics who deny any common tendency, we accept that there has been identifiable change in both the architectural structure of Anglophone states and in the governance mechanisms through which NPM states operate. Latter-day experiments, for example in 'networked governance' and 'public value governance' are based on the broad framework of these changes. In this section then, we will begin with early accounts of structural NPM reforms and the managerial processes of the NPM state, before describing later modifications, particularly the UK modernisation agenda.

An Early Model

Running through all accounts of NPM is an apparent tension between centralising and devolutionary or 'small government' tendencies. The concept of depoliticisation helps to explain this tension. The state has not been diminishing itself: rather, state controls have been distanced or displaced in the manner of Foucault's (1984) capillary power. Thus, the necessary concomitant or prerequisite for structural decentralisation or operational devolution is the establishment of mechanisms guaranteeing central control. Changes resulting in heightened political control of institutions that had previously enjoyed a level of autonomy, such as Australia's former Conciliation and Arbitration Commission or its Public Service Boards, have preceded the subsequent NPM processes of devolution. Corporatisation and privatisation, and the NPM culture of contracts, performance review and audit, make sense only as the two moments of the depoliticisation process.

Hood (1991) is credited with coining the term 'New Public Management'. He identified seven defining characteristics:

- the breaking-up of parts of the public sector into agencies that relate to one another on a user-pays principle;
- an emphasis on increased competitive pressures within the public sector through tendering processes; the development of quasi-markets (public corporations and government businesses) for those areas not privatised and the introduction of short-term contracts of employment;
- increased freedom for a professional elite of public sector managers to manage in place of the traditional primacy given to policy skills;
- an increased emphasis on introducing management techniques and practices from the private sector and on increasing management's ability to hire and fire and reward public service workers individually rather than through collective processes;
- a focus on the measurement of performance through the establishment of goals, targets and quantitative indicators;
- Increased control over outputs, with an emphasis on the results achieved rather than the process involved; and
- an emphasis on cost cutting and rationalisation, or 'doing more with less' (1991: 4–5).

In the United Kingdom during the 1980s and in the 1990s in Australia, there began a shift from large, hierarchical and unified public service organisations to a more fragmented and specialised set of institutional arrangements. These changes were reflected in the moves towards agencies and contractually determined relationships, as exemplified by the creation of Jobcentre Plus, as well as the history of its predecessors, such as the Benefits Agency. Established in April 2002, following a merger between the former Employment Service and those parts of the Benefits Agency that provided services to working-age claimants, it is an executive agency of the Department for Work and Pensions (DWP). Of the DWPs 113,000 full-time equivalent staff in 2007, 71,000 were employed in Jobcentre Plus. The senior levels of the department consist of a departmental board with three non-executive directors and an Executive Team, comprising the heads of the agencies, corporate services and client groups (who lead on policy).

More decentralised relationships and smaller scale organisations were seen as facilitating a more responsive and rapid delivery of services. Hood (1995: 96) explained the 'unbundling' and specialisation of agency functions and the introduction of purchaser/provider arrangements among cost centres as an accountability measure, allowing the assignment of blame for poor performance. The studies edited by Christensen and Lægreid (2006) identify a range of 'agencification' models, including non-departmental public bodies and quangos. Following Pollitt and Talbot (2004), Christensen and Lægreid (2006: 12) define agencies as national bodies that are structurally dis-aggregated and formally separated from ministries, although staffed by public servants. In Australia the term 'agency' was applied more generally, both to departments with secretaries, typically on five-year contracts, and to bodies such as Centrelink, governed by a Chief Executive Officer (CEO) and a Board of Management.

Centrelink, a statutory agency established by the Customer Service Delivery Act 1997, has a formally devolved relationship with government. It is the largest agency in the APS, with approximately 27,000 employees, or about 25 per cent of all employees in the APS. Over 400 Centrelink offices are located around Australia, with a central call centre taking over 20 million calls a year and a range of mobile and remote-link services based in rural areas and the regions. Service provision is funded, not by direct budget appropriations, but through interagency funding transfers, based on submissions by the 'purchasing agencies' to the Department of Finance and Deregulation.

The creation of agencies was a distancing process, thought to align administrative arrangements more closely with the private sector models espoused by neo-liberal agendas. Activities thus 'unbundled' have been co-ordinated variously through contractual or quasi-contractual relationships, marketisation and outright privatisation. Pollitt and Bouckaert (2004: 98) see a defining element of NPM as the creation of 'a large role for private sector forms and techniques in the process of restructuring the public sector'. They identify two elements to this process: a rapid and extensive pursuit of mar-ketising and privatising strategies; and a minimisation of the administrative arrangements of the state (Pollitt and Bouckaert, 2004: 187–9; Pollit, 2007: 17). This second point is to be understood, not in terms of small govern-ment, but in terms of a process of de-bureaucratisation. Pollitt (1993) notes in relation to the UK and the USA: 'the central civil service has borne a large share of political and popular discontent with "bureaucracy"' (p. 37). This discontent has helped gain electoral support for policies to 'reform' the civil services in these states. In fact, the demand has been for 'value for money', rather than for the shrinking of state services. Relationships amongst autonomised agencies have been monetarised, and competitive tendering processes have pitted public sector units against private sector counterparts in delivering 'best value'. Marketisation has been driven by a belief in competition as a driver of standards (Hood, 1995: 96). Whilst the outright privatisation of agencies and service delivery has occurred, marketisation has been a more far-reaching process, based on an 'exit' model of customer choice, particularly associated with conservative governments in the United Kingdom and Australia.

The realignment and depoliticisation of administrative arrangements was achieved through the rise of managerialism. This 'reform' has been defined as the introduction of forms of active 'management' (rather than passive 'administration') into state services (Pollitt, 1993: 1–10, Pollitt and Bouckaert, 2004). Counterbalancing the autonomy of managers within NPM models is their accountability for organisational performance. The focus on efficiency, cost-effectiveness and productivity is described as a response by governments to the problem of ever-increasing demands by citizens for quality public services in the context of declining revenues (Aucoin, 1995: 9–10). NPM's output focus and its emphasis on measurement is an instance of the replacement of discretion by conformity to rules and targets (Hood 1995: 96). We have already noted the use of rules as a key depoliticisation strategy. This focus on rules and on audit mechanisms has been criticised as contributing to loss of creativity, policy disasters and diminished capacity to solve 'wicked' problems (Ferlie *et al.*, 1996; Power, 1997; Strathern, 2000). In place of planning (a concept distrusted in neo-liberal ideology), NPM has erected an edifice of performance controls based on quantification (Hood, 1991) and a cascading array of financial and human resource management techniques.

Variations on the Model

The NPM models represent a marriage between economic theories (public choice theory, transaction cost theory and principal-agent theory) and a variety of private sector management techniques that have been introduced into public sector environments, both in the delivery of public services and the administrative services of the state (Hood, 1991: 5). The former emphasise notions of user choice and transparency while the latter assume the portability of professional managerial knowledge and promote increased freedom for public service managers to generate results and improve organisational performance. Different parts of the model have been dominant in different English-speaking countries and within countries at varying times, and under differing governments. Writing of the United Kingdom, Ferlie and others (1996) have identified the following variations in emphasis:

- The 'Efficiency Drive' model of the early 1980s introduced private sector management practices such as increased financial controls, performance monitoring, benchmarking, customer focus, a shift in power from professionals to management and attempts to marginalise trade unions.
- The 'Downsizing and Decentralisation' model involved reducing workforce numbers, decentralisation of financial budgets, contracting-out, a greater focus on quasi-markets and sharper distinctions between purchaser and provider organisations.
- The 'In Search of Excellence' model focused on changing organisational culture, whether through a 'top-down' approach based on charismatic leadership or a 'bottom-up' approach emphasising organisational development concepts such as the 'learning organisation'.
- The 'Public Service Orientation' model included Osborne and Gaebler's (1992) 'reinvention' approach, exhorting managers to be more

entrepreneurial, results-oriented and mission-driven. Total quality management initiatives focused on citizens rather than customers, and proponents were critical of market-based solutions. (Ferlie *et al.*, 1996: 13–15).

These models fit comfortably into the general neo-liberal direction of public policy in the Anglo states in the 1980s and 1990s. Not every aspect of NPM was introduced in each state; rather the multiplicity of changes that can be identified as constituting NPM were introduced to meet differing demands and ideological agendas in the various states. The direction was the same, but the range of measures, and the intensity of implementation varied.

Modernisation – How New a Direction?

In the UK from 1997, the 'New Labour' government promoted a 'modernising' version of public management (Prime Minister and the Minister for the Cabinet Office, 1999; Cabinet Office, 2000). Retaining the Thatcherite concept of the enterprising and sceptical consumer-citizen, it proclaimed a new, supposedly non-ideological pragmatism, based on the use of either state or market mechanisms according to 'what works' in achieving national economic development. This 'third way' model reaffirmed the communal values famously repudiated by Thatcherism, whilst making citizenship and social inclusion conditional on individuals' contribution to the national goal of competitiveness in the global economy (Clarke *et al.*, 2000; Newman, 2000). How different was this model from what went before, and from the neo-liberal and neo-conservative changes promoted at the same time by the Howard government in Australia?

In 1998, while hosting a conference of European social democratic governments on economics and social justice, Blair offered a new 'third way;

> Without [centre-left] values, globalisation would feel simply intolerable to too many ordinary people, and would fail ... We need to train, to educate, to break open access to capital and labour markets, to promote competition in key markets, and to make sure our countries have excellent infrastructure ...
>
> (Blair, 1998)

Third way advocates, such as Hutton and Giddens (2000), wrote of a post-NPM 'network governance model', based on the European communitarian values with which Blair sought to align New Labour (for an analysis, see Rhodes, 2003). Similarly, Australians Steane and Carroll (2001) outlined hopes that the network governance model might be a 'post-NPM form', better able to deal with social complexity: the central state would play an influencing and coordinating, rather than a directing role. However, Andresani and Ferlie (2006: 424–6) strongly argue that both NPM and 'network governance' emanated from a similar neo-liberal position (libertarianism and utilitarianism). They claim that that the network governance model lacked both the European tradition of communal self-governance, and the Weberian tradition of probity and predictability that differentiated continental European public management reform from Anglophone models. These two authors are highly critical of the thinned-out, transactional concept of stakeholders – a concept which they see as the basis of third way and network governance ideals.

The New Labour model of NPM had a distinctive side to it. Clarke and others (2000: 12) identify certain divergences between New Labour and Conservative models of NPM. The New Labour model proposed:

- a more welcoming view of Europe and of globalisation;
- a discourse of modernisation and improvement;
- a pragmatism as between state and market, based on 'what works'; and
- a discourse of social inclusion and diversity (but not inequality).

On the other hand, they identify the following continuities of approach:

- Public spending control, and a limited conception of social reform;
- a low taxing, high choice government, freeing the enterprising consumer-citizen from state paternalism;
- national competitiveness;
- moral authoritarianism; and
- a heavy emphasis on public sector reform.

The New Labour approach involved the promotion of NPM as central to the modernisation agenda. The Blair government thus attempted to address some of the organisational problems associated with agency specialisation and fragmentation by developing a set of coordinating measures under the label of 'joined up government'. This emphasis generated a battery of instruments to ensure both accountability to and control by these governments. In like manner, Australian governments established performance measures across the range of public services, in an effort to co-ordinate fragmented organisational provisions. In both countries, there was a steadily increasing emphasis on target setting and auditing as the means to achieve coherence of policy (Pollitt and Bouckaert, 2004: 83–9; see also Pollitt and Talbot, 2004). It is thus hard to escape the conclusion, reached by Andresani and Ferlie (2006: 417), that NPM is 'here to stay'.

Managerialism and its Dimensions

While NPM programmes have been about desired futures, the detail has been more prosaic. The core aspects of NPM have included financial management reform, and the introduction of 'strategic' human resource management practices (rather than process-oriented personnel management), particularly performance measurement (Pollitt and Bouckaert, 2004: 66–96).

Financial management reform has centred on the restructuring and reorganisation of budgets, resulting from pressures to restrict public expenditure and to improve performance (Pollitt and Bouckaert, 2004: 67). Under NPM, financial management eventually became an end in itself. Managers increasingly took on such responsibilities, and thereby became *de facto* financial managers. Both Australia and the UK attempted to link performance information to budget allocations. While these goals are very difficult to achieve, because of the political and practical difficulties of securing reciprocal and accountable relations between measurement and allocation, nonetheless there has been a sustained attempt to secure this link (Pollitt, 2001). These measures were accompanied by the introduction of more complex and comprehensive accounting systems, in particular accrual accounting based on performance-related information (Pollitt *et al.*, 1999). The corollary of all of these initiatives has been closer management of the performance of state workers.

It has been a feature of the Anglo-American countries that financial reorganisation was associated with a devolution of many management functions to agencies, including personnel management (on Australia, see Halligan and Power (1993): 101–2). Much of this activity was shaped by a sequential set of legislation and related decrees:

> Australia: Amendment of the Public Service Act, 1983; Guidelines on Official Conduct of Commonwealth Public Servants, 1987, 1993, 1995; Guidelines on Appraisal of Performance of Senior Executive Service (SES), 1990; Public Service Act, 1999; Hilmer Report, *National Competition Policy*, 1993; Public Service Act 1999.
>
> UK: *Financial Management in Government Departments*, 1983; Progress in Financial Management in Government Departments, 1984; Civil Service (Management Functions) Act 1992; Civil Service Management Code, 1993; Cabinet Office, 1994; Cabinet Office, 1995.

A particular feature of NPM has been a preoccupation with senior public service personnel. In the debates about NPM implementation, there has this been a focus on the tensions, difficulties and prospects faced by senior executive staff (e.g. Pusey, 1991; Halligan, 1996: 86–7). Shifts in managerial responsibility were accompanied by a restructuring of externally based and generated monitoring, auditing and regulatory processes. In effect, a managerial cadre now defines senior layers of the public services in the Anglo-American countries, one that is increasingly mobile within these states as well as beyond. The assumption, in the United Kingdom, has been that the stereotyped civil servant, a tenured careerist and a generalist, is no longer up to the demands of a modernised and reformed public service. In Australia, the quest has been for generalist public sector managers, people whose loyalty is to those above them and to their peers at the same echelon in other agencies, and whose lack of specialist knowledge of the area they were managing prevented policy capture: 'content-free' management.

The ideological underpinnings of the NPM model involve a reaffirmation of the rights and prerogatives of managers. Advocates of the NPM reforms emphasise the similarities between managerial work in the public and private sectors, arguing that management skills are generic and transferable in an unproblematic way from the private to the public sector (Bryson, 1987: 270; Pollitt, 1993: 7–8; Pusey, 1991: 121; Sinclair, 1989: 382). This is a view of management techniques and practices as context free, value neutral and applicable regardless of the political objectives of governments (Bryson, 1987: 260; Gray and Jenkins, 1995: 86; Sinclair, 1989: 383).

The models for public managers were seen as self-evident. As Peter Shergold, a former Australian Public Service and Merit Protection Commissioner, stated:

> As public servants we need to walk the same fields and gaze the same blue skies that inspire innovation in the private sector. Central to that is the need to bring our employment arrangements more into line with the wider Australian community. Does anyone really believe that, protected by a monopoly status and inadequate scrutiny, we can defend an approach to management that we now know is at least twice as expensive as best practice?
>
> (Shergold, 1997: 33)

Shergold presented a view of traditional public sector employment arrangements as dated and costly; neither transparent nor open to competition. Managerialism emphasised flexibility in employment arrangements instead of tenure of appointment, and, as already noted, rewards and progression were based on quantifiable performance outcomes (Painter, 1997: 39). Proponents of managerialism also challenged the autonomy of professionals employed in the public sector, typically by underlining the 'failure' of traditional service providers.

While such views have driven policies in the Anglo-American states, it is also important to remember that governments in those countries also presided over a large number of low paid, often part-time and untenured civil and public service workers. Thus, it is case that managerialist views have often been framed in ways that did not address the material and experiential circumstances of civil and public service work.

Performance Management

Despite the appearance that public managers appeared to have discretionary authority, at least over operational matters, they have been subjected to an array of performance indicators, targets and monitoring arrangements (Hood *et al.*, 1999). Thus, managers have been limited in their capacities, particularly over resources, as well as becoming increasingly liable when things go wrong (Pollitt and Bouckaert, 2004: 147).

The stated aims of governments have been to secure a more skilled and less numerous workforce, able to operate in flexible and responsive ways: 'to do more with less'. Thus, there has been strong pressure on managers to control and monitor their staff, both through policy prescription and by performance measures. Complementing this reconstitution of senior public service staff, there has been a succession of experiments in restructuring the state labour process and refocusing job tasks. Concerted attention has been paid to the relationships between state workers and those who use or are dependent on state services, based on the notion of citizen 'empowerment' (e.g. Cabinet Office, 1991). Such measures were designed to reverse apparently declining trust in public goods and services, although the evidence did not always support this hope (Pollitt and Bouckaert, 2004: 131–4). So, not only were workforces subject to greater managerial demands, they were also enjoined to meet the requirements of those who rely on the state or who have dealings with state employees, as students, patients, or taxpayers. These twin demands defined the parameters of state work, often in contradictory and confusing ways (Pollitt, 2004: Chapter 4).

Some commentators have attempted to portray NPM reforms as a 'high commitment approach' to labour management. In a 'reformed' or 'modernised' public sector, 'commitment' was equated with the internalisation of managerial norms, particularly those relating to performance. For example, in 1998, the Australian Minister Assisting the Prime Minister for the Public Service described the role of HRM in aligning public sector workers to high performance work systems:

> Reform of public administration has been a key part of the government's micro-economic reform agenda ... Public sector organisations, through their strong performance culture ... are increasingly seeking to become high performance organisations ... People who work in high performance organisations ... feel a sense of ownership of changes occurring within their organisation, and are committed to the external success of their organisation. This sense of ownership, and commitment to success, leads to a motivated and innovative workforce.
>
> (Kemp, 1998)

The high performance NPM worker was to be flexible, skilled, responsive and highly motivated (for the United Kingdom, see Cabinet Office, 1994: 26). The so-called traditional civil service employee was said to have been cushioned from the pressures and the state labour process was said to have required recasting to secure a 'new' worker, one able to meet the challenges of the NPM programme. In both the United Kingdom and Australia, the use of performance indicators and performance measurement were central to the creation of the conditions for the 'new' state worker.

Under New Labour in the United Kingdom, public service reform was cast in the language of continuous improvement, based on best value projects, comprehensive performance assessments, and public service agreements. One commentator observed:

> No public sector employee has escaped the ever-extending reach of performance evaluation schemes. The pressure to meet targets or performance standards, whether hospital waiting lists, school exam results, crime clear-up rates or university research ratings – has introduced profound changes in public organisations. As PIs [Performance Indicators] have become increasingly linked to resource allocation and individual financial rewards, so organisational cultures and individual behaviours have been transformed.
>
> (Carter, 1998: 177)

Hodgson and others (2007: 358) describe the Best Value policy, introduced in 2000, as requiring improvement, based on 'a combination of economy, efficiency and effectiveness', together with quality, equity, and the involvement of service users. They argue that Best Value further 'strengthened' the performance management framework, through an elaborate apparatus of standards, targets and external audits. Public service agreements were accompanied by sanctions such as the threat of loss of resources, and were backed by interventions in cases of 'performance failure'. Yet, as Hodgson and colleagues note (2007: 357), improvement lay in the eyes of the stakeholder-customer, and was an elusive concept. Moreover, there was no decisive evidence about the relative effectiveness of various approaches to improvement, whether one-off or ongoing, and whether based on external regulation or intervention, market discipline, resource injection, managerial leadership, or internal reorganisation (Ibid. 374–8).

Likewise, in Australia, performance management measures were introduced in the 1980s, and strengthened under subsequent conservative coalition governments (McGuire, 2004). The Howard Coalition government viewed performance management as a central element of its agenda to bring public service employment arrangements more in line with its vision of private sector practice (Reith, 1996). This approach involved reducing administrative appeals and other forms of bureaucratic 'red tape' that were believed to be restricting the ability of public service managers to manage their human resources effectively. The Coalition government during the late 1990s and early 2000s adopted a confrontationist approach to public sector workers generally and to public sector unions specifically. Its conception of the state and state workers resembled those of the Thatcherite experiment, but Australian constitutional arrangements prevented a Thatcher-style sweeping away of public sector industrial relations processes. The government thus experimented with alternatives to the collective regulation of state sector employment. It emphasised individual employment agreements and non-union 'collective' agreements. While the Rudd Labor government has reintroduced collective bargaining with unions as the primary form of agency level regulation, one of its earliest actions on gaining office was to cut staff numbers as part of a broader efficiency drive, while also increasing state functions and thus the pressure on the public sector to respond effectively.

State Sector Workers and their Unions

The process of civil and public service 'reform' focused on the position and place of civil and public service workers. Complementing the emphasis on performance measures, accountability and the individuation of work relations, the collective regulation of state sector employment was transformed. However, this dimension of the depoliticisation process is seldom mentioned and is therefore less theorised. Our focus is on worker and union-organised responses to managerialism, NPM and depoliticisation agendas. We therefore conclude this chapter by providing an overview of ways of theorising such collective response.

Workers contested these reforms. A range of studies of worker responses to NPM identify the contested nature of managerial reforms, and suggest that worker resistance could not be stamped out by unitarist attempts to repress or bypass state sector unions. Ackroyd and others (2004) suggest that professional and para-professional workers resisted both managerial control and a productivist redefinition of the welfare state, by appealing to a traditional public service ethic of accountability and integrity and a professional ethic of vocation and altruism (Ackroyd *et al.*, 2004: 40–2). In Australia, similarly, managerialism has sparked state sector worker resistance, both individual and collective (see for example Junor *et al.*, 2009). But, it remains unclear how such resistance has been shaped and developed by state trade unions.

Unions face a difficult moment in their history. Many of the past political and economic certainties no longer apply. This situation has arisen, in part because of a range of structural factors, such as changes in the labour market during the 1980s and 1990s, involving deregulation, increasingly flexible patterns of employment and the recomposition and reorganisation of various employment sectors. The wider political shifts affecting these relations include political advocacy of neo-liberal ideologies and associated practices, the promotion of strategies to encourage competitiveness, and restrictions on direct economic intervention. At the same time, there has been a recomposition of working populations, in term of ethnicity, gender, migration and other factors.

State sector unions have developed in the context of standardised employment and industrial arrangements, largely characterised by national level pay bargaining in the United Kingdom and service-wide arrangements in Australia mediated through Public Service Boards and the compulsory conciliation and arbitration system. The more agency focus of public service reform and the reconstitution of managerial structures presented a challenge to unions in both countries. Public service reforms in the United Kingdom were a reflection of a wider exclusion of unions and a radical recasting of labour market regulation. In contrast, in Australia, it occurred initially within a context of the managed decentralisation of the industrial relations system that was predicated on unions co-operating in work reorganisation in exchange for wage increases. On the surface, the system in Australia was more benign for unions, whereas in the United Kingdom, unions were challenged and were put much more on the defensive in their relations with managers and successive governments. On closer examination the picture is, however, more complicated.

In the context of the profound restructuring of the social relations of service and public sector provision, the conditions and circumstances of union organisation and practice also shifted. Against the backdrop of leadership-focused forms of union organisation in the public sector, and given the specificity of the restructuring of social relations, there was, consequently the possibility of the emergence of different forms of unionism. However, it is also possible that the basis for a localised and active form of unionism could be denied, as union members and their leaders acceded to the apparent inevitability and dominance of public sector restructuring.

Faced with membership decline and economic restructuring, the uncertainty about prevailing patterns of representation and organisation, and changing patterns of work and employment, many unions began to review the way they organised and operated. Over the last few years, these difficulties, and union responses, have been discussed and examined extensively (e.g. Bronfenbrenner *et al.*, 1998; Kelly, 1998; Peetz, 1998; Nissen, 1999; Hyman, 2001; Turner *et al.*, 2001; Fairbrother and Yates, 2003b; Milkman and Voss, 2004; Fantasia and Voss, 2004; and Lopez, 2004). However, what is unclear is how unions might begin to address these uncertainties in an active manner and in the process identify some of the conditions for union survival and renewal (Voss and Sherman, 2003; Lopez, 2004).

One view is that employers have the option either to accommodate union concerns and interests via partnerships or to marginalise unions in this process of change (Turner, 2006). Unions are thus subject to the logic of participation, which may stimulate to develop innovative organising and representational strategies. This suggests a process of renewal that begins to break away from the more common emphasis on stability and path dependency (Thelen, 2001). What is absent in this account, however, is a consideration of time and the way unions adjust and adapt and challenge in ongoing ways. It may be that there is an overemphasis in much of the writing on union renewal on the 'here and now' and not the way in which processes of renewal are part of ongoing restructuring of class relations (Frege and Kelly, 2003; on class composition, see Carchedi, 1987).

Two sets of analyses are relevant here. The first set focuses on the conditions for union renewal, focusing on the preconditions for change (Fairbrother, 2000; Voss and Sherman, 2003). Thus, union renewal is seen as part of a process of addressing the forms and practices of internal organisation (Voss and

Sherman, 2000). Renewal applies to the ongoing way in which unions organise and operate as collective bodies in the established and contested workplace and settings in which unions operate. There are five key organisational aspects to the process of union renewal: recruitment and extension of the membership base; replenishment of new generations of activist members; building workplace- and community-relevant structures and activity; mutually supportive relations between layered levels of representation; and the combination of the local with the global.

The term 'renewal' is defined as an organised response to the challenges faced by unions. The key attribute is a form of unionism where processes of union mobilisation rest on participative, and often by implication more democratic, procedures and practices. However, one weakness in these accounts is that there is little reference to the bases and processes of campaigning. Simms and Wills (2004), with their idea of reciprocal community unionism, take an initial step in this direction. Further, it is also the case that the protagonists in these debates have not centre-staged questions relating to union democracy.

A complementary analysis focuses on union capacity (Lévesque and Murray, 2002). Here the primary focus is on 'power resources' and the way they are used, drawing attention to the shaping of union agenda and forms of solidarity (pp. 45–6). One way of extending these analyses is to draw attention to questions relating to union capacity. Here the focus is on the 'power resources' available to unions, covering the development and implementation of union agenda, internal solidarity, exemplified by forms of democracy within union organisations, and external solidarity, namely the 'embeddedness' of unions within their communities (Lévesque and Murray, 2002: 45–6; see also Simms and Wills, 2004). For unions, one difficulty is how to go beyond the assumption that leaders (at all levels) have the capacity to shape union objectives in the context of growing social, economic and political complexity, and recognise the centrality of democratic (participative/accountable) practice.

The task then is to explore not only the capacities of unions, but also the ways in which unions, often in difficult circumstances, make use of them. First, some unions have long sought to refocus and rebuild the ways they organise and operate in relation to members. These processes are always in a state of flux and uncertainty. Second, for unions to focus on the implications of economic restructuring and political innovation, it is critical that these developments are crystallised in the form of a threat or, as some have argued, 'crisis' (Voss and Sherman, 2003). To illustrate, as states redraw the boundaries between private and public ownership, opportunities are provided, paradoxically, for unions to recast themselves in seemingly unlikely circumstances. And third, unions should be in a position to draw on internal and, increasingly, external resources when dealing with the impact and outcomes of managerial decisions. The circumstances for union renewal that are implied are threefold. First, union leaderships must have tools at their disposal to create the opportunities for union membership involvement and participation in rebuilding the union (Lopez, 2004). Second, the conditions for union renewal involve a set of relations involving the character of local leadership and the identification of problems as a 'crisis' that may require external union support (Voss and Sherman, 2003). Third, unions must have both internal and external capacities available to meet the challenges of managerial actions (Lévesque and Murray, 2002).

The relationship between state restructuring and union responses is complex and contradictory, predicated on attempts by governments to reposition the state administration in the context of economic globalisation (Tickell and Peck, 2003); and the ways unions in the state sector organise and operate. In the first instance, governments have sought to redraw the boundaries of state activity (privatisation) and restructure state administration in more flexible and compliant ways (see Fairbrother *et al.*, 2002). One aim is to recast the terms and conditions of the employment of state workers and their work relations in ways that underwrite a more compliant and flexible workforce. While these processes can take a number of forms, the outcomes are broadly similar. State sector unions respond to these developments and undertake initiatives that are grounded both in the detail of state restructuring, but also in the way union organisation and mobilisation builds on past relationships and addresses current dilemmas. In this respect, trade unions may pursue different pathways to similar ends.

STATE POLICY, MANAGERIALISM AND UNIONS

This consideration of the literature highlights a number of relationships that shape the ways in which public sector managers and state workers operate in the evolving liberal democratic state. It would appear that the state sector (at least in the liberal democracies) has been reorganised and now operates differently from the past. A state labour process has been forged and shaped in terms of the manager-worker relation evident in other sectors of the economy. Our contention is that these relationships have been constructed as part of the process of depoliticisation evident in states that have embraced a neo-liberal approach to governance and economic relations. In the context of the state sector, governments have promoted versions of NPM, reflected in the texture of relations between state managers and workers, work organisation and activity, often promoted as creating a flexible and compliant state workforce.

At the same time, the prevailing form of collective organisation by state workers, has faced challenges created by these developments. In most liberal democracies state workers have long been unionised and these unions have often become an integral part of the developing welfare states of yesteryear. With the embrace of neo-liberal agenda and the reshaping of the state sector in line with this agenda, state unions have begun to review the way they organise and operate. While most attention has been given to unions outside the state sector, there is no logical reason why the same type of analysis cannot be applied to state sector unions. If this is so, then there is a complex set of relations emerging in the state sector, focused on the development of a distinct form of state managerialsim and involving government, state managers, state unions and citizens.

In an attempt to explore these complex relations we present a tentative outline of the types of relationships that may have developed in the state sector in liberal democratic states over the last thirty years (presented schematically in Figure 2.1). Our claim is that to explain the last thirty years of state 'reform' requires a central focus on state management, state workers and their labour organisations. These relationships are part of a dynamic development of the employment relationship and the processes of collective organisation in the state sector. Indeed it would appear that there is a direct link between employment policy and union form. In practice, this can be a rather messy process that is worked out by unions in complex ways. Nonetheless, the critical issue is the determinant relation between government policy and the parameters of restructuring the administrative functions of the modern state. The porosity of these relations, however, means that unions may be able to act in active ways, opening up possibilities of new ways of operating. The restructuring of state employment may create

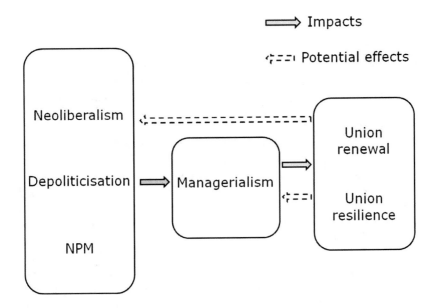

Figure 2.1 The Interrelationships between State Management and State Workers in Liberal States

conditions for a different model of state unionism. The problem, however, is to understand how and why this possibility is translated into a transformed model unionism, or whether it is merely a pragmatic, coping set of responses that may, over time, lead to a more comprehensive model of renewed unionism. Nevertheless, what may appear as a pragmatic response to particular challenges can aggregate into an emergent strategy that has consequences that go beyond the merely reactive.

CONCLUSION

The process of public service reform and change is complex and diverse. It is not straightforward to explain and characterise the main elements of these process. The neo-liberal project has a long pedigree, and has been articulated and elaborated in a range of forums. What is not clear from these accounts is how and in what directions the public services will and should be restructured and reformed. In addition, there is no single restructuring project. There are varied projects in place, with a range of implications for the public services. NPM reforms have been dominant in the Anglo-American states. To an important extent, the embrace of these types of reforms is a distinguishing feature of the last thirty years. Nonetheless, as many have noted, different states have had a varied engagement with these measures (e.g. Rhodes and Weller, 2003).

Developments in public sector management have been shaped by the national contexts in which they have occurred. One dimension of context is the constitutional arrangements that define the administrative structures of different states, federalism (decentralisation) in the case of Australia and a unitary state (centralisation) in the case of the United Kingdom. Such arrangements set limits on the scale and scope of reform policies and programmes. Moreover, the ethos of neutrality and non-partisanship within public and civil services provides a key reference point for the introduction and elaboration of new policies.

Nevertheless, underlying the specificity of particular arrangements, it is important to locate the ways in which governments in distinct contexts have pursued the same broad objectives. Under governments of different political complexion, the overall concerns appear to have been the same: namely how to recast the central administrative arrangements in each country, to achieve a closer alignment between service provision and the national economies. Operational relations have been redefined in terms of a managerial stratum and a managed workforce. In each case, the aim was to secure a more accountable and responsive, but more malleable and compliant state workforce.

Patterns of reorganisation played out differently in each state, depending on both the government in office and the overall structure of the state. Such reorganisation is partly to do with the distinctive constitutional, institutional and related arrangements that distinguish one state from another.

Nevertheless, it also has to do with the focus of these models, namely labour–management relations in the public sector. Public sector reform is shaped in a variety of ways. One neglected dimension involves state trade unions. It is one of the distinctive features of the public services is the long-standing and relatively high level of unionism. State restructuring has posed many and varied challenges to these unions. Often developing out of quiescent and compliant backgrounds, they have faced a daunting scale of change. Nonetheless, they can be key players in these processes, either defending existing conditions through mobilising their membership base or negotiating a 'new' settlement to meet the changing work exigencies.

In our comparative exploration of the changing administrative and managerial functions of the state, we seek to uncover the underlying processes, examining the dimensions of 'depoliticisation'. The first task is to present a more elaborated account of the history of public sector management change in each country.

3 Pathways to Change: The Restructuring of the Administrative State

The history of public administration in the United Kingdom and Australia is rooted in the colonial past. From these beginnings, each state moved beyond the colonial heritage to establish two parallel yet distinctive public administrations. Nonetheless, beginning in the 1970s a new round of debates about public service organisation and operation came to the fore. The rhetoric in each case was of public sector management 'reform' and 'modernisation', rationalised by the need to reposition the national economies more effectively in an increasingly globalised world (Fairbrother and O'Brien, 2000). Nonetheless, there were differences over time and place in the ways in which neo-liberal agendas were adopted and adapted (Peck, 2004; Larner, 2005). In this chapter we focus on the recomposition of state sector workforces, tracing out the varied approaches to this task in social democratic contexts (Australia: 1983–96 and 2007–10; United Kingdom: 1997–2009) and in neo-conservative ones (United Kingdom: 1979–97; Australia: 1996–2007). In both countries, this characterisation of governments became more difficult with the election of a Conservative-led minority government in the United Kingdom in 2010 and Labor led one in Australia in 2010.

From the 1980s onwards, restructuring and re-organisation of the state sector has occurred in many parts of the world. Despite the difficulty of capturing the complexity and diversity of change, both the United Kingdom and Australia belong to a group of nations in which changes to the state apparatus and machinery of government has commonly been dubbed 'New Public Management' (NPM). Whilst one element of NPM has been the embrace of key features from selected areas of private sector practice (Hood, 1995: 96), it has nevertheless seemed critically important to maintain the distinctive features of public administration, and practice. Thus, the Australian Public Service Act 1999 legislated a set of Australian Public Service Values (Australian Public Service Commission, 2003). Similarly in the United Kingdom, a Civil Service Code was promulgated in 1996 and revised in 2006 (United Kingdom Civil Service, 2009). Both promoted values such as integrity, honesty, objectivity and impartiality.

This chapter, thus, is about the process of institutional change, comparing Australia and the United Kingdom (on this type of comparative analysis, see

Barton and Turnbull, 2002: 2–5). Our focus is not on the way in which the forces of globalisation have shaped outcomes at a national or sectoral level (on this aspect, see Burawoy *et al.*, 2000). Rather, the chapter is a study of the various ways in which government pursuit of a set of policies, has shaped specific relationships between managerial agents and organised state labour.

Much of the academic literature and practitioner commentary on the impacts of NPM has focused on the re-organisation of administrative structures around a set of managerial relations. The managerial aspects of NPM have been well-documented and critiqued (e.g. Zifcak, 1994; Rees and Rodley, 1995; Clarke *et al.*, 2000). In this chapter, however, our focus goes beyond the reconstitution of managers at various levels, to changes to the labour process and employment relationship affecting a state sector proletariat. In this respect, we build on recent literature, where there has been a more concerted attempt to place changes in employment relations in the broader context of state restructuring (e.g. Carter *et al.*, 2002; O'Brien and O'Donnell, 2002). Our thesis is that underlying apparently 'depoliticised' labour-management relations, both the United Kingdom and Australian governments set tight parameters around the operational activity of state sector managers, in their dealings with their workforce.

The analysis of these processes of depoliticisation should be extended. Labour management is a feature of a modernised public sector, in which the state no longer has direct discretionary involvement with its employees, but is subject to a more distanced and disembodied form of regulation via financial control (Burnham, 1999a and 1999b; Pollitt, 1993). This argument, however, overlooks the dynamic aspect of change, between 'depoliticised' relationships and 'politicised' ones. As a governing strategy depoliticisation is intensely political. The other side of the process is one of repoliticisation, as governments seek to regulate state policy and practice via highly mediated policies of intervention and involvement in the organisation and operation of state and civil society (for details, see Rainnie and Fairbrother, 2005). The term 'politicisation' has greater currency in Australia. It refers specifically to the measures taken to make the public service more accountable to government, for example through limited term employment contracts for department heads. As with depoliticisation, this is another aspect of the management strategies pursued by governments (Curnow and Page, 1989; Halligan and Power, 1992).

In exploring the interplay of depoliticisation and politicisation, this chapter concentrates on the administrative and managerial functions of the state. To map complex patterns of recomposed relations between a new stratum of state managers and state employees, it presents a historically-informed account of the past thirty years in each country. We focus on three sets of developments:

- putting managers in place;
- fragmenting the state apparatus; and
- recentralising the operational activity of the state.

In this way, the distinctiveness of these reforms in each state is drawn out.

THE CONTEXT

The starting point for the comparison is the contextualisation of the two countries and their state administration. Against a colonial background, the British and Australian states are both long-standing liberal democracies, with established administrative structures for the provision and implementation of state policy over defence, social security, revenue collection and monitoring, and other related state functions. Both sets of administrative arrangements were historically characterised by 'bureaucratic' relations, indicated by formal hierarchy, tiered employment relations and rule-bound behaviour (e.g. on Australia see Caiden, 1967 and the United Kingdom, see Dunleavy, 1989). In both societies, the administrative services were seen as professional, trained and independent, providing necessary policy and administrative support to successive governments (Caiden, 1967: 27–43). The two states have a relatively close historical relationship, in part derived from the colonial past (Caiden, 1967: 28–9). The relationship remains close, with evidence that senior administrators and government officers in the two countries exchange knowledge over approaches to state restructuring (Rhodes, 2005; Rhodes and Weller, 2005; Zicfak, 1994).

The most obvious difference between Australia and the United Kingdom is that the former is a federal state, while the latter has been for a considerable part of its history a unitary state, albeit subject in the late 1990s to devolutionary processes in Scotland, Wales and in a rather more fraught manner in Northern Ireland. In Australia, services such as education, health and law and order are largely conducted by, and substantially funded, at state government level, with the federal government having a shared and increasing role in financing these services. In the education field, for instance, non-government school education and higher education are largely funded by the federal government, although the states remain formally responsible for education. In the United Kingdom, services are funded from Westminster, although delivered by a variety of local organisations such as councils, local education authorities and National Health Service Trusts and more recently devolved governments in Wales and Scotland. Nevertheless, both the British Westminster government and the Australian federal government are primarily responsible for state welfare services such as pensions, student assistance and employment benefits. Despite this centralisation, in both countries, recent measures to depoliticise service functions have meant that the agency model has been used for delivery of some services – Centrelink in Australia and Jobcentre Plus in the United Kingdom being prime examples of this phenomenon. Australia has gone one step further by contracting out employment services, although not the transfer of benefit entitlements, to the private and community sectors through the Jobs Network. For the most part, however, welfare services are delivered by employees classified as direct employees of the state – civil servants in the United Kingdom and federal public servants in Australia. It is these respective groups that are the focus of this chapter, whilst the book as a whole also look at state sector workers engaged in the assessment and collection of tax revenue.

A CHANGED PUBLIC SECTOR WORKFORCE

Over the last thirty years, the civil service in the United Kingdom and the Australian Public Service (APS) were both institutionally reorganised. Before proceeding to analyse these processes it is necessary to present an overview of the numerical changes that took place, thereby providing a statistical template of the changes during this period (see Figure 3.1).

In the United Kingdom, after more than a quarter-century of restructuring, the civil service was considerably reduced in size. The privatisation process had led to a reduction in the number of blue-collar workers (originally called 'industrials' in the United Kingdom). From a high point of 751,000 in 1976, the British civil service had dropped in numbers to 494,000 by 1996. The 'Competing for Quality' program, for example, meant the outsourcing of 34,800 posts lost to the private sector between 1992 and 1995 (HM Treasury, 1996: 8). Under the Labour governments first elected in 1987, staffing levels rose to 534,400 in 2004 before falling to 490,000 full-time equivalent in 2009 (Office for National Statistics, 2010). In Australia, the

Figure 3.1 Changes to Employee Numbers, UK Civil Service and Australian Public Service, 1976–2009

number of staff employed under the Public Service Act, after increasing from 155,000 to 180,000 between 1983 and 1989, was cut back between that year and 1991 to 161,000, largely as a result of the outsourcing of 12,600 jobs. Cuts continued under Labor governments until in 1997, there were 118,600 staff. Under the Coalition government, numbers declined to a low of 113,000 in 1999 and then rose steadily to 155,000 by 2007. Despite the incoming Labor government's announced job cuts, by June 2008 the 160,000 APS staff had returned to 1990 levels. (Task Force on Management Improvement, 1992; Verspaakdank, 2000; PSMPC/APSC, various years).

In both the United Kingdom and Australia, the restructuring of the 1980s meant a streamlining of 'non-industrial' classifications into a simple hierarchical structure. In the United Kingdom this consisted of Administrative Assistants (AA) and Administrative Officers (AO), then Executive Officers (EO), Higher Executive Officers (HEO), and the higher echelons of Senior and Principal Executives (HM Treasury, 1984). In Australia, the new office structures that emerged following the 1984 abolition of the divisional structure, were implemented through the restructuring of industrial awards (the wage and employment agreements characteristic of the Australian industrial relations system). They involved the creation of six generic Administrative Service Officer grades (ASO, later APS 1–6), three and later two middle management positions (Senior Officer or Executive Level) and three Senior Executive Service Bands. After 1994 there was a massive decline in the numbers of APS1 and 2 staff, to the extent that by 2008 they accounted for only 0.7 per cent and 3.5 per cent respectively of APS employment.

The hiving-off of blue-collar work increased the female density of the public sector workforce in both countries, and the application of Equal Employment Opportunity (EEO) merit principles to grade progression ensured slow increases over time in the proportion of women and other equity groups in higher grades. In the United Kingdom by 2008, in a workforce of whom 52 per cent were women, the proportion of female EOs was 55 per cent compared with 47 per cent in 1996 and 29 per cent in 1984. The proportion of women in managerial ranks rose from 7 per cent in 1984 and 22 per cent in 1996 to a point where in 2008, women filled 44 per cent of HEO and 33 per cent of senior civil service positions. By 2008, the proportion of civil servants from ethnic minority backgrounds (8.9 per cent) and with disabilities (7.1 per cent) remained low (Office for National Statistics, 2010; Government Statistics Service, 1996; HM Treasury, 1984). In Australia, similarly, by 2003 the APS was 53 per cent female and by 2008 the figure was 58 per cent. In 2008, women made up 45 per cent of the Executive Level (EL) middle manager grades and 37 per cent of the Senior Executive Service (SES). Indigenous workers (2.1 per cent) and people with disabilities (3.1 per cent) were still a small minority in 2008. Between 1991 and 2008, the proportion staff on non-ongoing appointments slowly declined from 12 per cent to 8 per cent (PSMPC/APSC, various years).

In both countries, the employment levels fluctuated, with declines in both countries, although more marked in the United Kingdom than in Australia (see Figure 3.1). This profile of employment was part of a process of reorganising grading structures in both countries, simplifying it and creating the conditions for a more comprehensive recomposition of managerial and related structures. It was accompanied by socio-demographic changes in civil and public service employment, with fewer blue-collar staff in employment and a higher percentage of women in civil and public service employment. These developments took place in the context of government promoted changes to the institutional organisation and arrangements in civil and public service employment in both countries. It is to this detail that we now turn.

BEFORE MANAGERIALISM

The origins of the civil service in the United Kingdom and the Australian public services date back to the pre-colonial period, when state administrations were established and developed. From beginnings characterised by coteries of court servants undertaking the equivalent of Treasury functions, collecting, recording and dispensing monies, the institutional basis of public administration were laid and refined (Hennessy, 1990: 17–18). Control shifted from the monarchical to the beginnings of parliamentary and government control over embryonic forms of state organisation and activity. During this long period of history, the form and ethics of a national civil service (and public service) were developed (Hennessy, 1990: 17–31).

One notable development occurred in the mid-nineteenth century, at the high point of the Victorian colonial period, with the Northcote-Trevelyan reforms of 1854. According to Hennessy (1990: 31), these reforms 'were the greatest single transformation the civil services has ever undergone, and, in their day, they were wholly beneficial'. In summary, the modern state bureaucracy was created as a 'politically neutral and permanent career civil service' (Hennessy, 1990: 5). It was transformed from an organisation characterised by patronage and influence into a structure and a mode of organisation that guaranteed rule by the emergent bourgeoisie.

The new bureaucratic principles of organisation, developed in the nineteenth century, reflected a concern amongst the emergent bourgeoisie, with the principles of impersonal rational organisation. The aim was to create a permanent and stable state workforce, recruited on the basis of merit and promoted on the grounds of ability and expertise. Northcote-Trevelyan (1854) recommended the introduction of competitive examinations to realise these principles of organisation. By 1870 such a system of competitive examinations had been introduced, complementing the formalised separation of the civil service from the government of the day. During the late nineteenth century, a succession of reports and enquiries laid the foundation for a civil service, characterised by universal grading structures, standardised rates of pay, and uniform conditions of employment (Playfair Commission, 1875–6; Ridley Commission, 1887–8). This model was exported to the colonies.

In the early twentieth century, a sequence of reforms further consolidated these arrangements in both the United Kingdom and Australia, which became a federal self-governing nation in 1901. For Britain, there was the MacDonnell Commission, 1912; Tomlin Commission, 1929, and especially the Fulton Report, 1968. In Australia by the late nineteenth century, most of the colonial governments that preceded today's states had established public services along Northcote-Trevelyan lines. Their practices were largely continued by the newly established Commonwealth (federal) government, with a Commonwealth Public Service Act being enacted in 1902. Initially a sole Public Service Commissioner acted as employer on behalf of the Commonwealth while retaining considerable autonomy in the recruitment, selection and promotion of federal public servants (Caiden, 1967: 2–3), Following a Royal Commission in 1918 into the federal public service, a comprehensive Public Service Act was passed in 1923, establishing a Public Service Board as the quasi–independent employment agency of the Commonwealth government. This framework remained largely in place until the 1980s (Caiden, 1965, 1967; Halligan and Power 1992: 77–8). The rationale for these arrangements was to make civil servants accountable to government, while permitting them to give 'fearless' advice to government without jeopardising their employment status.

A core focus of these measures was the creation of an administrative staff, formally appointed on the basis of merit. Nonetheless, class differences continued to prevail in the public service. In the case of Britain, senior civil servants were recruited predominantly from the educational elites of Oxford and Cambridge, while routine copyists or writers and other functionaries were recruited from a broader class base. By contrast, in Australia, most senior public servants arose from the ranks. It was only during the Second World War that graduates were employed in the federal public service. This trend accelerated in the post-war period. Since the 1980s there has been a feminisation of the Australian Public Service including in the most senior ranks. Criticism has been made in more recent times that senior officials in the key policy departments have tended to be drawn from a rather narrow neo-classical economic background (Pusey, 1991).

By the late nineteenth century in both countries, employment conditions had been standardised for all lower grade civil servants. This standardisation applied to salaries, of hours, of sick leave and holidays. It was followed by the introduction of more comprehensive and inclusive grading structures in the early twentieth century. Nevertheless, the civil and public services in each country were marked by social division and exclusivity until the 1970s. Moreover the bar on married women being permanent officers persisted until the mid-1970s. Thus, the civil service was a closed and seemingly immutable world for much of its modern history. It reflected a notion of rule where those from privileged backgrounds would maintain an influence over the way the state was organised and operated. It was not until the 1970s that these rigidities of movement between the grades or classes were eventually ended by the creation of a unified administration group, replacing the previously exclusive groupings of administrative, executive and clerical staffs.

In Australia graduate recruitment to the federal public service accelerated in the post-war period, particularly in the key policy departments such as the Treasury, the Prime Minister's Department and the Department of Foreign Affairs and Trade, although many of the middle ranking public servants in the service delivery agencies were usually non-graduates, at least at the point of recruitment. Following the contracting out and privatisation of many Commonwealth functions in the 1980s and 1990s the recruitment of base grade officers virtually ceased so that current recruitment to the Common-wealth is largely from graduate ranks. (*Task Force on Management Improvement*, 1992: 169–70). By 2006 some 52 per cent of all federal public servants were graduates (Public Service Commissioner, 2006).

Thus, these administrative bodies emerged out of particular backgrounds. The first noteworthy point is the survival until recent times of legacies of the colonial past, and the elements of continuity and transfer that char-acterised these arrangements in both countries. It is also important to note, however, the way in which these two administrative bodies diverged, parti-cularly in the post-colonial period. In part, the salience of class remained a critical dimension to recruitment in Britain and the United Kingdom more generally, whereas religious divisions marked the Australian experience, with some departments regarded as largely Catholic and others as largely Protestant in character. These divisions have been much less significant in the last thirty years. Nonetheless, the differences between the two countries were neither definitive nor enduring, and the two administrative services are marked by strong parallels in their organisation, focus and relations with governments.

THE BEGINNINGS OF 'ACCOUNTABLE MANAGEMENT'

Central government in the United Kingdom has been subject to a long history of re-organisation, marked in particular with the Fulton enquiry in the 1960s (Fulton Report, 1968) and its subsequent partial implementation. This resulted in a move toward centralised decision-making, complex mechanisms of control, simplified grading structures and a fragmentation of jobs toward either specialisation or deskilling. In some respects, this was the high point of the trends towards the centralisation of the civil service.

During the 1960s and 1970s, successive governments acted to consolidate and centralise the civil service structure. These reforms were based on the assumption that the current organisation and operation of state institutions created barriers to the ready implementation of government policies. The foundations for later reforms in both countries were laid in this early period, albeit more systematically in the UK than in Australia. From the late 1960s, the introduction of managerial techniques and procedures was seen as a necessary condition for a more effective civil service.

United Kingdom

In the United Kingdom, the concern with 'management' is not a new one. From the early 1960s culminating with the publication of the Report of the Fulton Committee (1968), the approach of civil service managers was identified as a major problem. The report stated that senior civil servants tended:

> to think of themselves as advisers on policy to people above them, rather than as managers of the administrative machinery below them.
>
> (Fulton Report, 1968, Vol. 1, para. 180)

Two important concepts came out of the report and the subsequent attempts to implement it. First, the principle of an 'accountable management', derived from General Motors and the USA was developed for the civil service. The key concepts in this were as follows:

• the measurement of achievement and performance in quantitative or financial terms;
• the measurement of performance in qualitative terms; and
• and management by objectives: a unit head agrees with superiors and subordinates on objectives, priorities and a timetable.

(Fulton Report, 1968)

These recommendations were a precursor of the types of proposals that were implemented more systematically and comprehensively in the 1980s. An embryonic form of agency organisation was introduced in this period. To a limited extent, departmental agencies came to be seen as a way of realising the principle of accountable management. Examples of the introduction of these forms of organisation included the Defence Procurement Executive created within the Ministry of Defence in 1971, with the function of providing defence equipment. In 1972 the Property Services Agency was set up within the Department of the Environment which had as part of its remit the maintenance of government buildings and the provision of equipment. Similarly, in 1972 the Employment Services Agency and the Training Services Agency were established, subsequently becoming part of the Manpower Services Commission (Drewry and Butcher, 1988).

The more developed form of departmental agencies, also recommended by Fulton, were based on the premise that 'hived off' activities could be separately established outside the civil service departments (Fulton Report, 1968, Vol. 1 para. 188–90 and Vol. 5(2) Proposals and Opinions, p. 507). Under this proposal, boards and corporations would be responsible for specific functions with powers delegated to them by the government. Examples of such agencies were the Civil Aviation Authority (1971), the Manpower Services Commission (1974), the Health and Safety Commission (1974) and the Advisory Conciliation and Arbitration Service (1970). Thus much of the content of later debates was laid down in an earlier period, particularly under the Conservative government (1970–4) but also under the Labour governments (1964–70 and 1974–9).

Complementing these institutional arrangements, distinctive management systems were implemented, most specifically the promotion of 'Management by Objectives' re-enforced by performance agreements between senior public servants and agency heads. Forty-four projects reported along these lines in 1974, although there was little evidence of any further development (Garrett, 1980: 135). As with the creation of agencies, the governments of this period experimented with some of the measures that acquired prominence in the 1980s.

Key to these reforms and increasingly emphasised during the 1970s was a concern with the introduction of managerial controls into areas of state employment in general, and the civil service in particular. This is evident in the steady introduction of forms of managerialism in local government during the 1970s (Cockburn, 1977). Initially these techniques were derived from understandings of the business and commercial worlds. It was assumed that managerial procedures and approaches could be grafted on to already established administrative structures. In public corporations such procedures have long been evident as these bodies have reorganised to operate in a commercial rather than a market context. From the 1960s, management structures were introduced into local government (Bains Report, 1972 and Cockburn, 1977).

Australia

In Australia, reforms during the 1970s focused on overcoming the perception that the public service operated as a quasi-autonomous instrument of governance. The problem was deemed to lie in a need to re-assert political control over the Australian Public Service. This need for control arose from the federal nature of the Australian state, with public administration organised and operating in six states and at a federal level, and no necessary correspondence between these domains.

Central to the reforms of the 1960s and 1970s was the re-casting of the semi-autonomous relationship between governments and senior public service staff. Historically there had been a strong disposition to place the responsibility for public administration, and in particular its organisation and operation, including employment relationships, in the hands of intermediate bodies, usually Public Service Boards (Caiden, 1965: 1–4; 1967). These boards generally played the role of employer of public service employees. The rationale for this arrangement was that public employees had a role in governance that was independent of changes in the political complexion of government (Caiden, 1967: 189). In the public service permanent employment was linked with the concept that public servants held an 'office' in a manner similar to statutory office holders. The concept of 'office' was the basis of security of tenure in public employment and the notion of a 'career' public service (McLeod, 1995).

Although ultimately subject to government, Public Service Boards became powerful instruments of governance, at both federal and state levels. One commentator noted that it was not 'an oversimplification' to say that the New South Wales 'Government does anything the Board tells it to' (*Sydney Morning Herald*, 14 January 1956). Indeed the New South Wales Public Service Board saw itself as an executive arm of government with considerable operational autonomy from the government of the day in the organisation of the provision of state services (New South Wales Public Service Board, 1954: 5). In a real sense the board provided continuity of governance in the state (Alaba, 1994: 50). This was also the case in other states and federally, although it is doubtful whether any of these bodies were quite as powerful as the New South Wales Public Service Board (Alaba, 1994: 42).

Two important reforms occurred during the brief term of the Whitlam Labor government (1972–5). They involved extending the concept of permanent employment in the Australian Public Service and recognising the industrial rights of public servants. In the mid-1970s the Royal Commission into Australian Government Administration argued for greater mainstreaming of employment arrangements as part of a general overhaul of the Australian Public Service (Royal Commission on Australian Government Administration 1976). However, the successor Fraser Coalition government (1974–83) initiated a major restructuring of federal government functions to meet its commitment to 'smaller government'. Hitherto, the principal source of labour flexibility within the APS had been use of 'temporary' public servants. These staff were used to deal with peaks and flows in labour demand; they were less useful for a major restructuring. The Fraser government introduced measures that made it easier to discipline and remove public servants: the Commonwealth Employees (Employment Provisions) Act 1977, the 'no work as directed – no pay' amendments to the Public Service Act (1978) and the Commonwealth Employees (Redeployment and Retirement) Act 1979 (Simms, 1987: 28–30). These measures were widely regarded as an attack on the concept of permanent employment in the public service, as well as on the industrial rights of public servants. Responses to them marked the beginning of the transformation of public service employee organisations from largely compliant staff associations to industrial unions prepared to use, albeit selectively, the full range of industrial tactics (Simms, 1987).

A third significant reform during the Whitlam period was to have a direct impact on the construction of employment relations in the Commonwealth sector. In 1974 the Whitlam Labor government established joint management-union consultative councils in federal departments. While these councils had no formal decision-making powers, they became a means whereby public service unions and their members could exercise some leverage on proposed management-initiated changes. They laid the foundation for subsequent experiments with industrial democracy in the public service workplace.

In the late 1970s, the relative autonomy of public employment authorities was called into question as governments began to wrestle with the emerging fiscal crisis of the state. The role and place of Public Service Boards were addressed by senior public servant Peter Wilenski when he conducted a review of the public service in New South Wales in the late 1970s (Wilenski, 1980). Wilenski argued that public administrative processes ought to be more directly responsive to ministerial direction. Wilenski not only advocated a change in the relations between politicians and the senior echelons of the public service, he also argued for greater involvement of public servants themselves in the workings of public service agencies (Wilenski, 1980). Both in New South Wales, and as the chair of the Commonwealth Public Service Board, Wilenski argued that the active recruitment, training and promotion of hitherto under-represented groups such as women, indigenous people and non-English speaking background people to and within the public service was not only a matter of social justice, but it was also 'good management' as it widened and deepened the pool of public sector managers (Wilenski, 1977: 179–245). The removal of the marriage bar from female federal public servants in the early 1970s and the increasing participation of women in higher education had a significant effect on the gender composition of the APS (Sawer, 1996).

Summary

The trajectories in each country during the 1960s and 1970s laid the foundation for different emphases in the 1980s. In the case of Britain there had already been experimentation with forms of managerial organisation in the civil service, complemented by the embryonic experiments with forms of agency-type organisation. This experiment had their roots in the Fulton enquiry (1968) and referred, in particular, to practices in Sweden. In contrast, the concern in Australia was to question the role and place of Public Service Boards in an already depoliticised relationship, and to replace them with more direct forms of political control. Complementing this focus, however, was the beginning of an analysis of the composition of the public service and the capacity of public service workers to influence and mould managerially initiated changes and policies.

PUTTING MANAGERS IN PLACE

The prime conditions for the transformation of core administrative arrangements were the introduction of managerialist practices. Whilst initially these were hesitant processes, they eventually amounted to an institutional re-organisation of the sector. The outcome was that the conditions for a restructured labour process and change in the dominant mode of control of labour in the sector were laid.

United Kingdom

The election of the first Thatcher government in 1979 provided a renewed impetus to restructure and reorganise the civil service along managerial lines. The government was committed to 'rolling back' the state and as part of this it was proposed that civil service posts be reduced. Between 1979 and 1991 there was a 24 per cent reduction of industrial and non-industrial civil service staff (full-time equivalent) (HM Treasury, 1991: 42).

Alongside staff reductions, the government undertook a major internal re-organisation of the civil service (for a full account, see Fairbrother, 1994, Chapter 2). One stated reason was 'to ensure value for money' (Drewry and Butcher, 1991: 201). Initially the main instrument for addressing cost effectiveness was the series of efficiency studies carried out under the auspices of Derek Rayner, via the so-called Rayner Unit (part of the Prime Minister's office). These studies looked at civil service activities and asked: 'What is it for?' 'What does it cost?' and 'What value does it add?' (Allen, 1981:10). Altogether 155 scrutiny exercises ('scrutinies') of departments were carried out between 1979 and 1983, with a number of multi-department studies. The effect of the scrutinies process was uneven but significant. In financial terms, however, the savings were quite limited. This should not be taken as indicating the ineffectiveness of such an exercise, because these scrutinies were an important element in the development of a managerial ethos. They were a landmark in the development of the view that what was required in the civil service was a major institutional re-organisation involving two elements: namely the need for control by ministers as elected representatives over their departments, and the creation, from a governance perspective, of an effective and efficient civil service.

The first step in the transformation of the civil service was the introduction of business-management techniques in order to both redefine and relocate the responsibilities of civil service management. A variety of programs was brought together in 1982 under the rubric of the Financial Management Initiative (FMI), developing a managerial form of organisation at a workplace level (Efficiency and Effectiveness in the Civil Service, 1982). During this period, management information systems and devolved forms or organisation, such as cost centres, became relatively widespread (Financial Management in Government Departments, 1983; Progress in Financial Management in Government Departments, 1984; Gray and Jenkins, 1985: 171–85). These initiatives were not welcomed throughout the civil service, however, and there was considerable debate about the direction of change at senior levels (Metcalfe and Richards, 1984; Drewry and Butcher, 1988: 204).

The FMI began with the publication of a White Paper in 1982 (Treasury and Civil Service Committee, 1982) and built upon reviews of financial management in a number of government departments. The policies associated with the FMI were put into effect throughout the civil service by a senior group consisting of officials from the Treasury and Management and Personnel Office, together with outside consultants. Central to the plans were the re-organisation of departments around cost centres and an increase in the delegated authority of line managers. Thus re-organisation had major implications for staff control and development. It meant devolution of management accountability and the redefinition of decision-making practice.

These developments were part of a process of restructuring that transformed the relations between state management and workers (for different accounts, see Drewry and Butcher 1991: 212; Gray and Jenkins, 1985: 171). The scrutinies, FMI and delegated budget procedures were the first step towards a comprehensive managerial civil service. They were limited 'reforms' aimed at managerial practice, particularly at the office level, and by implication, at the relations between managers and their staff. While staff at the office level had always been organised hierarchically, such organisation had been on a relatively rule-bound basis, with little discretion available to office 'managers'. Nonetheless, these 'reforms' did not yet involve the structural reorganisation of the civil service sufficient to allow the conception of a managerial civil service to be realised in full. Such a development, which was to come later, would require breaking the link between the civil service as an operational institution responsible for the direct provision of goods and services, and the civil service as a policy formulator and adviser of governments and as a contract manager for the privatised delivery of services.

During this period, the civil service in the United Kingdom was reconstituted via an extended process of institutional reorganisation that involved the beginnings of an extensive recomposition of work relations, creating a managerial stratum and associated state workforce. In the course of these developments, the Conservative governments of the time promoted the appearance of a more distanced and remote relationship with the civil service. The claim was that 'managers should manage'. A range of associated measures was implemented to reinforce this objective, annual reporting, business plans, cost centre reorganisation and the appointment of executive and management personnel. The appearance was that governments would coordinate and set objectives while the civil service provided services, creating the conditions for a set of depoliticised relationships.

Australia

While the primary restructuring of the United Kingdom civil service took place under a Conservative government, many similar changes in Australia were initiated by a Labor government, operating within a framework of a Laborist conception of social democracy, but with an accelerating movement in a neo-liberal direction. One of the most influential figures of the time was Peter Wilenski – a former adviser to the Whitlam government and former senior public servant – who endeavoured to articulate a social democratic model of the role of public bureaucracy.

In the late 1970s and early 1980s, Wilenski, then at Australia's leading business school, the Australian Graduate School of Management, articulated the view that a changed relationship between minister and senior public servants was central to a more explicitly social democratic model of public administration. This model emphasised responsiveness to government in place of the traditional quasi-independent role of the public service in overall governance. In his review of the New South Wales Public Service in the late 1970s, Wilenski argued that ministers should expect that the relative autonomy of administration should not hinder the exercise of overall policy responsibility by government. While Public Service Boards should retain general responsibility for personnel policies and industrial relations processes, more immediate activities should be undertaken by individual agencies (Wilenski, 1977, 1982). This would enable them to respond more flexibly to ministerial direction. In the early 1980s, during the period of the Wran Labor government from 1976 until 1988, the coordinating role of the Public Service Board was diminished in favour of the Premier's department. This centralisation of control occurred rather than 'empowerment' of individual agencies, although they assumed many of the personnel and other powers hitherto exercised by the Public Service Board. Indeed the Premier's department under the leadership of Gerry Gleeson (himself a former member of the Public Service Board) arguably became the strongest central agency in the nation (Halligan and Power, 1992: 122; Alaba, 1994: 22). By the mid-1990s all of the states had abandoned the Public Service Board model of central coordination. At the Commonwealth level department secretaries (no 'longer permanent heads') assumed responsibility for the classification of public servants, while the Department of Finance was given the role of advising on staff establishments. These changes laid the groundwork for the abolition of the federal Public Service Board in 1987 as part of a restructuring of ministerial departments under coordinating Cabinet ministers. The board's remaining functions were distributed among the Departments of Finance and Industrial Relations and the (new) Public Service Commission that took on responsibilities for monitoring developments within the Australian Public Service as well as training for the elite Senior Executive Service, though it has never played the dominant role that had been exercised by the Public Service Board. This recentralisation of control over managers and employees was a necessary basis for any subsequent devolution, and illustrates our argument that repoliticisation was the necessary precursor to the distancing strategies that we refer to as 'depoliticisation' (Chapter 2).

The initial impetus of the Federal Labor government after 1983 was thus to re-assert political control over the public service that had, hitherto, operated as a quasi-autonomous instrument of governance. One of the first actions of the new Labor government in 1983 was to institute a major re-casting of the Commonwealth Public Service Act 1922. A White Paper on the Australian Public Service stated that 'the balance of power and influence has tipped too far in favour of permanent rather than elected office holders' (Commonwealth Public Service Board, 1983). It announced the adoption of changes that emphasised Cabinet priority-setting, ministerial control and input from partisan, as well as public service sources (Halligan and Power, 1992). In the period 1984–7 the focus shifted towards more explicitly managerialist modes of public service. Managerialism was principally manifested through extensive reforms of budgetary processes that would enable 'ministers to involve themselves in the allocation of resources' (Commonwealth Public Service Board, 1983–4: 4).

The assertion of more explicit political control over the public service was symbolised by the redesignation of permanent heads of government agencies as 'secretaries' and the creation of a Senior Executive Service (SES) designed to provide a more mobile, but less secure, stratum of senior public servants. These initiatives simultaneously asserted political control while creating a management elite more consciously separated from the rest of the public service, through the institution of a Senior Executive Service replacing the strata of elite first and Second Division Officers of the previous regime (O'Brien, 1999, 2006). These developments were characterised at the time as a 'politicisation' of the public service which would lead, it was argued, to less fearless advice being given to government. At the other end of the scale the boundaries between the two lowest divisions, the third (officers) and fourth (employees) were dissolved in the late 1980s. These initiatives were reinforced by a number of financial measures that were designed to increase managerial accountability of the public sector, with an emphasis on a shift from compliance to a greater degree of performance control (FMIP Diagnostic Study, 1984: 37). To this end a comprehensive Financial Management Improvement Program was implemented that included the standard managerialist line-up: corporate and program management, program budgeting, corporate planning and performance evaluation together with a general Management Improvement Program (Halligan *et al.*, 1996).

For the broad mass of public servants this meant significant changes at the workplace. The emphasis became more focused on accountability to ministerial direction via the department secretary, on the efficient and effective management of both financial and staff resources, and a greater emphasis on outputs rather than input. Managers were expected to manage these resources with less inputs ('doing more with less') that was enforced by the requirement that each agency would deliver an efficiency dividend to government each year – a practice that has continued until today. The greater responsibilities of agency management were accompanied by greater accountability to the centre, exercised less by an overarching central agency, but through financial control directly exercised by government with the central agencies acting more directly as an agent of government in matters of staff establishments and industrial relations. In the name of 'responsiveness' to government, public servants were now subject to multiple account-abilities. The catch-cry of 'let the managers manage' was realised within a framework of increased accountability to government and its key regulatory agencies. This catch-cry perfectly captures the politicised basis of depoliticisation – the appearance of arm's-length governance, based on an autonomised and automatically-responsive machinery of government.

Summary

The 1980s and early 1990s was the moment in both countries when managerial structures were put in place in each core administrative service. These institutional rearrangements laid the foundation for a depoliticised set of relations between governments and the civil and public services in each country. Core administrative arrangements were transformed in each country via the introduction of managerialist structures and practices. These changes were driven in an explicit way by conservative governments in the United Kingdom, publicly seeking to introduce managerial practices supposedly modelled on the private corporate sector. In the case of Australia a more nuanced and complicated process took place, where the Labor governments were both concerned to introduce the foundation for a managerial reorganisation of the APS as well as securing a measure of more explicit control over the APS, and particularly the senior staff. In both cases, a depoliticised set of relations were promoted, developing the appearance (but not the reality) that governments were no longer directly responsible and accountable for the operational activity of the civil service in the United Kingdom and the APS in Australia.

FRAGMENTING THE STATE APPARATUS

The introduction of relatively limited sets of managerial practices, with the beginnings of a redefinition of work relations, set the scene for the transformation of the sector. This shift was accomplished through the introduction of decentralised forms of administration. The task was both to develop a system of devolved operational responsibility and to ensure continued centralised control over the financial bases of the administration. It was a way of ensuring that governments remained in control while enabling a degree of managerial autonomy, the crux of a process of depoliticisation.

United Kingdom

In the United Kingdom, the decisive step in consolidating the managerial bases of the civil service came with the publication and subsequent implementation of the Ibbs Report in 1988 (Jenkins *et al.*, 1988). The Ibbs

Report, popularly titled 'The Next Steps', addressed the question of the conditions for the creation of a managerial civil service, proposing the establishment of a series of semi-autonomous management units, known as agencies, working to the parent departments (Jenkins *et al.*, 1988). These agencies were organised as enterprises with their own management strata, recruitment policies and terms and conditions of employment. After a hesitant start, agencies were established throughout the 1990s. By April 1999, there were 107 agencies covering more than 356,520 permanent employees, 77 per cent of the civil service workforce (Government Statistical Services, 2000).

Building on earlier reforms, around FMI, the government began, under the late 1980s Next Steps initiative, to promote institutional decentralisation in the form of agencies and Executive Offices (reorganised as if they were agencies but formally remaining part of the department). These agencies had quasi-contractual relationships with the core or parent department. However, governments via the Treasury in particular, retained control over the exercise of these delegated powers, while laying the foundation for a more operationally devolved civil service. To this extent, these developments indicate an attempt to lay the foundation for a more directly controlled and increasingly fragmented workforce. The Treasury clearly retained an interest in remaining a decisive influence over the terms and conditions of employment within agencies as well as the resource allocation to any particular agency.

Thus, there has been devolution of lines of authority in the civil service, reflected institutionally by the establishment of agencies, and implemented in practice through managerial restructuring and reorganisation within these agencies. Nonetheless, the government retained the threads of control via public expenditure decisions. As the Next Steps Project Manager observed:

> I think that public expenditure will remain the essential piece of 'glue'.
> There is one banker; and we remain with that.
>
> (cited in Dowding, 1995: 73)

This is a form of control which circumscribes the degree to which agencies can act independently of central government requirements and concerns.

One control mechanism was the use of Framework Agreements. Of note, the Framework Agreements set the output and performance targets to be met by the relevant agency. The determination of these targets, however, was not the sole responsibility of the agencies; rather, the Treasury was actively involved in drawing up these output and performance measures for agencies. Thus, the independence of the agencies remained circumscribed. In this way, the Treasury remained a major determinant in the restructuring of the civil service, reinforcing its traditional role of influencing the structural reorganisation of the civil service, without undermining its authority within the civil service (Pliatzky, 1989). At the same time, agency managements gained considerably more autonomy over the organisation and operation of their activities, including financial disbursement. This framework of loose-tight central determination was the operational basis through which the structural form of depoliticisation called '*agencification*' was managed.

The initiation of the Next Steps programme began a process whereby department ministers would no longer be responsible for the operational activity of sections of their department; instead ministerial responsibility was more narrowly circumscribed as being concerned with policy formulation and development. As the Fraser Report, set up to review the progress of the Next Steps initiative, indicated:

> The aim of Next Steps is to improve quality and efficiency of government services through better management. It is for ministers, with the help of their department, to set policy objectives for their agencies. Chief Executives must propose, for the minister's approval, targets which reflect, within the resources allocated, the required performance of the Agency and its progress in meeting those objectives.
>
> (Efficiency Unit, 1991: 3)

The difficulty has been where to draw this demarcation of responsibility in practice.

The agency structure is thus a management model characterised by target-setting and a hierarchical management structure, based on a chief executive and associated managerial arrangements. By analogy with the private sector, the department was seen as the parent company whilst agencies became its wholly owned subsidiaries. This was a management model where the Chief Executive and senior staff constituted the 'Board of Management', that had both the incentive and authority to manage the agency.

This structure, and the governance arrangements through which it operated, was a response to concerns with the working patterns evident in the civil service, such those expressed in the Mueller Report (1987). Drawing on models of employment practice in the private sector, this report argued that the inflexibility of traditional civil service employment practice, was reflected in the limited application of varied modes of employment, such as part-time, period contracts and home working. Devolution of staffing budgets to agencies was seen as providing an incentive for managers to consider these varied forms of employment much more actively. Increasingly, it was acknowledged that if more flexible forms of employment were to be introduced into the civil service then this was most likely to occur at a local level, with local managers pursuing the most financially expedient policies at an office level.

Agencies and Executive Offices utilised flexible forms of employment and working procedures. They experimented with different forms of employment contract, particularly the use of temporary contracts (Potter, 1987). Multi-task forms of working were also introduced, often utilising computerised technologies and procedures. Performance-related pay schemes, market testing, team working, human resource management techniques and performance monitoring, both at the agency and individual level, were among the managerialist initiatives introduced.

A further development took place under the Labour government elected in 1997 with its continued extension of the Next Steps programme: namely the break-up of uniform wage levels and standard terms and conditions of employment. With the establishment of agencies and agency-type arrangements, there was a marked organisational fragmentation of the civil service via the establishment of quasi-markets. Pay determination arrangements, for example, were recast via agencies and non-departmental public bodies (NDPB) rather than the civil service as a whole (see White and Hatchett, 2001). These changes indicated the end of uniform and standardised conditions of civil sector work and employment.

Each civil service department and agency (and NDPB) negotiated pay with trade unions for its own staff, below the level of senior civil service (3,800 civil servants out of a total 500,000). Significantly, these arrangements were characterised by a complex inter-relationship between a centrally-constructed set of arrangements and delegated managerial decisions about the detailed arrangements. Departments, agencies and NDPBs were obliged to set the terms and conditions of employment for their staff within the framework set by the centrally-decided civil service Management Code. Accompanying these arrangements there was a near-universal application of individual performance pay. The outcome was a form of centralised negotiations, by department, agency and NDPB, where the terms and conditions of these areas of employment were set.

Thus, decisive steps have been taken to reconstruct the civil service in line with a model of a more flexibly-based civil service labour process. Local managers had considerably more autonomy but also greater accountability than in the past. Procedures were introduced to encourage these managers to look for ways of utilising their resources in more cost effective ways. In these respects, this marks the development of a more managerialist civil service. At the same time, however, the government via the Treasury, and departments, retained control over finance and overall objectives of each devolved area of the civil service. Increasingly these mechanisms of control acquired an opaqueness, in the form of performance measurement and audit.

Australia

The restructuring of the Australian federal administration did not follow the agency model of the United Kingdom. The major services delivered by the Commonwealth such as pensions, student assistance and employment services were delivered by a range of departments, such as Social Security. In 1993, the Keating Labor government (1991–6) began the process of outsourcing employment services to a Jobs Network that consisted of both for-profit and not-for-profit organisations that bid for contracts to carry out job seeking and assistance services, while the determination of benefit eligibility remained with the Department of Social Security. In 1996, the succeeding Coalition conservative government brought most welfare services under the control of single agency – Centrelink. This agency had a board drawn from government departments and the private sector, with a Chief Executive Officer responsible to both the board and the relevant minister. This minister was initially from the Department of Social Security and subsequently Health and Community Services and more recently the Minister for Finance. Centrelink also received funding from government departments such as the Department of Employment and Workplace Relations and Health and Community Services to deliver welfare-related services hitherto delivered by Departments of Social Security (Vardon, 1999: 178). Indeed the first Chief Executive of Centrelink described it as 'a unique model of public administration in human services in the world' (Vardon, 1999: 178). Nevertheless, the Centrelink model was the exception rather than the template for the federal public service.

To appreciate the novelty of the Centrelink developments, however, and the way reforms elsewhere were mainstreamed, it is necessary to go back in time and note that the initial the restructuring of the APS took on a quasi-social democratic flavour. In 1984 the Public Service Reform Act required agencies to develop Industrial Democracy Plans. While the public service unions were supportive of these developments, they insisted, successfully, that they remain the single channel of formal communication between employees and departmental managements (Dickenson, 1986). On the management side there was growing concern that unions were using industrial democracy processes as an additional means for the pursuit of industrial objectives, rather than a mechanism for the facilitation of a new style of participative management (Public Service Board, 1987: 15). Unions for their part suggested that some managers were seeking to isolate industrial democracy processes from the mainstream of decision-making in agencies (Keir, 1987). Although some departments such as the Tax Office and the Department of Social Security used industrial democracy processes to introduce major restructuring programs, by the late 1980s government enthusiasm for industrial democracy had waned. Both business organisations and unions were also cautious about the applicability of industrial democracy in the private sector (O'Brien, 2006). Indeed a joint statement by the Australian Chamber of Commerce and Industry and the Australian Council of Trade Unions agreed on little more than generalities (Confederation of Australian Industry – Australian Council of Trade Unions, 1988). The lack of progress outside a few Commonwealth Departments led the government to give the issue low priority. This was symbolised by the fact the Green Paper on Industrial Democracy issued by the Commonwealth in 1986 (Department of Employment and Industrial Relations, 1986) was never succeeded by a White Paper.

It was, the industrial relations system itself, however, that became the site of significant changes to the regulation of public sector labour in the

Commonwealth sector, rather than the further extension of industrial democracy processes. The industrial relations arena was well understood by all parties. It was not characterised by the contradictions and uncertainties of industrial democracy. The subsequent changes to the structure of the Australian Public Service employment arrangements were largely achieved by a combination of government fiat and negotiation through the industrial relations system (O'Brien 1999, 2006).

In 1994 a Labor government-appointed committee recommended a major revision of the Public Service Act. Its key recommendation was to abolish the concept of 'office' (McLeod, 1995). Tenure of office, derived from the Weberian notion of the ethical bureaucrat as occupying a role of trust, impersonally and impartially upholding due process (Du Gay, 2008). Protection from political pressure was seen as requiring that APS officers could be removed from their posts only via some procedural difficulty, unless the office itself was abolished. The McLeod Committee further proposed that APS personnel should be seen as employees, and that the industrial regulation of their employment should be along the same lines as those of private sector workers (McLeod, 1995). Before these changes to the Public Service Act could be implemented, however, the government changed in 1996. In fact, federal public servants had already entered the industrial relations mainstream, and indeed both the Keating and subsequent Howard governments used industrial bargaining with their own workforces as an exemplar for their economy-wide industrial relations agenda (O'Brien, 2006). The Public Service [(Act)] was finally passed, weakening employment security, and making the maintenance of public service values a matter of managerial responsibility.

Summary

During the 1990s and into the 2000s, governments in both countries took the changes proposed for their core administrative sectors and ensured that the institutional reconfiguration initiated in an earlier decade was completed. In effect, this formalised the relationships between governments and these sectors; functions were provided through various forms of 'agencification'. Nevertheless, this formalisation secured the appearance of separation, both sets of governments retained and indeed consolidated their controls over the new set of arrangements.

In the case of the United Kingdom, the process was relatively straightforward. Here governments promoted the establishment of agencies and related forms of organisation. These bodies consolidated the trends towards managerialism within the civil service. State managers acquired a degree of autonomy over operational and related matters which allowed them to tailor wages and terms and conditions of employment over time. The outcome was a managerialist civil service.

Australia followed a distinctive trajectory. The first stage of the reorganisation involved experiments with industrial democracy, promoting a degree of managerial autonomy and responsibility but within the benign climate often associated with such practices. However, utilising a combination of government fiat and industrial relations negotiation, successive governments embarked on a process of promoting change in the APS via these more traditional avenues.

BEYOND THE FRAGMENTS

The two broad programmes of reform – the introduction of managerial practices and relations, and the partial fragmentation of the administrative services in each country – had broadly been completed by the mid-1990s. Governments in both countries began to look to the mechanisms and ways of ensuring administrative compliance, on the one hand, and malleability of administrative structures, including labour markets, on the other.

The change of government in each country – in Australia, from Labor to Coalition in 1996 and in Britain from Conservative to Labour in 1997 – makes it possible to trace the pursuit of similar policies in distinctive ways. In the case of Australia, the Coalition government exercised tight and increasing control over the public service labour market; in Britain primary reliance was placed on performance management and audited budgetary control. Nonetheless, in both countries the broad trend was to re-assert central control over a managerial state, albeit within a framework of devolved responsibility.

United Kingdom

While restructuring initiatives were taken in the United Kingdom by Conservative governments during the 1980s and first half of the 1990s, the restructuring of the civil service intensified with the election of the so-called New Labour party in 1997. There was further privatisation of civil service operations, and the Next Steps project continued, but of even more significance was the elaboration of the Modernising Government Program (Prime Minister and the Minister for the Cabinet Office, 1999). The program outlined a form of public service management that rested on an adaptation of private sector business practices ('What business are we in?'). These reforms involved competition for senior civil service management positions, the introduction of more comprehensive performance management and performance-related pay systems, and a re-examination of business planning systems in the main departments (Cabinet Office, 2000). The result was an attempt to graft on to the civil service a process of governance that encompassed a form of public administration cast as being more responsive, both to citizen-'customers', also to 'business' itself, a further development of earlier debates and policies in relation to the citizen increasingly seen as the customer. This twin focus guides the continued construction of the managerial state under New Labour.

There was recognition by the New Labour government that the reforms of the Conservative period had been positive, even if cast in a framework that was hostile to the public sector. Thus the White Paper on modernising government stated:

> Public service has for too long been neglected, undervalued and denigrated. It has suffered from a perception that the private sector was always best and the public sector was always inefficient. The government rejects these prejudices. But their legacy remains.
>
> Despite that, public services have responded. The reforms of the last two decades in the civil service, for example, have done much to develop a more managerial culture. The quality of management has improved, there is a better focus on developing people to deliver improved performance and there is greater professionalism.
>
> (Prime Minister and the Minister for the Cabinet Office,
> 1999; Chapter 6, Sections 4 and 5)

For Prime Minister Blair:

> Modernising government is a vital part of our programme of renewal for Britain. The old arguments about government are now outdated – big government against small government, interventionism against laissez-faire. The new issues are the right issues: modernising government, better government, getting government right.
>
> (Prime Minister and Minister for the Cabinet Office,
> 1999; Foreword)

It was noted that ten years later, this 'what works' approach was still being described as 'new' by Democratic US President Obama in his inauguration speech:

> What the cynics fail to understand is that the ground has shifted beneath them, that the stale political arguments that have consumed us for so long no longer apply. The question we ask today is not whether our government is too big or too small, but whether it works.
>
> (President of the United States, 2009)

Labour governments have pursued a strongly interventionist (politicised) programme of public service reform, to 'direct and monitor performance' (Bach, 2002: 326). These governments remain committed to the managerial changes initiated under Conservative governments, and to principles of labour management based on individual accountability for system outcomes, performance-related pay and pay delegation. Nonetheless, there has been some refinement of these processes. In the UK, the incoming Blair government commissioned three reports to address various aspects of the working of these arrangements: the Wilson Report, (1999); the Bichard Report (1999);

and the Makinson Report (2000). These reports recommended reviews of the performance management systems in place (Wilson, 1999), increased use of incentives and improved performance management (Bichard Report), and the separation of performance from base pay as well as altered funding arrangements (Makinson, 2000; see also Bach, 2002: 335). Central to these policies was a strengthening of the link between performance management systems and individual or team-based pay arrangements (Bach, 2002: 334). It was notable, however, that for the civil service, unlike other areas of the public services, the Labour government maintained a policy of pay determination that is delegated, albeit centralised (within each administrative area).

In 2003, the Labour government, building on earlier investigations, commissioned an enquiry into the operation and composition of the civil service. This, in part, heralded a return to the efficiency scrutiny of the 1980s, but in the context that the government was also prepared to intervene directly in the construction and operation of the civil service (Bach, 2002). The aim was to shift the balance between 'front line' and 'back office' activities, as if one set of activities did not depend on the other (Gershon Report, 2004: 3). A second report recommended the move of 20,000 jobs out of London with a concomitant loss of 7,000 jobs (Lyons Report, 2007). The approach can best be characterised as a form of guided democracy. What the public was perceived to want was transferred into a policy that bore directly on the organisation and operation of the civil service, as if civil service workers were objects rather than subjects. Not surprisingly the unions responded to this report in a generally antagonistic way, since the cost in terms of jobs was of the order of 84,150 posts plus extensive relocation, with further job reductions of 20,000 foreshadowed in the devolved administrations by 2008 (*Hansard*, 12 July 2004, Column 1130).

In the early part of the twenty-first century the government recognised that wholesale privatisation of public services was not popular and thus advocated the notion of public value: a pragmatic 'what works' philosophy, presented as largely neutral about whether many services were provided by private, public or third sector. Public value discourses were popularised by writers such Mark Moore (1995) in the US, whose oft-cited parable of the librarian and the latch-key children encouraged public sector workers at all levels to use entrepreneurial imagination in finding new ways to meet community needs. Philosophy was presented as largely neutral about whether many services were provided by private, public or third sector the discourse of public value, as articulated by UK think tanks such as the Demos Foundation and Will Hutton's Work Foundation (Horner *et al.*, 2006). This discourse was based on arguments that choice and market mechanisms constituted citizens as passive consumers. Instead, public managers had the obligation, less to meet centrally-imposed targets, than to respect citizens' democratic rights to what the public valued most. It advocated forms of measurement based on sustained engagement with stakeholders, a renewed focus on ensuring the political legitimacy and operationally feasibility of projects, and on creating maximum value from taxation through cost containment. Rather than imitating private sector organisations, government agencies were enjoined to work in partnership with them and with the 'third sector' in responding to community demands. Performance improvement now took on a moral dimension, with rewards and sanctions based on public shaming: for example 'failing' schools and hospitals were to be restructured by partners from the business community (du Gay, 2000; Fergusson, 2000; Tomlinson, 2001).

Such reforms are indicative of the guided administrative approach pursued by UK Labour governments, building upon the platform laid by the Conservative administrations between 1979 and 1997. While there are clearly differences in emphasis between the two types of government, for the trade unions the outcome has been broadly the same: a fragmented but guided administration and governments committed to job reduction by *diktat*.

Australia

The newly elected 1996 conservative Coalition government attempted radically to recast the Public Service Act, using the McLeod Committee's recommendations as the basis of the changes. The Senate, which was not controlled by the government, rejected the changes in 1997, although modified legislation was passed in 1999. This new legislation stripped away much of the procedural regulation that had characterised the Act hitherto, particularly in relation to the work of public servants, and relied more on the notion of a code of public service ethics rather than close regulation of public service work. In the meantime, however, the government relied on the new agreement-making provisions under the Workplace Relations Act 1996 to as prime instrument of 'cultural change' within the APS (O'Brien and O'Donnell, 2001).

The minister responsible for the Australian Public Service, David Kemp, said that public servants' work would be characterised by high performance that would be

- customer focused;
- have clear directions and strong, committed leadership;
- exhibit and promote a strong strategic vision;
- continually benchmarking and improving their performance;
- values-based, rather than rules-based; and
- see themselves as public sector enterprises, judged by results, operating in a competitive environment.

To this end there would be a radical new regime of workplace relations within the APS whose features would include:

- variation in pay outcomes among agencies;
- terms and conditions designed to reflect the particular needs of individual workplaces;

- the replacement of automatic increments by productivity and performance linked salary progression;
- the negotiation of more flexible hours of work and working arrangements which will enable significantly improved and more readily accessible service to clients;
- the broadbanding and flattening of the public service job hierarchies;
- very significant simplification of leave provisions;
- the removal of specific penalty provisions for working overtime, or at higher duties; and
- removal of the restrictions on the numbers and hours of employment of permanent part-time employment.(Kemp, 1998)

Thus, the re-casting of the Public Service Act and the new regime of workplace relations were seen as integrally related in the quest to mould a new 'high performance' public service. Indeed Public Service and Merit Protection Commissioner Peter Shergold, a Labor appointee who survived the purge of department secretaries that followed the election of the new government, became an enthusiastic advocate of the slimmed down public service model run along private business lines, arguing

> a need to remove central control that is premised on the false assumption that the APS is a single labour market in which every decision is driven by the relentless pursuit of uniformity. We need to free ourselves from the red tape that binds management decisions in layers of prescription. We need to wind back the cumbersome mechanisms of bureaucratic control.
>
> (Shergold, 1997)

The 'public' identity of the APS should be maintained, he argued, through adherence to public service ethics. Moreover he attempted to put some of the government's preferred employment structures in place via a collective agreement with his own staff in the Public Service and Merit Protection Commission, with somewhat mixed success (Bennett and Shergold, 1998; Shergold, 2000; O'Brien and O'Donnell, 1999).

Agency-level agreement making under the new *Workplace Relations Act 1996* was the prime arena for the articulation of the 'new public management' arrangements in the APS. Indeed the Chief Executive of Centrelink saw the devolved agreement-making arrangements as an ideal opportunity to 'buy' a 'new organisation', although she was aware that the government was concerned about the shape of the agreement in the largest and most unionised of the government agencies (interview with Chief Executive, Centrelink, 22 October, 2002). The 1999 code of 'public service values' largely replaced direct supervision by the Public Service and Merit Commission, although direct financial control was maintained by the Department of Finance. The detailed regulation of public servants' behaviour that had characterised the rule of the former all powerful Public Service Board was replaced by a set of ethical standards that amounted to form a 'light touch' regulation administered by a Public Service Commission whose powers were minimal compared to its Public Service Board predecessor (Weeks, 2007: 26–7).

The current Labor government has made no changes to these arrangements, although unlike its predecessor it did not remove any departmental secretaries from office when it came to power. In September 2009, however, the government established an Advisory Group under the leadership of the Secretary of the Prime Minister's Department to advise the government on public service reform and how the APS might promote a 'values driven culture that retains public trust' (Department of Prime Minister and Cabinet 2009a). A discussion paper was issued and the group reported in 2010 (Department of Prime Minister and Cabinet 2009b; Advisory Group on Reform of Australian Government Administration, 2010). The Moran Report advocated streamlining enterprise bargaining and creating a more unified APS. It supported efforts to promote common APS-wide terms and conditions of employment and the retention of some role for agency-level agreements (Advisory Group on the Reform of Australian Government Administration, 2010: 55). Further, The Finance Department and Public Service Commission has acquired a renewed significance following the report.

Summary

In this final period, both sets of governments, for very different reasons and rationales, committed themselves to strongly interventionist programmes of public service reform. For state workers the outcomes were surprisingly similar in that they faced established managements defining civil and public service employee relations in particular ways, involving performance management systems, bonus-based pay systems, varied pay levels and terms and conditions of employment and the individuation of employee relations. In addition, governments were increasingly likely to reconstruct work practices, for example in the United Kingdom with the emphasis on 'front line' rather than back office jobs. In Australia, the objective was to introduce and graft on to the APS private business practices. Once again governments were concerned with appearance rather than the substance of service delivery.

Nonetheless there were significant differences of emphasis between the two states The Labour government of the United Kingdom increasingly emphasised forms of public private partnership and public value criteria in the assessment of service delivery. At the same time governments promoted increasing degrees of performance measurement and the related audit practices that have become a mark of neo-liberal employment relations. In Australia, there was a move to redefine workplace relations within the APS and thus to mainstream public service employee relations within the broad ambit of the Australian industrial relations system. Nevertheless, in both countries the broad texture of employment practices and features bore a striking resemblance to each other.

CONCLUSION

The restructuring of the state apparatus in both the United Kingdom and Australia took place over a thirty year period. It occurred against a background where the state played an active and interventionist role in the economy and in the provision of services. There were differences of emphasis between the two countries, and state forms were structured in terms of long-standing constitutional settlements in each country, along federal lines in Australia and broadly centralised ones in the United Kingdom. Administrative structures in both countries bore a legacy of layered and rule-based, governance, and were subject to direct political control. In the context of the economic and political problems in the 1970s, both states took steps to remould their administrative structures, and recast social relations within their civil services in managerialist and depoliticised or arm's-length ways.

From the late 1970s, governments sought to impose a sharper financial regime on state services and to further the imposition of direct managerial control of work processes, even whilst appearing to distance themselves from rules embedded in automatic technical processes and from agencies with varying degrees of 'autonomy'. Successive governments transformed areas of state activity from a bureaucratised set of institutions, characterised by standardised conditions of work and employment, becoming in the process a more managerially-oriented and selectively commercialised employer.

These developments in both countries involved trends towards increasingly centralised control of the civil and public services, via devolved accountability. The assumption was that public servants should be able to work with any government in an efficient and responsive way. In order to realise this objective there had long been a concern by different governments with the structure and organisation of the civil and public services. Until the end of the 1980s, there was a pattern of increasing centralisation and the reaffirmation of formal Treasury control over the civil and public services. The form this took was that of introducing managerial practices, giving senior staff more managerial responsibility. As part of these arrangements, it was assumed that ministers, as the parliamentary heads of departments should be directly accountable for the conduct of department business. Towards the end of the 1980s, this link became less clear, as the civil service was reorganised, as a semi-detached wing of government. With the institutional fragmentation of the civil and public service in both countries, relative autonomy of agency management, at least for operational and budgetary implementation, was affirmed.

Not only did governments seek to dismantle and then rearrange state structures, but long-standing terms and conditions of employment were challenged. These changes were introduced from the top down, and were often cast in the rhetoric of responsiveness to citizen needs, albeit with relatively little evidence to support these claims (e.g. Osborne and Gaebler, 1992). In both countries, governments sought to redefine public service management *qua* management and secure a more compliant and flexibly organised workforce.

While the trajectories and rhetoric were different in each country, the intent and the destination were the same. The catchphrases in Australia were 'improvement' and 'reform' rather than 'modernisation' (Task Force on Management Improvement, 1992). Nevertheless in both countries political control and managerial accountability were intensified. The initiatives taken during the 1980s particularly in relation to financial control and managerialist modes of control bore considerable resemblance to changes to the Australian Public Service under a Labor government. The more far reaching changes in employment relations in Australia had to wait for the election of a right-leaning government, following a path wrought by its Conservative counterpart in the United Kingdom. In both countries, governments distanced themselves from political responsibility while ensuring that its policies were enforced more effectively. The 'depoliticisation' was of operation; the 'politicisation' was one of increased control. The *architecture* of control had changed but not its source. It was a 'loose-tight' framework permitting tolerable convergence in implementation, but insisting on required policy 'outcomes' from its managerial agents. In both countries, the direction was part of more general neo-liberal project, albeit somewhat differently constructed in each state. These transformations had significant effects on labour relations and trade unionism: the focus of the next chapter.

4   Trade Unions Addressing Change

The changes to the administrative state in the United Kingdom and Australia provided the occasion for unions to reorganise and reposition themselves. Within the emerging state structures, employees were often at the frontline of these changes. While employees can react to, accommodate, and sometimes resist, changes in less organised ways, discontent is often channelled through unions, particularly in the public sector. Over the last thirty years, unions in the state sector have reorganised and refocused the ways they organise and operate to address the developments of the last thirty years.

Civil service unions in the United Kingdom and the federal public service in Australia recast themselves with a workplace focus to their activities. It is also the case, however, that the Australian union is now more centralised than it has ever been in the past. These somewhat paradoxical processes are analysed in relation to the reorganisation and restructuring of the two states over the last thirty years. The conclusion that emerges from this account is that the processes of union renewal and revitalisation involve a complex and apparently contradictory set of relationships between union members and their leaderships. Whilst the recomposition of managerial hierarchies and government promotion of managerialism redefined the context of unionism, the major unions confronted these developments through a complex and uneven process of re-focusing union organisation and representation. This entailed the promotion of more active unions that sought to encourage member activism, while at the same time centralising resources to address a more decentralised bargaining environment.

The chapter is organised as follows. The first section begins with an overview of the two industrial relations systems that characterise each country. This is followed by a brief history of the United Kingdom civil service unions, tracing the institutional reorganisation of the last twenty-five years. A similar account is then provided of the developments among the public service unions in Australia. These themes are brought together in the third section with a comparative evaluation of civil and public service trade unionism and of the industrial relations systems in each country. In the fourth section a brief conclusion to this history is provided.

TRADE UNIONISM AND INDUSTRIAL RELATIONS IN TWO COUNTRIES

The way in which industrial relations evolved in each country was marked by the particularities of their history and politics. In the case of the United Kingdom, this history was grounded in the clashes, compromises and settlements between an emergent working class and a powerful ruling class. Australia, by contrast, developed out of a colonial past, but in ways that reflected the political arrangements that had begun to develop in the colonies that had come together in federation in 1901. In both cases, the 1980s and 1990s were decades when these arrangements came under challenge from government.

United Kingdom

The distinctiveness of the development of United Kingdom unions is based on two features. First, the state has played a relatively non-interventionist role in the regulation of industrial relations for most of the twentieth century. Second, the focus of union activity, outside the state sector and parts of the private service sector, such as manufacturing, was on the workplace. The role of the state was predicated on an assumption that trade unions should seek to pursue their lawful industrial goals via collective bargaining, without direct state intervention. Broadly, and particularly in the engineering sector, unions negotiated with managements at a local level.

The origins of this form of social regulation lay in the nineteenth century, which saw labour laws developed on the assumption that, while worker organisation was a potential threat to the stability of the employment relations, such organisation was best contained rather than suppressed. The outcome was a sequence of legislation that provided for immunity from prosecution in the event of industrial action. The state became the guarantor of the rule of law, providing a legal framework defining the relationships between employers and unions (Kahn-Freund, 1972). The philosophy was that industrial relations was organised by a process of voluntary regulation of employment, involving both employers and workers. A voluntarist approach to industrial relations can be defined as one where there was limited state intervention in the process of regulating relations between unions and employers. The role of the state was confined to the maintenance of law, rather than to legal prescription about processes, with limited involvement of the judiciary in employment regulation. Employers were not obliged to bargain with unions and collective agreements were not legally enforceable. The emphasis on the absence of the state from the process of industrial relations can however be overstated (McIlroy, 1995: 67–8). There was not a positive right to strike, rather there was a limited immunity for strikers from legal redress; employers were not obliged to bargain with unions and collective agreements were not legally enforceable.

One of the key features of the unionism that developed under this approach was the shop steward. The steward was the work group representative who embodied the union at the workplace, speaking on behalf of members and negotiating work rules with local management. The key area for this type of representation was in the engineering industry, where it emerged out of disputes in the late nineteenth century. Nonetheless, until the 1960s, this was a relatively unusual and restricted form of organisation in the economy as a whole. It was in this period that the steward form of organisation was extended, beyond craft workers and into the large factories in manufacturing. The result in many unions, particularly in larger workplaces, was that the steward form of organisation acquired a degree of independence from official union hierarchies and where national union leaderships began to develop ways of incorporating these representatives formally into union structures.

A key dimension of the voluntarist tradition was the inability of governments to address the emerging structural problems of the United Kingdom economy after the Second World War. The difficulties faced by governments had their roots in the long-term decline of the economy, which saw a shift from a major exporting economy in the early 1950s to a net importer of manufactured goods by the mid-1980s. This was an economy characterised by low rates of growth, rising unit labour costs and low productivity. In order to deal with recurring economic crises, a succession of governments embraced corporatist type policies. Shortly after the Second World War, attempts were made to regulate the wage bargaining system via incomes policies (Clegg, 1979). While in part such policies rested on the compliance of union leaders in limiting union demands for wage increases, the political accommodation required, particularly from the unions, was often too costly, both economically and socially.

Before the 1970s, bargaining arrangements in the civil service were based on a set of national joint committees, defined by function, and organised hierarchically, in an arrangement known as the Whitley system. Under this arrangement, trade unions participated as the staff side in a series of joint committees. One feature of the system was the emergence of tensions about to pay comparability, particularly between public and private sector employment, as well as stark differentials within the civil service. To address these problems, the Priestley Commission recommended a system of civil service pay determination based on 'fair comparisons' with salary levels in comparable sectors, on the basis of investigations conducted by the civil service's own Pay Research Unit (Priestley Report, 1955). In turn, these arrangements came under strain as government ministers sought to minimise the costs that comparability studies often implied, thus frustrating expectations and underwriting the discontent felt by this highly-unionised workforce (Fry, 1974).

The highpoint of these accommodative type policies came in the 1970s with the initiation of the 'Social Contract' from 1975 to 1979. This programme was an agreement between the Labour government and the Trades Union Congress (TUC), formalising the long-standing partnership between the Labour Party and the trade union confederation (Flanders, 1970). Briefly this 'quasi-contractual exchange' was a political accommodation where 'wage moderation was exchanged for tax concessions and other benefits in the field of labour legislation' (Edwards and Elger, 1999: 7). This was very much an alliance between a number of national union leaders and the Labour government, and in this respect was a corporatist settlement in a very partial sense in contrast to Western Europe where employers were often parties to corporatist arrangements. It was part of an attempt by key labour leaders to lay the foundation for social legislation and wage restraint. It was also partial in another sense, in that the burden of wage restraint was borne by the public sector and in 1978/79 a number of public sector unions became involved in strikes (along with some private sector unions) as part of the 'winter of discontent'.

For the public sector unions this period was an important coming of age. Most of these unions had a history of quiescence and compliance with government policy. Historically, they had turned to negotiation and bargaining, often within the framework of consensual arrangements that had been established for a number of decades. In the 1970s, these arrangements were found wanting and the public sector unions began to turn to more active forms of representation to pursue their interests (Fairbrother, 1989). The result was a challenge to government policy and a questioning of the broad direction of a Labour government's economic programme. It was the beginning of a shift in the locus and focus of union relations with the Labour Party that came to fruition in the 1980s.

With the election of a Conservative government in 1979 there was a rejection of the politics of accommodation. The government was committed to an emerging neo-liberal agenda of economic management and pursued a policy of legislative intervention that ended the voluntarist tradition of British industrial relations in significant ways. The 1980s and 1990s was a period where legislative changes had a noticeable impact on the incidence and conduct of industrial action. This legislation included the Trade Union Act 1984, Employment Act 1988, Employment Act 1990 and the Trade Union Reform and Employment Rights Act 1993 requiring unions to hold ballots before conducting industrial action, placing restrictions on unofficial action, and giving notice of industrial action. More generally, the import of the legislation during this period was that unions found themselves in relationships that were legislatively restricted.

This legislation was introduced incrementally, in large part as a reaction against the corporatist compromise between the state and unions in the 1970s. Conservative governments aimed to reverse the seeming success that many union leaders had achieved in prosecuting their aims and objectives. This neo-liberal agenda of deregulation was buttressed by legislation that defined unions as a problem (McIlroy, 1995: 245–50; Dickens and Hall,

1995). Increasingly, the focus of the legislation was on the replacement of collective bargaining with the individual contract of employment. In this world, there was a very limited formal role for trade unions. The policies attempted to lay the conditions for the marginalisation of union organisation and action. The approach taken was to create the legal conditions for the encouragement of a climate whereby managements would be empowered to marginalise trade unions, narrowing their legitimate concerns and restricting union members' capacity to act collectively.

The election of a 'New' Labour government in 1997 did not modify these arrangements, although the adversarial relationship between government and union movement was replaced by a policy of interest group representation. From the mid-1980s onwards there was a distancing in the previously close relationship between the Labour Party and the trade union movement. This relationship had formerly entailed the formal involvement of affiliated trade unions in the policy formation, administration and finance of the Labour Party. While there had always been tensions in this relationship, it had been a relatively close and effective partnership between the two wings of Labour (Flanders, 1970). During the 1970s this relationship came under strain. However, it was not until the 1980s that moderate elements within the trade union movement became willing to accept the 'new realism' of a looser relationship, as the cost they had to pay for a more 'electable' (New) Labour Party. This reassessment was accompanied by the beginnings of a party acceptance of the broad contours of Conservative economic policy and industrial relations programme, although not explicitly stated at that stage. In the lead-up to the 1997 election the party indicated that it would not reverse the labour legislation of the 1980s. It also took the first steps to formally distance itself from affiliated unions, by reducing the voting powers of the unions at the Labour Party's annual conference, and related measures.

With the election of the Labour government in 1997, trade unions, including the TUC, faced a contradictory situation. The passage of the Fairness at Work legislation (Employment Relations Act, 1999) and the introduction of a Statutory Minimum Wage gave some comfort to trade unions, which had long campaigned for such legislation. These measures represented the partial achievement of union aspirations relating to worker and trade union rights, although the detail was much less than had been hoped for prior to the election. At the same time, the Labour government made it clear that the trade union movement, including the TUC, would not have privileged access to the government and that the old notion of labour movement partnership no longer applied (McIlroy, 1995: 299–304, 410–11).

Even so, unions increasingly looked to legislation and state regulation more generally, as a solution to the problems they faced in representing the interests of their members. Such a strategy assumes that governments will be responsive to these requests. The problem for British unions is that the traditional ally of the trade unions, the Labour Party, has distanced itself from the unions and seems unlikely to reverse this stance, at least in the short to medium term. Where the Labour government has taken steps to implement legislation in support of union rights, union recognition, minimum wage, and the acceptance of EU directives, this has usually been in terms of providing specific rights at a minimal level. It has not been in terms of the broad range of concerns facing union members, irrespective of government in office (for a comprehensive overview, see Daniels and McIlroy, 2009).

Australia

For observers outside Australia and New Zealand, the industrial relations systems of these countries, until relatively recently, seemed quite unlike those of most other advanced industrial countries. A system of compulsory conciliation and arbitration was used in various parts of the world for specific groups of employees, usually in the public sector, who were denied the right to bargain collectively. No where else outside Australia and New Zealand did the system cover such a high proportion of employees. By the early part of the twenty-first century, New Zealand had abandoned the system altogether and in the Australian federal jurisdiction there were only remnants left, although some of the Australian states still have functioning conciliation and arbitration systems. The Coalition government sought to transfer most state-regulated employees to a national system in 2005, a decision not fundamentally challenged by the Labor government on its election in 2007 (Rudd and Gillard, 2007; Williams, 2007).

Australian exceptionalism can be explained as follows. In the run up to the formation of the Australian Commonwealth in 1901, there had been considerable disagreement about the extent to which the Commonwealth should exercise industrial relations powers. At the final federation convention the colonial delegates decided that the industrial relations powers of the Commonwealth should be confined to the right to establish conciliation and arbitration machinery for the prevention and settlement of industrial disputes 'beyond the borders of one state'. This formulation was reflected in section 51 of the constitution which set out the powers to be exercised by the Commonwealth.

While the precise meaning of these words in the federal constitution was the subject of considerable deliberation by the High Court, particularly in relation to the meaning of interstate dispute and the nature of an industrial dispute, over time the Commonwealth's role in industrial relations expanded. Nevertheless, the Commonwealth was still largely confined to establishing machinery, rather than legislating directly for employees other than its own employees and those in the federal territories. Sitting alongside the Commonwealth system were strong conciliation and arbitration systems in the states of New South Wales, South Australia, Queensland and Western Australia. The other two states – Victoria and Tasmania – had systems of wages boards whose powers were much more limited than those of the systems in the other states and the Commonwealth. Only in the 1980s did Victoria and Tasmania set up fully fledged conciliation and arbitration systems.

Compulsory conciliation and arbitration in Australia worked on the basis that disputes between unions and employers were usually resolved through conciliation, whereby an industrial tribunal would seek to encourage the parties to agree on a resolution. If the matter could not be resolved then the commission would arbitrate the dispute, sometimes against the express wishes of the parties. The resolution often resulted in the commission making an award that could set wage rates for particular categories of workers. Over time, however, awards became very comprehensive documents setting out in considerable detail the wage rates attached to particular employee classifications. Outside the purview of the commissions sat the phenomenon of over-award bargaining, where unions and employers would agree to wage rates higher than those set by the award. Over-award bargaining often involved the use of industrial action which was strictly unlawful and parties, usually unions, faced the prospect of fines if they took unlawful industrial action. Thus the system in Australia became one of collective bargaining within an arbitral framework (Niland, 1978). The advantage for unions was that the system afforded monopoly representation rights for specified categories of employees; although it has also been argued that this was also a source of weakness for unions (Howard, 1977).

While the conciliation and arbitration system was not favoured by many employers and some unions, until the 1980s there was a rough consensus among peak union bodies, employer organisations and governments that the system was satisfactory. Nevertheless, many adjustments were made to it throughout the twentieth century. The last major public enquiry into the federal system was held in 1983–5 under the chairmanship of Professor Keith Hancock, a leading labour market economist (Hancock, 1985). Very few of the submissions made to that enquiry opposed the maintenance of the system overall, although many called for significant changes. The enquiry found that the 'weight of history' was so strong that it would not be practicable to abolish the system and replace it with another. When the Hancock enquiry reported in 1985, criticism was mooted but in the following years various organisations began a systematic assault on conciliation and arbitration. These organisations included the Business Council of Australia, the Chief Executives of the Australia's largest 100 companies, and an influential New Right 'ginger' group called the HR Nicholls Society that ran conferences with titles like *Arbitration in Contempt*. By the early 1990s the federal opposition parties had formulated an industrial policy calling for the downgrading of the role of 'third parties' (unions and industrial relations commissions) and the facilitation of direct 'bargaining' between employees and employers at the enterprise level (Liberal and National Parties, 1992).

At the same time, elements within the union movement became disaffected with the role of the commission in preventing bargaining outside its control. This disquiet had come about as a consequence of the role of federal

Industrial Relations Commission in maintaining the wage determination system within the neo–corporatist framework established by the Labor government (1983–96) and the Australian Council of Trade Unions (ACTU), involving the so-called Accord agreements about wage rates and related matters. While the commission was not bound to follow the recommendations of these agreements, it generally did so and insisted that once a decision had been made the parties (especially unions) could make no further claims. This meant that the system of over-award bargaining had been effectively suspended, with additional claims being restricted after 1987 to localised productivity trade-offs. By 1991, the leadership of the ACTU began to argue for an extension of the system of enterprise or workplace productivity bargaining to supplement the National Wage Case decisions of the commission. Such a proposition was supported by most employer organisations and the federal government. After initial rejection of the proposal, the commission acceded to the wishes of the main parties and instituted a system of workplace bargaining albeit under the control of the commission. Its right to certify or reject agreements that it deemed to be of overall disadvantage to employees was enshrined in the 1993 legislation whereby the Labor government established an industrial relations system that gave primacy to decentralised bargaining. By 1993, agreements were a part of the lexicon and practice of industrial relations. In its 1993 legislation the Labor government opened a small door to the making of agreements between employees and employers without the necessary involvement of unions. To do this the government used another power in the constitution: a power permitting it to regulate the affairs of corporations.

When the conservative Coalition parties were elected to government in 1996, they made extensive use of the corporations' power to establish a regime of agreement-making between employees and employers, rather than between unions and employers. In addition, the Workplace Relations Act 1996 permitted the making of agreements between individual employees and employers in the form of individual contracts called Australian Workplace Agreements (AWAs). Although awards were retained, they were restricted to a minimal set of employment entitlements, with, agreements between employers and employees or unions becoming the principal form of regulation for workers with any bargaining power. Although agreements had a specific nominal duration, they remained in force until varied by the parties. In legislation subsequently passed in 2005 this provision was further weakened by permitting employers to revert to the relevant award when the agreement's nominal date of expiry was reached. During the bargaining period when new agreements were being negotiated, the parties were permitted to take industrial action in support of their objectives, but any such action outside that period remained unlawful. The 2005 legislation, however, limited the capacity of unions to take industrial action by the requirement that complicated balloting procedures had to be undertaken before action was taken. Many but not all of these provisions were maintained by the incoming Labor government although AWAs were abolished and collective bargaining was promoted as the preferred form of agreement-making (Fair Work Act 2009)

Thus in the course of thirteen years the federal industrial relations system has gone from one relying primarily on the making of awards between unions and employers, to a system where awards are marginal and there are now a number of agreement models that can be utilised by the parties. Unions and industrial tribunals formerly played a central role in the compulsory conciliation and arbitration system. Under the Coalition government, the Industrial Relations Commission was largely reduced to a conciliation role, while unions faced a range of restrictions on their activities. Even the commission's traditional role in setting minimum wages passed to another body, the Fair Pay Commission, a panel of economic and social policy experts whose brief was to have regard to the impact of wage movements on inflation and unemployment – a role that assumed the neoliberal doctrine of the market-clearing wage and the non-inflation rate of unemployment. The Rudd Labor government was elected to office in November 2007 on a tide of discontent over the impacts of de-collectivising employment relations. It legislated to phase in a new system to be fully operational by January 2010, phasing out AWAs, deregulating collective bargaining, and modernising awards. The last-named task was the final role of the Industrial Relations Commission, before its incorporation into a new body entitled Fair Work Australia from July 2009 (Fair Work Act 2009). While the Rudd government dispensed with the distinction between agreements with employees and those with unions and favoured collective bargaining, it did not give collective bargaining exclusivity as a means of reaching agreements between employees and employers.

TRADE UNIONISM IN THE CIVIL AND PUBLIC SERVICES

Civil and public service unionism has a long history in both the United Kingdom and Australia. A number of the early public sector unions were functionally-based, representing grades and/or departments. Over time, these unions, often forms of staff association, merged to create the main public sector unions in each country, the Community and Public Sector Union (CPSU) in Australia and the Public and Commercial Services Union (PCS) in the United Kingdom. From the first part of the twentieth century, each state tacitly encouraged unionism in this sector and the result was an accommodative unionism. It was only in the 1970s that some unions began to assert themselves and develop more aggressive capacities in relation to the government of the day.

A Brief History of Civil Service Unionism in the United Kingdom

The marketisation of central and local state administrations has had a diverse impact. Marketisation had considerable implications for labour representation and collective state worker activity. Significant changes were evident within the civil service labour process, with the explicit definition of a 'frontier of control' between a 'new' stratum of managers and a more proletarianised workforce, comprising both the manual workforce and the lower stratum of the non-managerial, non-manual workforce. In this respect, the 'frontier of control' was made more explicit. With private capital accumulation running into increasing difficulty, developing trade union militancy and a shift in government ideology, governments since 1979 sought to impose a sharper financial regime on state services and re-structure the control of the work process. State structures were fragmented, so that the unities of the past no longer apply. The responsibilities of middle and junior managers have been recast to enforce an acceptance of responsibility and accountability. From relatively anonymous positions within extended administratively controlled hierarchies, managers became highly visible and identifiable actors involved less in a collective (albeit hierarchically-organised) labour process and more in the control and supervision of the work of others.

This reconfiguration of the state apparatus aimed, in part, to undermine the basis of collective organisation, thereby weakening trade union influence within the state. During the 1970s and the 1980s public sector unions had emerged as potentially powerful and influential groupings, reflected in the patterning of major disputes. Almost without exception, these occurred in the public rather than the private sector. In view of this, one of the prime objectives of the governments during this period was to undermine and marginalise unions in the state sector. This was reflected in successive legislation during the 1980s and into the 1990s aimed at restricting the activity of unions as well as recasting their organisational structures, via rules governing union elections, and other related arrangements. A second strand was to create public sector enterprises where managerial modes of work organisation prevailed and union influence was necessarily minimised.

The central point of these observations is that in the context of the profound restructuring of the social relations of service and public sector provision, the conditions and circumstances of union organisation and practice also shifted. Against the backdrop of highly centralised forms of union organisation in the public sector, and given the specificity of the restructuring of social relations, there was, as a consequence, a possibility of the emergence of distinctive and different forms of unionism. Nevertheless, it was also possible that the basis for a localised and active form of unionism would be denied, as union memberships and their leaders bowed to the apparent inevitability and dominance of public sector restructuring. These are the issues that will now be explored.

In the United Kingdom during the 1980s there was an explicit intention to marginalise state sector unions (Smith and Moreton, 1993 and 2001). This marginalisation took the form of cumulative legislative restriction throughout the 1980s and a strong affirmation of managerial responsibility and accountability for operational activity. It placed management in a stronger position in relation to trade unions at a local level, and assisted in the maintenance of centralised control over budgetary and financial arrangements. In this circumstance, unions were forced to confine themselves to narrowly focused economistic issues, the pursuit of which would be restricted by the legislative obligations placed on them (Kelly, 1996). The unions were not, however, compliant in this process. They began a process of reorganisation and laid the foundations for a different form of unionism.

As the restructuring of the United Kingdom civil service proceeded, the prospects for unions went through some dramatic shifts. Initially, the devolution of managerial responsibility to the office level opened up the prospect of wider bargaining opportunities at this level of organisation. This prospect was embraced by the only department-based union – the Inland Revenue Staff Federation (IRSF). It was regarded sceptically by the two main unions at the time (National Union of Civil and Public Servants – NUCPS and Civil and Public Services Association – CPSA), both under the control and influence of political machines, of the left and right respectively, who were committed to maintenance of centralised forms of bargaining as the condition for maintaining political control over the membership. As a result, moves to broaden the bargaining agenda at a local level took place in the absence of national leadership involvement, and occasionally, in the face of this leadership's outright hostility. Local initiatives were thus a semi-detached process of union reorganisation.

The first stage of union response to restructuring produced a new generation of members, who became used to a more direct involvement in union affairs at the local level. It coincided with a series of reviews within the civil service unions of the ways they should organise and operate (Drake *et al.* 1980 and 1982). The aim of these reviews was to reorganise the unions so as to provide the basis for a better prepared and more sustained mobilisation of members in the face of increasingly hostile governments. In doing so, the model of the workplace steward was both encouraged and promoted, although often against a background of debate about how to best direct the activity of such representatives (Fairbrother, 1984: 88–95). Just as importantly, this was a period in which local bargaining and disputes became more common, accompanied by the emergence of activist workplace stewards in greater numbers than previously (Fairbrother, 1994). The density of the unions in question was maintained during this period. At the workplace level, unions became part of representative structures, and office-based negotiations became common, particularly over working conditions (Carter and Fairbrother, 1995; Fairbrother, 1994 and 1996).

It was only with the second stage of reform, under the auspices of the post-1988 *Next Steps* programme and the associated fragmentation of the civil service, that these embryonic workplace-based representative structures came into their own as the basis for the aggregation of union interests. Centralised bargaining arrangements were broken up department by department, and replaced by agency-based arrangements. Memberships were thus able to continue the uneven process of developing forms of unionism in which interest representation could operate effectively at agency level. There was an episodic aspect to this process of union reorganisation, focused on particular issues and involving sections of the memberships. Nevertheless, the foundation has been laid for effective mobilisation and the organisational articulation of interests in the relatively harsh conditions of civil service reform during the 1980s and 1990s. Even so, devolved bargaining was still largely conducted by paid union officials, although elected lay officials found themselves with greater responsibilities for pursuing workplace issues and personal grievances on behalf of members (interviews, Public and Commercial Services Union officers, 5 and 17 September 2001; for a more developed account, see Fairbrother, 1994 and 1996).

Nevertheless, these developments must be viewed against simultaneous pressure for older forms of union activity to reassert themselves. A feature of unionism in the United Kingdom, that has had important consequences for the eventual developments within unions, was an apparent inability to achieve an effective integration of local union organisation within broader national union structures. Nevertheless, the devolution of managerial hierarchies and the fragmentation of civil service institutions created the conditions for more varied and localised union initiatives, and thus provided the basis for union recovery and renewal. It was possible that unions in the civil service could begin to reorganise and refocus their activities both structurally and ideologically, developing union forms where the emphasis was on local initiative. In this way, members might be able, and be encouraged, to participate, and the balance between local and national leaderships might shift towards the former rather than the latter (Fairbrother, 1996 and 2000). In practice, such a rebalancing of relationships went some distance, but ran up against the entrenched power of centralised national leaderships, who continued to suffer the illusion that the parochialism and localism of the workplace was such that it was the responsibility of national union leaderships to retain their authority.

With the election of the 'New' Labour government in 1997, two notable steps were taken. The Employment Relations Act 1999 provided a legal framework for securing union recognition (formal acknowledgement of the right of unions to recruit members and negotiate on their behalf). This legislation, together with the Statutory Minimum Wage, provided a limited basis for worker and trade union rights, although less than had been hoped for by unions prior to the election. Nonetheless, the focus of the reforms laid the groundwork for a partnership agreement between the government and the civil service (Public and Commercial Services Union, 2000). This approach has to be seen in the context of the Blair government's focus on reform of the civil service. Central to the realisation of this objective was the programme outlined in the White paper on government modernisation and the reform strategy developed in 1999 and 2000 (Prime Minister and the Minister for the Cabinet Office, 1999 and Cabinet Office, 2000).

Towards the end of the 1990s, pay determination arrangements were recast, based on the agencies and Non-Departmental Public Bodies (NDPB) rather than the civil service as a whole (see White and Hatchett, 2001). These changes challenged uniform and standardised conditions of public sector work and employment (Bach, 2002). In this context, the prospect of partnership-style industrial relations appeared to signify a new and less confrontational approach under New Labour. Subsequent experience has been rather different. The agreement of March 2000 between the Cabinet Office, the civil service unions and the CCSU (Council of Civil Service Unions) formed part of the modernising strategy advocated by the government (Cabinet Office, 2000). In the language of such agreements, the document committed the employer to 'valuing' civil servants, while committing the unions to co-operation based on a number of objectives. Significant amongst these was the need for 'continuous improvement' in order to ensure that the civil service remained 'the supplier of choice for the services and functions that are required by government' (Cabinet Office, 2000).

'Partnership' is a confusing concept. In some cases, partnership has been associated with major union concessions, while, in others it is little more than an employer-friendly rebranding of fairly routine forms of collective bargaining (Oxenbridge and Brown, 2004; Johnstone *et al.*, 2009). Certainly, the agreement of 2000 contained little to suggest an aggressive employer stance; on the contrary, it has been taken as a sign of 'restoration of the good and model employer traditions that were eroded during the Thatcher years' (Duncan, 2001: 33). At the time, the agreement was seen as the means to secure the position of the unions nationally, as well as providing the basis for influencing the modernisation process, at a time when many unions expressed disquiet about the government's agenda for the public sector, particularly the extension of public-private initiatives in the delivery of public services.

Whilst it could be argued that the civil service unions saw social partnership as part of a programme of co-operation with the government, the reality of Labour in power highlighted the limited scope for the possibility of a social democratic imperative. Part of the problem for the unions was there was little evidence that the Labour government was prepared to accept anything beyond a limited agenda of industrial citizenship. Moreover, it could be argued that the Labour government's reform agenda undermined any more radical view of social partnership. Social partnership presupposes effective union organisation, otherwise such relations are unequal and the unions become supplicants rather than active partners.

One response is that partnership can only be evaluated in terms of 'what works': that is judging it by its substantive outcomes (Johnstone *et al.*, 2009.) The problem is that agreements themselves do not *cause* anything and various other factors trump procedural detail in determining outcomes (Jenkins, 2007.) For PCS, the period since 2000 has been one of unremitting struggle against a government strategy that has, at times, been openly hostile and spurred on by a cross-party consensus concerning public sector 'bureaucrats.' The continuation of the rhetoric of 'partnership', albeit in a restricted sense, creates dilemmas, first, whether unions stand to gain more by remaining notional partners while their members are made redundant and, second, how to maintain and legitimate this position in the face of growing membership disquiet and militancy The solution for many was the promotion of a managerialist unionism, centralised and professional, as necessary to securing the benefits of partnership while maintaining the union integrity. This perspective emphasised the importance of centralised, effective union organisation, achieving a fruitful and productive balance between active workplace unionism and forward-thinking centralised leaderships (see Heery and Kelly, 1994; Terry, 1996; and McIlroy and Daniels, 2009).

The PCS, in particular, faced a choice, to underwrite forms of managerial unionism, as the organisational condition for partnership arrangements, or to continue to develop a participative and mobilised union membership, building on the foundations laid in the late 1980s and 1990s (Fairbrother, 2000). During early 2000, after a bitter leadership struggle within the PCS, a left leadership was elected, committed to reinvigorating the union, and shaping the public debate about the 'modernisation' of the civil service. Union activists and members through elections and campaigns began to challenge the government's modernisation strategy, going beyond narrow defensive arguments to set out a positive agenda for a different form of 'modernisation', one that centre-staged the workforce. Equally importantly, this challenge was accompanied by an elaboration of terms and conditions of employment that if realised, would signify the return of the civil service as a model employer.

Overall, throughout the twenty-five years plus of state 'reform', the PCS, and to a lesser extent, other unions have gone through a complex process of workplace activism, retrenchment and nationally-led union renewal (see Fairbrother, 2000: 244–81) in a manner that defies simplistic typologies of union organisation and strategy. Of the three main unions, the PCS has, on the one hand, developed an active and confident steward network, and this development has, to a significant extent, been driven by the need to respond to a changing bargaining environment of fragmentation and devolution. On the other hand, the union has campaigned most publicly for a return to centralised forms of pay determination and concurrently for an end to delegation and performance pay (PCS, 2003a). The union presents its case in terms of equity and fairness (PCS, 2003a). In 2005, the two leading unions, PCS and Prospect, launched a further stage of the campaign, calling for a return to a single national pay arrangement (Taylor, 2005). More generally, the PCS has increasingly spelt out alternative visions for public service organisation and delivery, contributing to political debate about public services, and the part the civil service should play in this process (e.g. PCS, 2003b). Central to this approach has been the slow evolution of the union as a campaigning union, beginning with organisational initiatives in the 1980s, experiments with different forms of leadership and the continued refinement of its critique of public policy and the presentation of alternatives (e.g. Davies, 2006).

A Brief History of Australian Public Service Unionism

Unions have long been active in administrative services in Australia, at both the state and the federal levels. Initially, they were relatively passive organisations, often designated and operating as staff associations. In Australia, unions were first founded in the late nineteenth century (see Caiden, 1967: 251 274). They mirrored many of the features of civil and public service employment, with an emphasis on consultation and 'responsibility', rather than adversarial actions. These unions often represented staff from particular grades and sections of the service, initially resulting in numerous organisations, distinguished in some cases by gender. Over time, these various associations and unions merged to produce the Community and Public Sector Union (CPSU), the major civil/public service union.

The CPSU was formed by a series of union amalgamations over the period 1989 to 1994. The first of these was the amalgamation of the Administrative and Clerical Officers' Association (ACOA), the union representing 'officers' in the APS and the Australian Public Service Association (APSA), representing the lowest graded clerical staff in the APS. These two unions formed the Public Sector Union (PSU), which still has an identity as the PSU Group within the wider CPSU. There followed mergers with the Australian Broadcasting Commission Staff Association, the Tax Office branch of the Clerks Union and the Commonwealth Scientific Industrial Research Organisation (CSIRO) Officers' Association, the latter representing staff in the Commonwealth Scientific and Industrial Research Association. In 1994, the CPSU took final shape, through a further amalgamation of the PSU with the State Public Service Federation, a federated union of state-based public service associations

Prior to amalgamation, the ACOA had gone through a period of radicalisation and politicisation in the late 1970s. It had shifted from being a conservative male-dominated organisation to a more militant and more feminised one willing and able to launch some level of mobilisation against the government (Simms, 1987). The amalgamations of the PSU and the APSA in the late 1980s contributed to a further radicalisation of the union, although most of the internal arguments in the union were about how far the leadership should comply with the wishes of the Labor government and how far it should confront the government (O'Brien, 2006). The change of government in 1996 left the union little choice but to mobilise members, if only selectively, and to present itself as an 'organising' rather than a service-oriented union. Despite significant losses of members in the late 1990s, it survived the continuing hostility of the conservative Coalition government and began to extend its membership beyond the core public sector (interviews with

Senior CPSU officer, 1998, 2004; interview with senior official, 2004). Nevertheless, the union never confronted the ideology or efficacy of private sector-oriented management, although many of its actions were designed to alleviate the impact of NPM on the working conditions of its members.

The federal public sector unions had entered the industrial relations mainstream by joining the ACTU in 1981. On the management side, during the 1980s, changes in personnel management in the Australian Public Service had tended to lag behind financial reforms. The Public Service Board continued operating until 1987, when a Public Service Commissioner and individual agency secretaries took over many of its personnel functions. In 1984, the Public Service Board embarked on a major review of the public service classification system. This process involved an extensive broad banding and simplification of the complicated classification systems that had developed in the Commonwealth sector (Dorrington, 1992; O'Brien, 1995). The size of this task was beyond the capacity of any single agency. Such a process required the active involvement of public service unions. It suited the government and the unions to negotiate centrally, although the new arrangements could subsequently be implemented to meet the specific requirements of individual agencies.

The 'managed decentralism' of the industrial relations system generally after 1987 enabled the processes within the Commonwealth sector to be integrated into broader regulatory changes. The beginning of localised over-award productivity bargaining in 1987 required unions to negotiate with employers on issues of efficiency and productivity in exchange for access to arbitrated wage adjustments. In August 1988 the implementation of the Structural Efficiency Principle resulted in the rationalisation of employment classifications from over 100 professional, technical and industrial grades to just eight. This collapsing of distinctions between professional staff and other employees in the APS meant that staff could also be expected to undertake a wider range of tasks at their classification level. It meant, among other things, that employees would be expected to undertake routine work such as photocopying, filing and keying in final drafts of documents in addition to their substantive tasks, and that, over time, a number of lower-level positions would no longer be required. This rationalisation of classifications therefore involved both a recomposition of public service labour and a process of task broadening (O'Brien, 1995). By tying management-initiated organisational changes to the wages system it was possible to incorporate unions into management agendas, while limiting the capacity of management to impose changes without negotiation. The industrial democracy model of consultative management, employee participation and limited codetermination, promoted during the 1980s, gave way to a more traditional industrial relations model of negotiated change via the wage determination system.

In 1991, both the Labor government and the ACTU argued for the institution of enterprise or workplace bargaining that would further develop the model of managed decentralism. Labor maintained a central place for unions in its decentralised model, and had a political imperative to demonstrate that this model was preferable to the union-hostile model being promoted by the Coalition parties. The Labor government thus needed to show that managed decentralism could work for its own employees. In December 1992 the government signed a framework agreement with twenty-seven unions with members in the APS. This agreement provided for the development of more flexible employment conditions at the agency level in exchange for an overall wage adjustment. Each agency management could seek to make an agreement with unions operating within that agency. Those agencies that managed to make an agreement were required to return some part of the savings achieved through the agreement to a central fund that would be used to pay wage increases to agencies that had not been able to reach an agreement. This arrangement became known as the 'foldback' mechanism. It suited the government as it could demonstrate its commitment to a more decentralised regime of industrial relations, by demonstrating that it had implemented this regime with its own employees. Labor was thus able to contrast its measured approach favourably with the much more radical approach being advocated by the Coalition parties. On the other hand, it mollified the public service unions. They would have preferred the maintenance of a completely centralised system, but they could live with a system that guaranteed that all public servants a share in a wage increase, even if it was not applied simultaneously to all agencies.

The Coalition government, elected in 1996, was determined to have 'real' agency-level agreements without allowing some agencies to rely on central funding arrangement beyond the normal annual level of wage supplementation of 1.3 per cent (Reith, 1997). Given its general policy direction in industrial relations, the new government could not appear to maintain a tight degree of control over its own employees. Yet it needed to ensure that its agencies conformed to its policy directions. Its instrument for appearing to loosen supervision, while maintaining overall control (a 'loose-tight model') lay in its parameters for agreement-making. The key provision of the parameters was that any agreement needed to be consistent with the government's general industrial relations policy. Significantly, unions were to lose their 'privileged' role as the exclusive bargaining agents for employees. Moreover, agreements were to be funded within the appropriations made to each agency, although the government loosened the severity of the efficiency dividend that had been part of funding arrangements since the early 1990s.

For the unions the problem was they had lost their monopoly as the representatives of staff generally. Public service unions and the CPSU, in particular, had to earn their right to be the principal, if not exclusive, representative of employees. Moreover, under the provisions of the Workplace Relations Act 1996, management representatives had no stronger obligation than to 'consult' unions. In agencies where unions had a strong presence, to the level of being the representative of a significant minority of staff, management could not really avoid dealing with relevant unions. Nevertheless, in agencies where unions had a significant, but minority presence, managements tried to establish bargaining arrangements where the union had to run candidates for positions as employee bargainers. In the Department of Employment, Education, Training and Youth Affairs, the union ran a ticket in the election for staff representatives and won all positions. In the Australian Bureau of Statistics (ABS) where union density was less than 50 per cent the management declined to establish any formal arrangements and instead used an elaborate system of employee consultation as a means of monitoring employee responses. Within that framework, the union was consulted and some *de facto* negotiations took place. At least in the short term, this process caused management some problems. The ABS had a strong tradition of rank and file activism (interview with union delegate 23 July 1988). This was instrumental in the union's successfully campaigning for rejection of the first draft agreement in a ballot of employees. Subsequently, the staff supported an amended draft agreement. The management regarded the union as less of a threat to its objectives than the rank and file activism that had long characterised the agency (Senior Manager, Australian Bureau of Statistics, 1999; see also O'Brien and O'Donnell, 1999, 2008).

In agencies where unions had a much stronger presence, the CPSU had less difficulty in asserting its claim to speak for most staff. In the Department of Workplace Relations and Small Business the Secretary attempted to establish an employee consultation mechanism that was designed to exclude union members. Ironically, the department found itself in breach of the 'freedom of association' provisions of the Workplace Relations Act in attempting to use such a mechanism to marginalise unions. Moreover, the Secretary was forced to deal with unions who were able to insist that the final agreement would be with the unions rather than with employees: an option widely used in agencies where unions had a weak presence. In Centrelink, where the CPSU had a majority presence, the management took the pragmatic decision to deal with the unions. Unlike many agencies where the unions had little capacity to resist the immediate imposition of performance pay systems, the management had to be content with an agreement to negotiate about the issue rather than proceed with its implementation as a key outcome of the agreement (interviews with management representatives, Centrelink, 16, 26 February, 1999). Nevertheless, the unions had little choice but to agree to such a system in the subsequent agreement, although they were able to insist on a significant degree of regulation in the process of performance assessment for pay purposes (Centrelink, 1999).

By contrast, in agencies where union presence was much weaker, unions were marginalised. In the Department of Finance and Administration, the union fought an unsuccessful campaign against the management draft agreement, having been largely excluded from the process of employee consultation that had produced the document. In the subsequent round, the management took the position that there was no need for a further collective agreement with employees. It insisted that the only mechanism for a pay increase would be through an individual contract, although management agreed to meet the CPSU after public pressure was put on it by the Senate Committee on Finance and Public Administration (Senate References Committee on Finance and Public Administration, 2000a: 210–11; Senate References Committee on Finance and Public Administration, 2000b: 30). In the Department of Foreign Affairs and Trade (DFAT), management was able to persuade a majority of staff to accept an agreement that incorporated a comprehensive performance management and pay scheme against strong union opposition. Considerable disaffection with the operation of the scheme emerged during the life of the agreement (O'Brien and O'Donnell, 1999, 2000). The CPSU was able to use that disaffection to negotiate a scheme with greater protection for employees in the subsequent agreement.

Indeed, the CPSU claimed to the 2000 Senate Finance and Public Administration References Committee enquiry on APS employment matters that it had been involved in the negotiation of most agreements even if it was not party to many of them, particularly in smaller agencies. While allowance must be made for a tendency to exaggerate its role, the union's claim indicates that it and the other public sector unions had not been excluded or marginalised in the overall process. Nevertheless, the fact that nearly half of the agreements in the first round were negotiated with employees rather than with unions indicates that the government had been successful in delegitimising the role of unions in the bargaining process. In doing so it had achieved one of the key objectives of its legislation – to reduce the role of unions from party principal to mere bargaining agent. Moreover, the unions could not impose a template across the APS, although it could modify the impact of management agendas in particular agencies where it had both presence and organisational capacity. If nothing else, these outcomes reinforced the arguments of the proponents of delegate activism that 'union organisation and bargaining capacity, rather than management style, are decisive elements in maintaining and extending the union membership base (Alexander *et al.*, 1998: 662; cf., Morehead *et al.*, 1997: 142; Waddington and Kerr, 1999: 164). Nevertheless, the CPSU lost significant membership as a consequence of the downsizing of the APS. In late 1999, it was beginning to think about whether it could maintain the level of services to APS agencies where it had low membership (Interview with senior industrial officer, CPSU, 1999). In 2009 the membership density in the APS had fallen to 40 per cent (Jones, 2009). It is worth noting in this context, that despite the great hostility of the Conservative government to British public service unions, that there had been no concerted attempt to cut unions out of pay determination processes. In this context the approach taken by its Coalition counterparts in Australia was perhaps more ideologically-driven than in the United Kingdom.

The key problem for Australian Public Service unions in this environment is the contradictory operation of managerial authority at the agency level.

On the one hand, public sector managers could legitimately exclude or marginalise unions from the bargaining process. On the other hand, the government, as the 'ultimate employer' of public servants limited the scope of agency managerial autonomy by ensuring that where unions had the capacity they were parties to the process. The unions, however, were forced to bargain at workplace level and not at the level of the public service as a whole. While it was possible for unions to reduce the impact of the government's mandated agenda in an agency where they had some strength, it was much more difficult for them to operate at a national level to modify the broad parameters laid down by the government for its managers in their agency-level negotiations. Public sector unions were reduced, therefore, to fighting defensive actions at the agency level while waiting for a change of government to bring about some shift in the macro-environment.

In December 2006, the Coalition government, having won majorities in both houses of Parliament, was able to make significant amendments to the Workplace Relations Act 1996. These changes had considerable implications for most Australian workplaces and for the APS, in particular. As far as public sector unions were concerned, union access to APS workplaces was further restricted. A strike could only occur during a bargaining period if a majority of voting employees supported the action in a secret ballot, with heavy financial penalties for industrial action outside these parameters. Collective agreements were to be lodged with the Employment Advocate (the name was later changed to the Workplace Authority), rather than certified by the Australian Industrial Relations Commission, a change that implied minimal regulatory oversight. The commission, moreover, would be largely reduced to a conciliation role, with the power to arbitrate on disputes only when all parties agreed. In addition, the Minister for Workplace Relations could veto any provision in agreements which he deemed opposed to government policy (Workplace Relations Amendment Act (Work Choices) Act 2005). In some respects, these provisions were similar to those that had operated in the APS since 1997, except that they would now have broader application. Indeed the Secretary of the Department of the Prime Minister and Cabinet, Dr Peter Shergold, considered that the provisions of the Work Choices legislation would have far less impact in the APS than in many other workplaces (CPSU, 2005a).

This view was contested by the CPSU. It warned its members that it would find it more difficult to service its members in the workplace. Moreover, when access to a workplace was granted, employers would be able to exercise greater control when and how staff met with union officials (Costello and Bolton, 2005). Indeed, there was a fear that the union would need to rely on telephone, email and out-of-work meetings for communicating with its members (CPSU, 2005b); these fears came to pass. Moreover, the safety net was reduced from the minimum standards set out in residual awards, to only five minimum standards set out in the Act (plus, where applicable a Fairness Test). To ensure that the agreements provided more comprehensive standards, union members were forced to bargain away some benefits or pay rise in order to maintain other provisions, such as redundancy protections. Redundancy provisions were not included in the five minimum standards but were particularly important for the APS where restructuring of agencies often meant loss of staff. In agencies where there were low levels of union-isation and where agreements were made with employees directly, unions faced even more restricted access to workplaces. As they were no longer able to gain the status of party to agreements made directly with employees, they lost the capacity to pursue disputes arising out of non-union agreements.

The greatest concern of the union, however, was the potential for government and agency managements to exploit this more difficult collective bargaining environment in order to promote AWAs. The worst-case scenario was in DoFA where more than 95 per cent of staff had individual agreements because the management had successfully refused to negotiate any kind of collective agreement since 1997. Although the CPSU had succeeded in thwarting a similar tactic being used by the management of the more highly-unionised environment of the Department of Employment and Workplace Relations in late 2005, the greater restrictions on industrial action would make a similar campaign more difficult in the new environment.

The CPSU was a significant contributor an ACTU-led 'Your Rights at Work' campaign that was undertaken in the eighteen months prior to the 2007 election. Although the Labor Party made no commitment about returning to a more centralised bargaining system its commitment to re-legitimising collective bargaining was sufficient for unions to back the return of a Labor government. Indeed the ALP (Australian Labor Party) won a significant, but not overwhelming, victory in the federal election in November 2007. One of its first actions was to order the cessation of individual contracts. In the resulting legislation primacy, but not exclusivity, was given to collective bargaining. In 2009, the CPSU leadership sought to affiliate with the ALP on a state by state basis, a decision that provoked a membership revolt in some quarters (*Canberra Times*, 1 March, 2009; CPSU, 2009a).

ASSESSMENT

Industrial relations were distinctive to each country. One important difference between the two countries is that unions in Australia were recognised by the federal Industrial Relations Commission which conferred a quasi-judicial status upon unions that was absent in the United Kingdom. In Australia it was open to governments to use the industrial relations machinery to implement change in the public sector. Public sector unions, in turn, could use the same machinery to influence the nature and direction of those chan-ges. No such opportunity was available in the United Kingdom. This dif-ference means that the institutional form of change and the themes addressed by each union movement were articulated in differentiated ways.

The unions in each country addressed these changes in distinctive ways. In Australia, the roots of union activism went back to the 1960s, with unions beginning to break from the traditions of consultation and relative passivity. The amalgamations of the PSU and the APSA in the late 1980s contributed to a further radicalisation of the union, although most of the internal arguments in the union were about how far the leadership should comply with the wishes of the Labor government and how far it should confront the government (O'Brien, 2006). The change of government in 1996 left the union little choice but to mobilise members, if only selectively, and to present itself as an 'organising' rather than a service-oriented union. Despite significant losses of members in the late 1990s, it has survived the continuing hostility of the conservative Coalition government and has begun to extend its membership beyond the core public sector (interviews with Senior CPSU officer, 1998, 2004; interview with senior official, 2004). Nevertheless, the union never confronted the ideology or efficacy of private sector-oriented management, although many of its actions were designed to alleviate the impact of NPM on the working conditions of its members.

Personnel matters and industrial relations negotiations were to take place at the agency level under parameters laid down by the Department of Employment and Workplace Relations (DEWR) on behalf of the government. The Department of Finance and Administration determined appropriations to agencies and the Public Service Commissioner had responsibility for general personnel policy and some training of senior public servants.

Industrial relations at the federal level was operationally decentralised but still closely regulated from the centre. By 2007 about 80 per cent of APS employees were covered by agreements between unions and agencies; the remaining collective agreements were between employees and agencies directly. Most members of the SES were on individual contracts as were some middle management in a number of agencies. The difference between individual contracts and collective agreements involved the former's more explicit focus on linking performance bonuses or advancement within classification scales more sharply to the achievement of performance goals outlined in individual performance agreements. Throughout the period of the Howard Coalition government the CPSU had retained its status as the prime representative of public servants negotiating collective agreements. In 2009, the union claimed to have represented over 100,000 APS employees in bargaining across dozens of agencies (Jones, 2009). Nevertheless, union density had declined to approximately 30 per cent of APS employees by December 2009 (55,000 CPSU members, with a substantial number employed by non-APS employers such as Telstra (Jones, 2009). In June 2009, the total APS workforce (including temporary staff) stood at 162, 009 (APSC, 2009)).

While private sector industrial relations in the United Kingdom had usually operated on the basis of collective bargaining between unions and employers, there is a history of 'special arrangements' being made for public employees. Until the 1980s, these were often Whitley – style consultative arrangements. In recent times wage determination has varied. Office-based arrangements have determined the pay and conditions of civil servants, albeit within a wage range set down by the Treasury. Specialist review bodies for teachers and local government workers make recommendations to government that may or may not be adopted. Moreover, unlike the situation in Australia there is no defined period for any particular set of agreements or determinations. Public sector unions usually campaigned for wage adjustments, since there is not a timetable for re-negotiating agreements as is the case in Australia. One effect is that union action is not confined to the circumscribed time during which it is allowed to open periods of bargaining for new collective agreements.

The UK union, the PCS arose out of a series of mergers during the 1980s and 1990s. While important in creating a major unified union in the civil service, it is equally of note that the union arose out of the recomposition that took place within the civil service employment hierarchies, dating back to the late 1960s. Over time, the differences between civil service grades was blurred and made more permeable. In addition, in the 1980s clearer distinctions were drawn between a managerial civil service stratum and a civil service workforce, with implications for the union form of organisation. Indeed, one of the solutions to this emerging managerial distinction was to provide the basis for civil servants, qua civil service state workers, to act collectively via their unions, irrespective of grades. The PCS, and the few remaining smaller unions, such as Prospect (covering scientific and related professional civil servants), increasingly emphasised their common concerns rather than their grade based distinctions. This reorganisation and the way it addressed the recomposition of civil service employment, enabled the PCS to become the major radical union force within the United Kingdom administrative sector, as well as within United Kingdom trade unionism more generally.

State sector unions in both countries had developed in the context of standardised employment and industrial arrangements, largely characterised by national level pay bargaining in the United Kingdom and service-wide arrangements in Australia, mediated through Public Service Boards and the compulsory conciliation and arbitration system. The greater agency focus of public service reform and the reconstitution of managerial structures presented a challenge to unions in both countries. In the United Kingdom the public service reforms were a reflection of a wider exclusion of unions and a radical recasting of labour market regulation. In Australia these reforms occurred within a context of the managed decentralisation of the industrial relations system. This decentralisation was predicated on unions co-operating in work reorganisation in exchange for wage increases. On the surface the system in Australia was more benign for unions, whereas in Britain unions were put much more on the defensive. On closer examination the picture is, however, more complicated.

In both countries, the reconfiguration of the state apparatus aimed, in part, to undermine the basis of collective organisation, thereby weakening trade union influence within the state. During the 1970s and the 1980s the public sector unions had emerged as potentially powerful and influential groupings, reflected in the patterning of major disputes: in the UK these, almost without exception, occurred in the public rather than the private sector. One of the prime objections of the governments during this period was to undermine and marginalise unions in the state sector. One strand to this approach was the successive legislation during the 1980s and into the 1990s aimed at restricting the activity of unions as well as recasting the organisational basis of unions, via rules relating to union elections, and other related arrangements. A second strand was to create public sector enterprises where managerial modes of work organisation prevailed and union influence was necessarily minimised.

Whilst public sector unions risked incorporation by being absorbed in the minutiae of decentralised bargaining, the alternative was a quest for more centralised and higher-level political influence that brought different risks of incorporation. In the UK, the PCS has been led since 2002 by a strongly-supported activist General Secretary whose political links are to the left of New Labour. There has been no question of attempting to influence government policy by political affiliation. While the unions were effectively marginalised in the Conservative period, they were able to use the more fluid environment of the post–1997 Labour government to contest a government agenda that was very similar to that of the Conservatives, but that mobilised an apparently more inclusive rhetoric to justify its policies. In particular, since 2002, the PCS has engaged in a more nationally co-ordinated form of resistance. A series of strikes in 2004 in response to government directed staff cuts are a case in point.

In Australia, in contrast, the CPSU since 2007 has seen its best hope of exerting political influence as lying in shifting Australian Labor Party policies from within. In the lead-up to the 2007 Australian federal election, the CPSU was a strong supporter of the broad-based Your Rights at Work campaign. Before its election, the Australian Labor Party made no specific commitment to public sector workers, beyond its general policy guarantee of a return to collective bargaining. At no point in 2007 or since has the Labor Party deviated from its policy adherence to the decentralised APS bargaining that has absorbed so much union energy. In the lead-up to the election, the CPSU made a crucial decision at its Governing Council: to seek affiliation with the ALP. The experience of eleven years of the Coalition government had convinced the leadership that, while it had survived industrially, most of the crucial decisions that affected its members were political, with the government determining the specific managerial climate within which public sector unions operated. The decision was easily carried, with delegates from the large Tax Office branch leading the opposition. Supporters argued that there was a greater chance for influence from within the party; opponents argued that the party had not come out in strong opposition to the Howard government's industrial relations policies until the wider union movement had organised mass protests. Affiliation proceeded state by state during 2008 and 2009, with some controversy. This episode illustrates the fundamental incorporation/marginalisation dilemma: will the union leaders now have more influence on government policy, or is the union, as an organisation, now less likely to mobilise against the government? (Bolton, 2007). In September 2009, the Rudd government introduced a new Australian Government Bargaining Framework for the Australian Public Service (APS) that restored and reaffirmed the representative role and rights of workplace union delegates (Australian Government, 2009).

The restructuring of the civil and public services over the last two decades stimulated unions in each country to re-assess the way they organise and operate. In the United Kingdom this involved an experiment with decentralised forms of representation and leadership during the 1980s and 1990s. However, with the election of the New Labour government in 1997, and with the more explicit promotion of managerialism, the national union leaderships succumbed to the temptations of partnership, with consequences for the initial steps towards union renewal. Nonetheless, by the mid-2000s the union had drawn limits around the partnership approach and had emerged as the major critic of government approaches to civil and public services in the United Kingdom. In Australia, the main union found itself in an increasingly hostile bargaining environment where the long-established forms of centralised unionism no longer sufficed. However, the reshaping of state management created a situation where unions faced managements with the authority, and encouragement from the Howard government, to limit and circumscribe the scope of union organisation and action, thereby attempting to limit the union's capacity to renew. For both unions, the organisational tension has been between pressures towards centralisation and participation; in both cases the unions have attempted to address both the devolution of managerial responsibility within the civil and public services as well as the recomposition of managerial and employment hierarchies.

CONCLUSION

The restructuring of the core state sector in both countries has been in progress for over two decades. These processes have involved the recomposition of two civil and public services that had long been organised in centralised and hierarchical ways. In the context of increasing difficulties with private capital accumulation, growing trade union militancy in the state sector and a shift in government ideology, governments began to impose more stringent financial regimes on state services and to re-structure control of the work process. However, the processes and trajectories of change were very different involving distinctive approaches to the perceived problem of labour inclusion or exclusion.

The reforms in the United Kingdom were driven from the centre and imposed from the top. They were premised on the marginalisation of trade unions and their members. Policies were implemented to reconstitute the forms of control and the organisation of the labour force in these sectors. There were three distinct but related stages to this process. In this first instance, there was a twin process of marginalising unions, via an incremental process of legislative reform, aimed at the trade union movement as a whole. Within the civil service, the government began a process of redefining the bureaucratic relations of the past in an explicitly managerial direction, initially giving supervisory layers of staff explicit managerial authority. In uneven and tentative ways a number of unions took the opportunity to promote workplace-based forms of representation and resistance. Second, the government towards the end of the 1980s and into the 1990s began to fragment the civil service, as part of the process of constructing semi-autonomous managerial hierarchies, with the capacity to embed a managerialist mode of state organisation. Whilst the unions were excluded from this process of organisation, and indeed governments saw such reorganisation as a way of marginalising unions further, workplace union groups were able to use decentralisation in order to consolidate the processes of union renewal that were underway. However, in the third period, under a Labour government, committed to securing the operation of the civil service as the core of the managerial state, the fragility of the moves towards union renewal were exposed. In this most recent period, central union leaderships succumbed to the beguiling prospects of working partnerships with a so-called reforming government. Whilst this may appear to be the end of the processes of union renewal it is worth noting that the complicated processes of managerial composition and recomposition are likely to force unions to continue re-examining the bases of collective organisation and action (Fairbrother and Poynter, 2001).

The pattern of change in Australia was different, reflecting the particular version of social democracy elaborated during the 1980s (Dow, 1993). Drawing on a long labourist tradition, the successive Labor governments during this period elaborated a view that the state should be responsive to the citizenry (Beilharz, 1994) and replace the stultifying and conservative practices of the past with a 'modern' public service. As part of this approach, managers in several departments, such as the Australian Taxation Office, were willing to enter into social partnership arrangements that provided an active role for workers and unions in the process of change. The election of the Coalition government in 1996, however, saw the emergence of a more determined path towards the managerial state predicated on the marginalisation, rather than the incorporation, of state sector unions. The Coalition government's public service reforms involved in many ways the application of its broader industrial relations to its own employees.

It is not that Labo(u)r governments are necessarily as hostile to unions as governments that have no historical association with organised labour.

Rather it is a more an issue of the nature of the state itself. Although the progress from a welfare state to a managerial state in both the United Kingdom and in Australia was contradictory, contested and uneven, there are strong grounds for suggesting that the nature of the state has shifted in a fundamental way. A managerial state may be hostile to organised labour, but it is within that hostility that lays the potential for counter mobilisation, more evident in the United Kingdom than in Australia at least until 2006. On the other hand, the welfare state has not passed away in its entirety. Indeed, there are tensions at the heart of the modern state as a managerial state, involving the organisation and provision of public services that provide the foundation for continued union organisation and action. As well as mobilising in the workplace, there is still a constituency for a defence of the provision of public services through public agencies. Union – community alliances, social unionism, may be much more useful political strategy than a return to the modified corporatism of the 1970s in the United Kingdom and the 1980s in Australia.

The stance of unions within the process of state restructuring is critical. In the United Kingdom, the greater hostility of governments to unions during the 1980s forced some state sector unions to re-assess their workplace organisation. Thus it could be suggested that with the change of government in 1997, unions had some experience of not relying too much on a nominally social democratic New Labour Party to come to their rescue. However, this was not to be so and in practice the unions turned away from the potential of the organisational reforms of the earlier period and moved towards a compromised social partnership. In Australia, however, the Labor Party's Fair Work Act has overturned many of the aspects of the Howard government's industrial relations legislation and promoted collective bargaining in 'good faith' as central features of its new legislation introduced in July, 2009. For the CPSU the legislation restored the rights of workplace union delegates to represent union members and to be consulted about workplace change (Jones, 2009). Under the New Labour governments of the late 1990s and early 2000s, state sector unions contended with such measures as Private Funding Initiatives in the provision of public services. Indeed they have been warned by the Prime Minister that they will have 'no veto' on further developments in this area. This is, perhaps, a warning for Australian public sector unions that waiting for Labor is not always the most fruitful approach to take in the renewal and restructuring of state sector unionism. In the next chapter we discuss management initiatives in re-moulding the state labour processes.

5 Remoulding the State Labour Process

Over the last three decades, governments have promoted a range of measures aimed at creating a 'modern' administrative service, each of which has had profound implications for the state labour process. These measures can be distinguished as redrawing state boundaries and reconstituting managerial hierarchies, creating wider divisions between state managers and workers, in order to restructure labour markets and promote greater individual responsibility in state sector work practices. Taken together they constitute a cluster of arrangements undertaken by governments to shape the state labour process in the context of a more globalised world. One key dimension of state restructuring has been a process of work reorganisation and outsourcing to lay the foundation for the provision of services and products more in line with private sector business practices than traditional patterns of organisation and operation (Ramanadham, 1988: 3–25; Whitfield, 1992: 65–104 and 127–69; Young, 1990: 537). Associated with these initiatives were attempts by successive governments to restructure the labour process so that it was no longer organised to provide goods and services to the public based on some notion of need or 'public good', but in terms of efficiency and cost effectiveness (Whitfield, 1992: 128–31). The legitimating discourse was that a traditional state labour process, predicated on formalised notions of consensual work and employment relations, job security and notions of the state as a model employer, was not sufficient for the commercialised climate of the 1980s and 1990s. Central to the restructuring of the state labour process was the devolution of management structures and the decentralisation of managerial accountability and responsibility (on the United Kingdom civil service, see Fairbrother, 1994; on the Australian Public Service see O'Brien, 2006).

The promotion of managerialism in the public services in the United Kingdom and Australia meant that the management of the employment relationship has become an increasingly strategic activity. In the United Kingdom, there has been considerable experimentation with performance appraisal and individual performance-related pay and more active management of issues such as absenteeism (Bach and della Rocca, 2000). There have also been a series of attempts to transform the Australian Public Service (APS) in line with a strategic human resource model, as management attempted to align individual staff contributions to agency missions and corporate objectives and placed a stronger focus on individualising the employment relationship (O'Brien and O'Donnell, 2001). In both states, governments have promoted a rhetoric of customer service and customer rights. Such a focus in relation to work tasks and work experience is also part of the recomposition of the state labour process.

This chapter explores the tensions between this rational approach to management and the potential for an emergent model of implementing management strategy in the public-sector (Mintzberg, 1993). These tensions are played out in relation to the politically determined objectives that public organisations pursue. The rhetoric of a public sector that is 'responsive' to 'stakeholders' entails the potential for political interference; this may include inappropriate intervention from government ministers, the influence exerted by political parties, the role of lobby groups, public opinion and the impact of parliamentary committee investigations. This set of relations is what Batstone and others (1984) referred to as 'political contingency'. It makes the task of strategy formulation more complex and indeterminate in the public sector. It also highlights the great difficulty in mimicking private sector management practices in an increasingly uncertain public-sector environment. Governments that initially championed customer-driven public-sector organisations in the 1980s and 1990s (Osborne and Gaebler, 1993), encountered tensions between a mantra of treating citizens as 'customers' and the need to contain budget deficits and to maximise the efficiency and cost-effectiveness of service delivery organisations, particularly in areas such as education, health and welfare services. For public-sector workers this manifested as an ongoing tension between management strategies that emphasised 'responsible autonomy' and a growing emphasis on 'direct control' (Friedman, 1977), deskilling and work intensification.

The focus of the chapter is on the state labour process and the way in which it has changed over the last twenty-five years. The chapter outlines two key managerialist strategies, explaining the role of each in reshaping the state and the public-sector labour process. These measures were: the redrawing state boundaries through privatisation and marketisation; and the restructuring of work processes by reconstituting the relationship between managers and workers and with 'customers'. The purpose is to document privatisation and managerialist processes in Britain and Australia, and to draw out their implications for the working lives of state sector employees.

REDRAWING THE BOUNDARIES OF THE STATE AND THE STATE SECTOR LABOUR MARKET

From the mid-1980s, the traditional boundaries of the state sector were redrawn, initially via privatisation policies and then via programmes aimed at outsourcing, public-private partnerships and most recently public-third sector partnerships. While these developments set the scene for the restructuring that took place, they also have an impact on forms of managerial control and the way these changes were played in relation to the organisation of work.

Privatisation, Contracting and Partnerships

The redrawing of state boundaries took three principal forms. First, in both countries sections of the core public services were privatised. Second, and probably of more significance, there has been a process of outsourcing, contracting-out and reorganising the relationship between the public and private sector in the provision of public services and the organisation of core administrative activity. One of the initial ways in which the state labour process was reshaped was through the privatisation of functions, or the outsourcing and the establishment of public-private partnerships (Grimshaw et al., 2002). There has been a broad debate about privatisation and its implications for work and employment relations, ranging from an exploration of the sale of public enterprises (Fairbrother et al., 2002) to the ways in which private sector organisations deliver public services (Montanheiro et al., 1998). Thus through the process of 'privatising' public services, including the core administrative areas of employment, the state labour process was recast.

There has been a long history of privatisation in Britain. Some of the privatisations have involved agencies whose links with the marketplace are not obvious, and whose policy sensitivity might call into question the appropriateness of their being in private hands. In 1996, the Capita group acquired the entire issued share capital of Recruitment and Assessment Services following the incorporation into that company of the Recruitment and Assessment Services Agency (RAS), an Executive Agency of the Cabinet Office (Office of Public Service). Based in Basingstoke and Whitehall, RAS employed 137 staff. It undertook recruitment of all grades in the civil service and other central government bodies and provided related consultancy work, including psychological assessment programmes, advice on recruitment requirements and use of career development centres. This was no loss-making agency: in the year ended 31 March 1996 RAS recorded a surplus on ordinary activities of £683,000 on an income of £9.7 million, with net assets at 31 March 1996 of £1.06 million (Commons 1996; PR Newswire Europe Ltd, 1996). In 2003, the government unveiled plans to privatise the United Kingdom's Forensic Science Service (FSS). The FSS became an Executive Agency of the Home Office on 1 April 1991. As such, it developed a business approach to forensic work, while operating under the delegated responsibilities and accountabilities of agency status. It was transferred from an Executive Agency to a government owned company in 2005 (Service, 2007). Since 1997, there have been sell-offs in the Ministry of Defence (including the Defence Evaluation and Research Agency and the Fleet Maintenance and Repair), and National Savings. National Air Traffic

Control Services was part privatised to a consortium of airlines with the government retaining a stake.

In Australia, sales also occurred from the early 1990s onwards. While most of the privatisations at a federal level involved transport, finance and statutory bodies, such as the Snowy Mountains Engineering Corporation, they also involved some equivalent bodies to those in the United Kingdom. In 1989/90 the Australian Industry Development Corporation was floated as a public company and sold in 1997/98. Similarly, the overseas tele-communication authority AUSSAT Pty Ltd established as a publicly owned company in 1979 and sold in 1991 to Optus Communications. Overall, it would appear that the Australian federal government has taken a more gradual approach toward privatisation than has been the case in Britain. Nonetheless, at the state level there have been privatisation of public infra-structure such as tramways and electricity generation (in Victoria) and cor-poratisation of other functions such as the provision of water (in NSW) (see Fairbrother *et al.*, 2002; for an accounting-based critique of privatisation see Funnell *et al.*, 2009).

In both countries however, the core administrative areas remained more or less in public ownership, with particular functions subject to private sector provision and related arrangements. Much more commonly in both countries, governments have outsourced core public functions. In particular, there has been an increased use of public-private partnerships (PPPs), invol-ving collaborations between public bodies, such as local authorities or cen-tral government, and private companies. This enabled governments to build new hospitals, schools and prisons without having to face heavy up-front costs although in the longer term there may be a greater debt burden or continuing need for public subsidy. The contractors, in turn, gained from design and construction costs, as well as from the 'rent' income, often for thirty years (Pollock *et al.*, 2007).

Outsourcing and contracting-out has long been a feature of state restruc-turing in the United Kingdom. In the 1980s and 1990s, it involved a wide range of services and had an immediate impact on particular government services, especially prisons. In the mid-1990s, the United Kingdom govern-ment awarded a contract to a Group-4 joint venture with Tarmac to design, construct, manage, and finance a 600-bed prison in Liverpool (Grout, 1997). Elsewhere, from the early 1990s onwards, institutions such as departmental libraries faced a regime of outsourcing via market testing. From 1992 onwards government library services were outsourced, and effectively privatised, department by department: the Department of Transport (1985), the Depart-ment of Health and Social Security (1992); the Ordnance Survey (1993); and the Department of Trade and Industry (1994) (Burge, 1998: 12–16).

These processes continued after the election of the Labour government. Despite government assurances to the contrary, in the mid-2000s, the out-sourcing of core front-line services in the Department for Work and Pensions continued. In 2000, Jobcentre Plus Action Teams (previously praised for their high performance) were closed down. The government announced that replacement employment services would be provided exclusively from the private sector. During the transition process, no in-house bids were allowed.

Similar arrangements were also promoted by Australian governments. These covered laboratories, research and innovation and similar activities. The evidence however, suggests that Australian privatisations have been narrower in focus and far less comprehensive than has been the case in the United Kingdom (Sharp and Tinsley, 2005). Of more significance has been the contracting-out of employment services (Ranald, 2002). Beginning in 1996, the federal government subjected all the services of the then Commonwealth Employment Service to competitive tendering. In this proposal, private- and public-sector providers competed to win tenders to provide employment-placement services to the unemployed. Employment National, the government owned service provider, was a successful tender in the first round. In 1999, however, this body lost its employment share to private providers and was eventually abolished (O'Brien and O'Donnell, 1999). Employment services are now provided exclusively by the private Employment Services Australia.

Centrelink delivers services on behalf of departments such as Family, Community Services, Housing and Indigenous Affairs, (the former Department of Social Security), Employment, Education and Workplace Relations and numerous other government agencies. These services include transfer payments to pensioners and students, the referral of jobseekers to Job Network providers, and the implementation of regulations based on government policy decisions. Service provision is funded, not by direct budget appropriations, but through interagency funding transfers, based on submissions by the 'purchasing agencies' to the Department of Finance and Deregulation. In its early years, in Centrelink and its client agencies, there was much debate as to which partner should carry the risks of meeting government policy objectives (Centrelink Board and Quality Committee, 1997–2004: June, 1997; 23 November, 1998; 21 September, 2001). Business Agreements with client agencies included performance and risk management standards, such as Business Assurance Frameworks, which were tightly monitored. This appearance of decentralised contracting-out in fact occurred within a centralised whole-of-government framework. It was a 'loose-tight' model of governance, that was adopted more widely across the Commonwealth government sector during the Howard years, leaving the agencies to deliver programs while the government made key policy decisions, such as the greater targeting of welfare payments. In the case of Centrelink, this process was taken one step further: the purchasing departments contracted to the provider, while exercising considerable control over how Centrelink met government policy objectives (Junor *et al.*, 2009).

In all cases, where contracting-out, outsourcing, and the related complex relations of public-private providers, there was a strong sense of a 'depoliticising' process at work: distancing the provision of services from government while at the same time strengthening government control. State employees and managers were not granted a full measure of autonomy, but were not in all cases closely supervised. They remained accountable for outcomes, not so much for processes. This arrangement involved the redrawing of state service boundaries and control mechanisms in a 'loose-tight' manner that sought to ensure a more compliant workforce providing core state services, albeit within a rhetorical framework of greater autonomy for front-line workers.

Emergent Managerial Control

At the centre of the new managerial approach in the United Kingdom and Australian public services was the emergence of a stratum of managers who acquired increased prerogatives and authority to lead their organisations and who, in turn, were expected to deliver higher levels of organisational per-formance. The devolution of responsibility was thus accompanied by an intensification of accountability within managerial hierarchies. In Australia, an 'economically rationalist' cadre of senior managers emerged in the 1980s focused on achieving results and managing their organisations in a cost effi-cient and effective manner (Pusey, 1991). In the United Kingdom, this was a more gradual process, highlighted by the reconstruction of the civil service with the establishment of agency forms of organisation in the 1990s, accompanied by managerial reforms.

Such reforms centred on a recomposition of the state labour process. The analysis begins with a consideration of the way that management seeks to convert workers' labour power into actual labour (Braverman, 1974: Chapter 1). Converting labour power into labour, however, represents a perpetual challenge for management because, unlike other factors of pro-duction, the productive capacity of labour is indeterminate. Managers seek to overcome such uncertainty by developing strategies to both control employees and to extract maximum effort from them at work (Braverman, 1974; Littler and Salaman, 1982).

The application of a labour process analysis to the public sector redefines public servants as workers who are subservient to processes of management control and supervision. Fairbrother (1994) contended that the introduction of private sector management techniques in to the United Kingdom's civil service was part of an agenda to reconstruct public servants, along with the public sector itself, in line with a private sector corporate model. As such public service workers:

> occupy class positions as wage labourers, subject to control and exploitation. In this respect, these workers are like other workers, selling their labour power in the context of a set of relations which constitute a specific labour process. This is a labour process which has its own specific forms and which has been reconstructed and reorganized over the last decade.
>
> (Fairbrother, 1994: 52)

The outcome was a restructured labour process and a change in the dominant mode of control of labour in this sector. A distinctive stratum of managers was established, based on a differentiation between a middle class and a working class (Carter and Fairbrother, 1995). This process of proletarianisation led to rising union density levels in the public sector but also coincided with government efforts to contain budget deficits and reduce public spending. Such budget cut backs were a significant factor in rising public-sector industrial unrest. Between 2000 and 2005, strikes by public-sector workers in the United Kingdom represented some 50 per cent of all strike activity and three-quarters of days lost because of strikes (ONS, 2011). Public-sector unions were aware of the political fall-out for governments of any disruption to public services. They were also successful in overturning certain managerialist initiatives, such as attempts to introduce performance pay for teachers in 1999. Nevertheless, the state in the United Kingdom responded to this vulnerability by making extensive changes to industrial relations processes over recent decades, for example through the decentralisation of bargaining, and by efforts to weaken the power and influence of public-sector trade unions. The fragmentation of public-sector organisations into agencies also enabled governments in the United Kingdom to intensify efforts to limit the role of public-sector unions and enhance the prerogatives of public-sector employers (Brown, 2008). In Australia, the Howard government's industrial relations legislation similarly aimed to marginalise the role of public-sector unions, by introducing non-union forms of collective bargaining and by promoting individual contracts (O'Brien and O'Donnell, 2007).

In both countries, managerialism went through oscillations between direct and indirect approaches to controlling state sector workforces. Whilst less stark in the United Kingdom than in Australia, two forms of managerialism remained in continuing tension during the three decades in question. This analytic point is best developed by referring to Friedman's (1977) theory of responsible autonomy, and to competing tendencies within the human resource management literature, which took shape during this period.

In contesting Braverman's (1974) original theory of the necessary tendency to deskilling and control in the capitalist labour process, Friedman (1977) argued that under controlled conditions, the skills of core workers could be harnessed by affording them a measure of 'responsible autonomy'. This concept was defined as referring to a labour process in which individual workers were afforded a degree of discretion over a range of tasks, by contrast with forms of direct managerial control involving close supervision over a narrow range of tasks. The contrast was one between the use of high-trust relations to secure worker commitment and a low-trust approach to securing compliance though direct control. Managerial approaches have either veered between these poles or tried to overcome their contradictions (Fox, 1974; Wright, 1985). Close supervision overlooks the independent and potentially hostile will of workers and generates resistance. Yet 'responsible autonomy' may mean that workers incompletely absorb the organisation's 'official' corporate culture or fail to remain consciously accountable for management's ultimate goal of profitability or cost containment (Friedman, 1990: 178).

While developed in relation to manufacturing and related labour processes, this analysis can be extended to work in the state sector. First, the intersection between pressures toward responsible autonomy and direct control need to be worked out in the context of government commitments to neo-liberal approaches to governance. Over the past two decades, the state as employer has embraced a range of strategies in relation to service delivery, attempting to lay down the basis for 'responsible autonomy' in the public services, albeit underpinned by highly mediated sets of control relations, usually based on financial measures. Second, debates about the labour process within the public service need to consider worker responses to NPM, including the reality of resistance, as a response to such control measures.

The standard strategic human resource management literature emerged together with the service economy. In this normative literature, 'employee alignment' is a central preoccupation, reflecting a tension between 'utilitarian instrumentalism' and 'developmental humanism' (Legge, 2005: 66). The former approach focuses on a headcount management of labour as a factor of production; the latter treats employees as valued assets, a source of competitive advantage through their commitment, adaptability, skills, and quality performance.

Labour Markets and Work Processes

These various forms of state restructuring were undertaken in line with the neo-liberal doctrine of the primacy of market relations. They were based on two structural adjustment dogmas: the alleged crowding-out of markets for goods and services by bloated and inefficient state sector agencies; and the inflexibility and inefficiency of state sector labour markets. Typically, structural adjustment agendas defined the state sector as characterised by over-staffing (a result of monopolistic service provision); over-generous pay, allowances and benefits (a result of weak budget constraints); inflexible labour markets, uncontrolled absenteeism and restrictive work practices (a result of high employment security); and low work intensity in terms of hours and pace of work (a result of over-regulated conditions of employment) (see for example OECD, 1989; Kikeri, 1998: 1–3).

Redrawing the boundaries of the state through privatisation, marketisation and public-private partnerships all had a direct impact on the labour process of workers in both sectors. Contestable funding drove labour market flexibility, ensuring cost-effectiveness if not outright cost-cutting efficiencies. Contracting-out brought with it the threat of downsizing, retrenchments and decreased job security. By removing alleged monopolies of provision, even in cases where there was no clear competitive market, the tendering process imposed budget constraints. These helped to push public-sector staff to do more with less, removing demarcation barriers between jobs, and intensifying the pace and duration of work. Private providers tended to have lower overheads. Living from contract to contract, they could offer their employees more limited job security, fewer paid training opportunities, and less in the way of fringe benefits. The effect was similar to an increase in direct managerial control, but this control was depoliticised, in the sense that employees disciplined themselves in order to remain competitive. We turn now to the shifting relationship between managerial forms of control and worker autonomy as played out in Australia and the United Kingdom.

CONTRADICTIONS OF MANAGERIALISM
AND WORKER AUTONOMY

One impact of the recomposition of the state labour process and the redrawing of state boundaries was to highlight the relations between managers and workers. In both cases the boundaries and focus of managerial authority were recast, in more discretionary ways. The impact on workers and the work process was profound, leading to increased work intensification and the individualisation of work relations.

Australia

The shifting patterns of managerial authority and employee self-management in Australia followed a complex trajectory between the early 1980s and the early years after 2000. In the early 1980s, a new Labor government inherited a rule-bound and hierarchical public service. It pursued a contradictory set of policies in relation to existing managerial hierarchies and practices in the public services. On the one hand, the government promoted an economic rationalist agenda in relation to public service elites (Pusey, 1991) and on the other it experimented with a version of industrial democracy, particularly in the Australian Taxation Office (ATO) and the Department of Social Security (DSS) (Mathews, 1989). By the beginning of the 1990s the experiment with industrial democracy had waned and was replaced by a process of decentralising managerial authority, coupled with organisation of the state labour process via industrial relations procedures, involving the resort to third parties (O'Brien, 1997).

The focus on industrial democracy in the late 1980s was associated with the promotion of a staff development approach and team working agenda (Mathews, 1992). These developments occurred in decentralised tax offices that served as data input and recording factories, with large clusters of workers in the lower grades undertaking the basic administrative work associated with taxation. There are three aspects to the changes that were made to the traditional hierarchical organisational arrangements. First, new technology was introduced. Second, the unions were brought into the relationship to secure agreement to change, and third, managerial hierarchies were recomposed, away from state-based offices to geographical offices.

As one leading trade union official reflected:

> The whole work place structure and job structure and job design fundamentally changed and the other area is the technology has fundamentally changed. The third area is the work environment and accommodation [which] has substantially changed so it is those three areas basically means everything has changed and in fact that is exactly what's happened.
>
> (State Union Official, CPSU, 1996)

The Commissioner of Taxation during this period commented that the problem was poor revenue collection, large clerical factories, without appropriate work procedures, and a seemingly dysfunctional set of relations between the management and unions (Interview, December, 1999). These changes, he said:

> coincided with a period where a lot of public service reforms here and early managerialism and I guess we [Taxation] focused more than I think others did at the time, on the people dimension and worked to achieve and to some extent did achieve, an integration between [them and] the introduction of technology.

It was in this context that the unions negotiated a version of industrial democracy as a positive work process measure and as a way of promoting the changes that were taking place.

> From a union point of view, I always felt that we had to look at some long term strategic issues about positioning the union and its members for the type of change that was coming. A lot of that change was fairly obvious, and has been obvious, I would have thought, for a long while. It involves basically, the use of technology to change and in some cases displace particularly clerical work which is repetitive in nature. So one of the tasks of the union was to try and recognise that that was a flow of direction for society and organisations.
>
> (Former Union Leader, CPSU, 1995)

While this represented a very moderate form of worker participation, it nonetheless should be acknowledged that even these developments were unusual in public services. The initiatives were ongoing and it was not long before the imperatives of management meant that the decentralisation associated with the industrial democracy experiment was restricted. As noted by one union leader:

The whole office has totally changed. It used to be capital city based and the other one is decentralization ... that's a physical decentralisation rather than a managerial centralisation. Well it was a managerial one too, some of that they're now regionalising so it's like it's gone from being totally centralized with state-based managers to totally decentralised in twenty-seven distinct little regions [and now] to coming back to all regions in management terms.

(Former Union Leader, CPSU, 1995)

In this respect, the elements that made up the state labour process were not static, and these managerial steps further reconstructed the relations between workers and managers, this time in a more hierarchical way than previously. Moreover, the scale of these experiments was relatively restricted, being confined to taxation and to a lesser extent social security, two well organised and active union areas.

While the industrial democracy experiment had become largely moribund by the end of the 1980s, as a general policy, in two agencies it had been used successfully as a means of facilitating organisational restructuring. In the light of subsequent events, this phase of participative management was short-lived. The next phase still incorporated unions but a more contestable industrial relations environment, albeit within the neo-corporatist framework. Although the late 1990s and earlier 2000s provided a harsher climate for the unions, nonetheless, they were successful in continuing to ameliorate the sharper edges of the managerial policies promoted, and in the course of that process they were able to influence management policy and practice.

The new managerial approaches of the late 1990s, and the embrace of NPM policies, are exemplified by developments in Centrelink between 1997 and 2004. These developments suggest experimentation with responsible autonomy throughout this period, followed after 2005 by a return to centralised control, task narrowing and managerial hierarchy. Centrelink was originally conceived as an all-purpose delivery agency, providing customer-contact services on behalf of 'client' departments. In 1997, it was set up as a statutory body with a Chief Executive Officer (CEO) and Board.

The first CEO moved to establish a strong, non-hierarchical service culture based on teamwork and local problem-solving. The classic managerialist 'loose-tight' paradox is illustrated by her central, top-down role in driving cultural change away from the hierarchical model:

when I arrived, we did a culture survey. We had groups of people sitting around who had come to Centrelink from various agencies ... [They wanted] open communication ... : 'We want to be empowered and we don't want to have too many rules' ... We [now] talk about servicing the customer. If anyone uses that language, 'from the top to the bottom', they are jumped on very quickly around the organisation ...

I don't think that people before that had that kind of experience. I think it was very hierarchical.

(CEO, Centrelink, 2004)

The CEO encouraged active participation of senior managers in monthly 'Guiding Coalition' meetings, and ensured careful analysis of six-monthly staff surveys. Nevertheless, there was no question that the purpose of consultation was to ensure commitment to the new high-performance culture: she described an exchange with an employee thus:

I said to her, 'How do you find Centrelink?' This is what I usually say to people. She said, 'It is all right'. I said, 'That is a bit half hearted. You obviously preferred it when we were a department'. 'Yes I did. I did not have to think and I was told what to do'. ... Now there is change all the time ... We are in a contestable environment. There are always people who talk about selling off Centrelink. A lot of the young ones love it. They have to meet KPIs. She is measured against them ... So the experience for her is uncomfortable.

(CEO, Centrelink, 2004)

Part of the cultural change involved a reconfiguration of the physical layout of the Centrelink offices. Open-plan customer bays replaced counters, and initially, queuing was replaced by a booked appointment system. The local Centrelink office was envisaged as a one-stop shop in which front-line staff worked in teams, adopting a problem-solving approach to anticipating and addressing client needs. Based on a 'Life Events' model, this holistic One Main Contact approach was described by an interviewee as 'Sue's biggest baby'. As outlined to Board members, it was a business process model enabling staff to be proactive in advising customers of their options and entitlements. Once customers identified their personal situations (for example losing a job), all available service options could be brought together and presented to them (Centrelink Board and Quality Committee, 1997–2004: 15 December, 1998; 20 July, 1999; Centrelink Guiding Coalition, 1998–2004: 15–16 May, 2000). This 'Life Events' model relied on the empowerment of front-line workers to solve complex problems (but also on the capacity of different IT systems to connect seamlessly). It was part of a wider discursive shift in the late 1990s, from the language of 'clients' or 'beneficiaries' to that of 'customers' (du Gay and Salaman, 1992). Vardon, the CEO, also instituted 'Value Creation Workshops' whereby customers were invited to meetings in Centrelink offices to discuss standards of customer service with local staff (Centrelink Guiding Coalition, 1998–2004: 20–1 September, 2001). In addition, regular customer surveys were conducted.

An aspect of customer service which was pursued with great vigour was 'workforce availability' – a concept that encompassed an extension of opening hours and a reduction in absenteeism. Like the ATO, Centrelink was highly unionised, and Vardon distanced herself from the Coalition government's anti-union agenda, saying that she was prepared to be 'looked down on' by 'other people in this town [Canberra]' for her willingness to 'work with the unions': given the magnitude of her reform agenda. 'I know which fronts to win.' (CEO, Centrelink, March, 2004). Nevertheless, she was fully supportive of the government's tough stance on industrial action, seeing strikes as antithetical to customer service.

In open-plan offices, flexible opening hours were a source of work intensification. Staff found it difficult to do follow-up work or gain training in rapidly-changing and increasingly complex benefit eligibility rules, without exposing themselves to the anger of customers waiting to be served. The incidence of aggression mounted, as waiting customers became abusive and even violent at the sight of staff exchanging information or doing paperwork. The problem escalated after the CEO's departure in late 2004. From that time, the geographical and spatial layout of Centrelink office became, not an expression of decentralised 'empowerment' but an arena in which a return to low-trust relations among government, client agencies, staff and customers was played out through heightened surveillance, customer aggression and employee absenteeism.

By 2005, the customer focus discourse was ringing increasingly hollow. In what was commonly called 'Welfare to Work', government policy revisions linked increasingly targeted welfare payments ever more tightly to proof of job-search activity. There was little customer 'choice' or sovereignty in the new role of Centrelink staff in determining eligibility for transfer payments and in enforcing the conditions attached to ongoing eligibility for those benefits. Inevitably, the front-line customer service officer bore the brunt of reactions to these changes. The customer service model implied direct contact between customers and Centrelink staff. Before 'Welfare to Work', the model had been one in which initial contact was with front-line staff, and subsequent reporting arrangements could be made on line or by phone. As the monitoring of the unemployed tightened and became more complex, face-to-face contact increased:

> What we're moving to now is something called the participation contact mode ... For a long, long time people who are more than 32km ... away from the office, have been allowed to fax or post their fortnightly application for payment for the dole form. As of now that's no longer the case. The rule now is if it's 90 minutes one way travel you will lodge in person ... .
>
> (Customer Service Adviser, Centrelink, 2006)

Offices became more crowded with disgruntled 'customers' increasingly feeling distrusted and coerced, increasing workload pressures on front-line staff who were now increasingly powerless to make decisions. This worker commented on the new checking process and its impact:

[We] get a lot of abuse now. Just suppose you were claiming payments, you'd contact Centrelink either over the phone or by coming into a customer service centre ... so now you come to Centrelink, you go to the Job Network, you come back to Centrelink and then you come back to Centrelink again.

(Customer Service Adviser, Centrelink, 2006)

The complications of the new eligibility checking process placed considerable demands on information technology, and it might take three visits and well over the mandated eighteen days before eligibility was confirmed. Dissatisfied customers took their frustrations out on staff (IT worker and CPSU Councillor, 2006). Moreover, as a condition for ongoing payment eligibility, front-line staff were required to check customers' job-search diaries, telephoning employers for confirmation. There was escalating stress for both customers and staff of sitting in an increasingly crowded open space, sometimes with 'kids riding their bikes around ... and playing football and things', advising customers that they had breached eligibility requirements, and 'could not get paid for two, three months' (Customer Service Adviser, November, 2006). The open-plan remnants of high-trust days meant that:

if aggression does become an issue, there is nowhere for staff members to withdraw to, that is effectively removed from the rest of the office ... the incidence of high-level aggression is spiking.

(IT Programmer, Centrelink, 2007)

After 2005, the growing number and complexity of decisions was addressed by a gradual return towards specialised 'back office' work through a process of Business Line Consolidation, reminiscent of that already described in the ATO. Call centre staff with five weeks' training were used to collect 'initial contact' data. But there was also a classic 'tight' managerialist explanation:

They're trying to get a line of sight from the client agencies and departments through to the customers. And they felt other structures [national office, area managers and customer service centres] there were a lot of breaks ... I think they saw that the departments were paying us money to provide services and they couldn't see where their money was going. ... [Now] if you are talking about Working Age Participation, that's DEWR [Department of Work and Employment Relations]. DEWR pays money to Centrelink to provide these services. Now you've got whole sites that are just Working Age Participation sites, so really all the staff in that site and what they're doing almost belongs to DEWR.

(Specialist Program Officer, Centrelink, 2006)

Indeed, after 2005, DEWR, now Centrelink's major client agency, adopted what a number of interviewees saw as an increasingly micro-managing role within Centrelink, in pursuing the government's reform agenda. First, it drove a hard value-for-money bargain, pitting Centrelink's cost structures against those of its private and community sector Job Network providers:

> DEWR have been right in there, ... putting pressure on ... : 'We have been into your offices and we have seen people doing this kind of work and we know it doesn't take as long as your model says it does.
>
> (Financial Officer, Centrelink, 2006)

Second, DEWR was responsible for ensuring that all government agencies complied with the government's 2005 WorkChoices amendments to the Workplace Relations Act 1996. These amendments strictly curtailed workplace union activity. Centrelink staff were engaged in a work process that increasingly cut across their own value systems:

> That is a requirement of Centrelink staff now, rather than being empathetic to the needs of the customer, that they actually support and implement government policy as their primary focus.
>
> (IT Worker, Centrelink, 2007)

The lack of trust implied in increasing surveillance and pressure to meet performance targets was insulting to those who work beyond contract, for example spending lunch-hours on behalf of especially disadvantaged customers. With no respite from an increasingly intensified and conflictual work process, and constrained from any overt form of collective action or show of mutual support, Centrelink staff increasingly took refuge in utilising the leave entitlements that they had been able to secure in their earlier collective agreements (Junor et al., 2009). As managers tried to clamp down on the use of leave entitlements, workers came to see absenteeism as a way of resisting control and affirming collective rights.

United Kingdom

In the United Kingdom, the working out of these processes took a different trajectory. Here the government promoted a decentralisation of managerial authority in the 1980s, as part of the process of enhancing managerial capacity within the offices (Fairbrother, 1994). These processes gave rise to an uneven pattern of managerialism, although the common feature was to enhance the immediate capacities of managerial staff at the local level. Towards the end of the 1980s, these developments were complemented by a fragmentation of the civil service structure with the establishment of Executive Offices and agencies, as part of a break-up of the formerly unified and interlinked civil service labour process (Fairbrother, 2006). While these dimensions continued to be promoted, the relation between national approaches and office politics increasingly affirmed management by diktat, by decisions made at a national level, increasingly at the senior level of the Executive Offices and the agencies.

The government initiatives in the early 1980s were aimed in part at creating a decentralised managerial structure, with the authority to manage offices in a more direct way than had previously been the case. This was a move towards creating a more malleable workforce, employed in terms of immediate work demands. This meant the end of standardised and uniform employment relations and a more authoritative local management, particularly at the office level.

Increasingly during the 1980s, a layer of staff – the district managers and other senior staff – were designated as responsible for budgets and people management. These managers increasingly exercised discretionary authority over the local budget, such as overtime worked and refurbishment of offices. In effect, this has meant redrawing the management-worker divide in these offices. At the same time, there was a formalisation of already existing divisions within offices, often gendered, with women on the lower grades and men as the 'new' managers. While the impetus for these changes came from outside the office, the way in which they were implemented depended crucially on the practices and commitments of the local management and workforce.

These developments were played out in stark ways in the Inland Revenue, at the time that the Australian Taxation Office began to experiment with forms of industrial democracy. By 1986 two key elements of Financial Management Initiative (FMI) had been announced for the Inland Revenue. First, building on earlier schemes a management information system was developed, using standardised indicators, to decide what work an office should achieve in designated time periods. Second, the Financial Management and Accounting System, was implemented, a method to provide information on what an office expects to spend and has spent, within designated time periods. Accompanying these initiatives there was a reorganisation of management structures with reference to cost centres at a local office, as well as regionally. Henceforth, each local office developed financial plans detailing how much money was available to run an office and how it would be spent. While these developments did not necessarily mean a change in managerial style there was evidence of managers feeling their way and in the course of so doing invoking a range of practices that had implications for the Inland Revenue workers. This restructuring was furthered with the consolidation of managerial structures, establishing a cadre of new line managers replacing functional managers.

These developments in the Inland Revenue were paralleled by similar moves in Social Security. During the 1980s, the department was divided into 800 cost centres. There was a manager for each cost centre, which had a budget covering staff and non-staff costs, with the staff budget the most significant since staff costs account for 70 per cent of department administrative costs. During the 1980s, flexibilities were introduced within the staff budgetary control. This involved a relaxation of the staff in post targets; variations in the grade mix; and movement of funds within the staff budget, particularly between permanent staff, casual workers, and overtime work.

Central to this process has been the devolution and redefinition of managerial authority and discretion. This created the opportunity for local management to exploit the polyvalent nature of civil service jobs, thereby underwriting a 'flexible' use of labour resources. With the changes in the 1980s calculation and administration of contributory benefit and subsequently supplementary benefit, modifications to work routines were introduced, with workers expected to acquire new skills, for example in computing, and to shift from one set of work routines to another. For the workers, these changes involved moves from one area of expertise and knowledge to new areas.

One union branch secretary from the social security area described the approach of managerial level staff in 1986 as follows:

> the manager has only got so many staff. The problem as far as they are concerned is that I ain't got enough staff. They can see that but they tend to attribute it to the other buggers having too many so they spend all their time fighting each other to get staff off each other without really being able to see that it is just lack of staff *per se*.
>
> (Executive Officer, Social Security, 1986)

This was an office in which staffing levels were determined centrally and where there was relatively little scope for managerial initiative in these matters.

With the shift during the 1980s to more devolved forms of management it became evident that local managements had begun to exploit the 'flexible' margins of their workforces. This involved a consideration of forms of numerical and time flexibility, the recruitment of temporary workers and the allocation of overtime. Local managements exercised their new-found discretions to relax staff-in-post targets, vary grading mixes, and move funds within staff budget headings. Thus, the devolution of decision-making to a local level meant that managers have been able to exercise hitherto unprecedented discretion on a range of matters to do with office conditions and management.

As part of the quest to engender a service or enterprise ethos, senior managements looked to various human resource management techniques, specifically total quality management, as potential work organisation models. Central to these initiatives was an attempt by management to recast employment relations in terms of the individual rather than the collective. To realise this objective it was common for line management to be given an enhanced role in dealing with their workforce, particularly in relation to promotion procedures, merit payments and the like. This involved the introduction of such practices as team briefings, quality circles and total quality management procedures. Similar experiments with total quality management were also evident in public-sector organisations in Australia.

Pay arrangements were also amended to include a performance or merit element. As a result, workers found that local management could exercise their discretion in what to some appeared to be arbitrary ways. This was illustrated in one office when one office secretary reported about the problems of obtaining performance-related payments for women who had been on maternity leave during the period:

> the main thing at the moment is that I am finding is that ... women who have been on maternity leave and really were back at work when their report should have been written but they were never ... written because the actual period that they were at work was less than four months ... Even though reports are not written, the HEO can say 'I deem a marking for that period' so that they can be awarded their performance pay. But what they are seeing is that ... they have to wait another a year. They are really being discriminated against for being off on maternity leave.
>
> (Office Secretary, Social Security, 1992)

Thus, accompanying the restructuring of management in these offices problems have begun to emerge which arise from individual mangers exercising their new-found discretion in ways that are seen by the workforce to be to their disadvantage.

The reordering of managerial structures was quite complicated and varied from area to area. Nonetheless there are general patterns across the civil service, indicated by a generalised concern with more devolved and decentralised forms of management. In this context, a range of initiatives has been introduced aimed at individualising employment relations as well as laying the foundation for a corporate or enterprise ethos. The other side of this is the attempt by management to restrict and redefine collective worker involvement in matters concerning the organisation and operation of offices. This has involved giving attention to staff motivation as well as recasting the role and scope of union action.

In this context, management began to take on a different face in the eyes of workers.

> Another thing: you had good and bad managers – us and them type managers. Some were quite good. They had a job to do, but you could work with them. Others are quite enlightened, and they would try to work things or get more staff.
>
> (Call Centre Operator, Benefits Agency, 1995)

But, management work within a very restrictive context that tends to underwrite the move towards more direct forms of control, rather than facilitating cooperative arrangements. Thus:

Now you've got this management that seems to be a massive ego and says 'I'm the boss'. They are even breaking their own rules, ... Before, theoretically, if a manager could see ... a situation with staffing, they could alter the budget, move staff around, reinforce a particular dept to take the strain, and focus the staff where it is needed. Now district managers don't have that. They have just been told 'you have got to lose this staff and this is your budget'.

(Call Centre Operator, Benefits Agency, 1995)

So increasingly the workers experienced the sharper edges of both direct and indirect forms of managerialism.

These practices were nuanced over the subsequent decade and a half. However, by the end of the 1990s and into the 2000s, these agencies had been transformed. First, government and senior agency management continued to issue requirements for the delivery of services and the organisation of work, underwriting the authority of the civil service management from local to senior levels. Second, the offices were reorganised, with an increasing emphasis on front-line staff rather than back room specialists and support. Third, new discourses were promoted, particularly focusing on 'customers' rather than 'claimants'.

These developments were clearly evident in Jobcentre Plus. Beginning in 2001, before the establishment of Jobcentre Plus, the DWP began setting up Pathfinder offices, initially located in the two agencies, Employment Service (ES) and the Benefits Agency (BA). These offices seek to provide an integrated and sequential process of work-welfare provision. The first Pathfinder offices were opened in October 2001 and by 2007 there were 272 offices, covering a quarter of Great Britain, providing a single point of delivery. Everyone of working age who enters the benefits system, including those who are economically inactive, see a Financial Assessor who checks their benefit claim form and a Personal Adviser who conducts a work focused interview. The national roll was completed by 2006 (Lissenburgh and Marsh, 2003). Accompanying this initiative, new integrated Jobcentre Plus offices were set up across twenty-four districts (some of which included Pathfinder offices) (Karagiannaki, 2006).

The Jobcentre Plus concept created the opportunity for efficiency savings and, at the same time, a reduction in inconvenience to jobseekers. Whilst these two aims were not necessarily antagonistic, the experience of job centre staff was that 'efficiency' took clear precedence over any measure of service delivery. The new arrangements brought together two sets of processes under one roof; it also made possible the centralisation of 'back office' functions as well as telephone enquiries. Clients now initiated claims by telephoning a regional contact centre. An appointment would then be made at the local job centre; this appointment was required before visiting the local office. The perceived efficiency gain from this move was termed a reduction of 'footfall'. Employees put these developments in more conventional terms: 'They didn't want people in job centres, so they centralised it' (Benefit Processor, Jobcentre Plus, 2005).

Reality, inevitably, was more complicated. First, the visibility and familiarity of local offices meant that they remained the first port of call when individuals wanted to discuss problems. As was noted:

> [Other departments], including pensions and Inland Revenue, say 'pop into your local job centre'. Because we are everywhere.
> (Business Manager, Jobcentre Plus, 2006)

Centralisation of services meant that they were less accessible. As indicated, Jobcentre offices were used even when queries were unrelated to the work of the job centre. The second complication was that, while the system itself was workable, it took little account of the nature of clients' needs:

> ... because, whilst the person will probably want to know about job opportunities available to them, they won't want to know that until their money is sorted out, because obviously they still need to eat.
> (Income Support Processor, Jobcentre Plus, 2006)

This concern – that the focus on procedural efficiency has been at the cost of quality of service – is widely shared. Another member of staff puts the point more strongly:

> There is a concerted effort to make the aspect of the benefits almost a secondary concern. But it's not. If the customer is desperate for money that's going to be their primary concern. The job can come later. They are making the receipt of benefits almost impossible.
> (Benefits Processor, Jobcentre Plus, 2005)

The rationale for such major changes to systems and working practices is inevitably more complex and less Machiavellian that this. Nevertheless, the impact on employees and the public was marked. For employees, the effect was to limit job roles and constrain individual discretion, while creating the framework for a more systematic approach to work intensification and monitoring. The procedure for appointments exemplifies an approach that some interviewees felt infantilises employees who are perfectly capable of exercising judgement. As one interviewee puts it:

> When [the claimant] actually gets to sit down with somebody face to face, what that person can discuss with them is really limited.
> (Income Support Processor, Jobcentre Plus, 2006)

The implications of these and other changes for employee relations are complex. One possibility is to view these developments as part of a changing 'frontier of control', between state managers and state workers. However, whilst local managers have been empowered, this is true only in a rather narrow sense. Office managers, for example, are now responsible for a range of human resources and 'business' issues that would, previously, have been specialist functions. At the same time, they themselves act within tightly specified parameters, with very little leeway to vary procedures. Thus, the label 'manager' needs to be treated with caution. One consequence of this is that, in 2006, PCS strike action was strongly supported by some groups of junior managers: 'people who line-manage staff are under the cosh as much as everybody else' (Branch Secretary, PCS, 2006). Thus, the 'frontier of control' refers to a fluid relationship and ongoing relationship between 'managers' qua managers and 'workers'.

The cuts to public spending announced by the Coalition government in May 2010, ostensibly in response to a record budget deficit, raised the prospect of a far more radical government approach to running the agency. Cuts of £62.5 billion have been scheduled to fall on those areas, such as benefits, deemed not in need of special protection, representing a 34 per cent reduction of financial support in these departments. By one estimate, a 34 per cent cut for the Department of Work and Pensions would be the equivalent of the entire Jobcentre Plus pay bill (Social Market Foundation, 2010). For PCS, in arguing for 'not a single penny cut, not a single job lost' (PCS, 2010), the recent history of the agency created a weakness and also, possibly, a new source of strength. Government could now certainly envisage the transfer of Jobcentre Plus – either wholesale or piecemeal – to the private sector. At the same time, collective action in defence of jobs seems likely. The routinisation of work, along with the introduction of more rigid approaches to performance management, meant that employees related differently to management and were now more likely to identify their own interests collectively.

ASSESSMENT

From the early 1980s onwards, state workers in both countries experienced a shifting pattern of managerialism, as governments have promoted the restructuring of state services, including the core administration. This involved the introduction of increased flexibility in the state sector labour market through the creation of increasingly fluid boundaries between the public and private sectors. It also involved a managerialist restructuring of the state sector labour process through the combination of aspects of direct (and indirect) control and responsible autonomy.

By the late 1990s the values of the 'audit society' (Power, 1997) had been embraced in both countries, within a social framework in which a neo-liberal governmental philosophy rested uneasily with highly restrictive practices and came into conflict with collective opposition from organisations like trade unions and professional bodies. While the British government of the early 1990s promoted more nuanced and indirect forms of control, their Australian counterparts promoted the sharp edge of these policies once the Howard Coalition government was elected and consolidated its political control. New work cultures were promoted in each country where the workplace became the site of a prevailing instrumentalist and managerialist mode of thinking, though there were several complex dimensions to this ascendancy (For further detail, see Fairbrother and Poynter, 2001).

Reflecting the changed role of the state in mediating the political relationship between capital and citizens, new public management restructured the state sector labour process in three main ways. First, modernisation involved an attempt to reshape public servants' identity, displacing traditional orientations – whether bureaucratic, welfarist or occupational/professional – through realignment with agency norms and with pragmatic values such as effectiveness. Second, managerialism, as a performance-based control system, held individual workers accountable for delivering the efficiencies required by the neo-liberal delegitimation of the welfare state. Third, public-sector workers, particularly those in the front line, were subject to contradictory performance management regimes. On the one hand they were accountable for serving and even 'delighting' citizens reconstituted as sovereign consumers in 'markets' for state services, but on the other hand they were required to administer the stringent economic criteria and workforce participation tests on which access to streamlined and rationalised services was increasingly contingent. When recipients of rationalised, standardised or coercive 'services' became disenchanted to the point of aggression, public-sector workers were held accountable for transforming the resulting abusiveness into consumer satisfaction. Several studies have identified the impacts of these three managerial principles – the attempted reshaping of public-sector worker identity, service rationalisation, and customer focus.

There is a relatively sparse literature on what such changes have meant for the organisation and operation of the state labour process, particularly that of front-line workers, although significant work has been done on public-sector professionals (see Ackroyd *et al.*, 2004 and Kirkpatrick *et al.*, 2007). Ackroyd and colleagues note an overarching sense of increasing managerial control, based on the increasingly interventionist role of politicians in determining the priorities of welfare services and delivery. The attack on 'producer dominance', with state sector workers 'on tap not on top', has resulted in those responsible for delivering services feeling caught between two 'empowered' groups, on the one hand, active, individualistic, managerial leaders, and on the other hand, users empowered by citizen's charters that offer both choice and voice (Bolton, 2002; Ackroyd *et al.*, 2004: 56–64; Korcynski and Bishop, 2008). Nevertheless, as the depoliticisation thesis argues, the power of both managers and consumers is circumscribed. Managers were operating within a 'homeostatic' (Ackroyd *et al.*, 2004: 68) control system based on accountability for best value goals. In work areas such as job centres, a rhetoric of 'customer sovereignty' rang hollow amongst those whose welfare eligibility was contingent on meeting work and job-search tests: such customers were likely to become difficult, demanding and even aggressive (Korczynski and Bishop, 2008).

Nevertheless, as Ackroyd and others (2004: 44–6) demonstrate, managers found that top-down control was always incomplete; policy was never adopted without compromise and modification, and the implementation of new techniques and practices was always negotiated. Forms of resistance, involving claims to autonomy and discretion, might involve the invocation of a distinctive public service ethos of altruism, vocation and willingness to work beyond contract. Over time, however managerial control became more attuned to financial realities, as new, generic managers replaced middle managers who had come up through the ranks and who recognised the difficulty of evaluating the complex, context-dependent and discretionary nature of front-line decisions (Power, 1997; Ackroyd *et al.*, 2004: 38–45). Front-line managers were still able resist this pressure, creating spaces for humane and dignified interaction with clients (Bolton and Houlihan, 2005; Bolton, 2007). Yet the costs of NPM took their toll. The intended consequence was work intensification; the unintended consequences included change fatigue, stress, demoralisation, increased absenteeism and higher turnover (Ackroyd, *et al.*, 2004).

Similarly, in Australia, public-sector workers reported greater loss of control over hours and greater work intensification (O'Donnell *et al.*, 2001). They felt less able to use discretion, and reported declining levels of information from their managers. Public-sector workers were twice as likely to report insecurity and lack of career opportunity, and indicated a dramatically higher incidence of stress, which they attributed to workload, organisational change and insecurity. Public-sector workers were also more likely to report deteriorating management-union relations and a stronger sense that downsizing was attributable to managerially-imposed financial restrictions, not to external market factors.

The clash of values between the new managerialism and an older public service ethos of vocation, integrity, impartiality and altruism has had the 'unintended consequences' – stress, demoralisation and high turnover (Ackroyd *et al.*, 2004: 42). They argue that a new generation of middle managers, who had not risen through the ranks, had little sense of the complexity and risk of welfare work, and inappropriately ignored process and discretion in the rigid imposition of outcomes-based performance standards. They note how the shift from universal citizenship to means-tested services clashed with rhetorics of citizens' charters and consumer choice. Public-sector welfare workers were supposedly empowered as active, individualistic, entrepreneurial leaders, strongly identified with the organisation, controlled by centrally-determined goals, and efficiently delivering best value (p. 69). At the same time, they were typecast by government rhetoric as inefficient and self-serving. Operating in a climate of financial retrenchment, user pays, rationing, and means testing, they struggled with increased caseloads and standardised and intensified work processes (pp. 107–9). Nevertheless, Ackroyd and colleagues (2004) argue that it would be a mistake to underestimate the resilience with which public-sector workers maintained a sense of identity, noting that the new management systems were never fully perfected, cautioning against claims of deskilling, and arguing the limited effectiveness of performance management (p. 113). Certainly, workers experienced:

> 'initiative fatigue' – in a succession of new policy initiatives, restructuring and downsizing, each changed organisational format seemed to be 'invented long before any rational assessment of its predecessor.
>
> (pp. 164–5)

Yet they learned to 'accommodate the mess' of mixed policy objectives with 'cynicism at all levels' (p. 166). Despite a sense of being 'driven not by what matters but what could be measured', public-sector values, remained 'surprisingly robust', because they reinforced key aspects of practice (p. 169).

In a sense, managerialism represented an attempt to apply neo-Taylorism to the public-sector labour process (Pollitt, 1993). The new calculus of economic efficiency requires workers to negotiate the clash between the conflicting 'temporalities' of service work and clock time (Cortis, 1999; Harvey, 1999), within staffing levels calculated on the basis of the duration of a 'standard' procedure or interaction. In desk-based work, there is reduced scope for problem-solving or follow-through. On the front-line, whether in case management, education or care work, customer contact is organised with scant respect for the 'process time' needed by clients who are young, frail or otherwise 'non-standard' (Davies, 1994). Bolton (2005) describes the difficulty of attempting:

> to maintain customer satisfaction in the face of unmet expectations. Nurses, teachers, and social workers find themselves unable to offer what they see as truly 'quality service'. The time available when they could offer their authentic self to patients and clients has been restricted.
>
> (Bolton, 2005: 159)

> In what Bolton describes as an increasingly 'unequal exchange', the gap has widened between workers' time-constrained capacity to meet clients' needs and managerial discourses of customer service, and this gap licenses customers to express indignation, even aggression.
>
> (Bolton, 2005: 6)

The remoulding and reshaping of the state labour process are best captured by the concept of 'customer oriented bureaucracy' (Korcsynksi, 2002: 1–15; see also Korczynski and Bishop, 2008). The term 'customer oriented bureacracy' captures the offer of an unachievable combination of efficiency, empathy and consumer control, through work organised and managed according to contradictory principles: a bureaucratic division of labour designed to maximise task efficiency; and a division of labour designed to enhance a customer relationship. On these contradictory logics a fragile social order is constructed through a human resource management approach that uses a language of shared values, based on identification with business strategies, teamwork and customer orientation. Worker interests are delegitimised by a denial that they can be separated from those of customers (Korczynski, 2002: 1–67). Thus, conflict and potential aggression are structurally embedded, not accidental. The 'indeterminacy of labour' – employers' incomplete control in translating labour power into labour – means that workers must be given some 'ownership' of customer interactions, even while the work process is rationalised and speeded up. As bureaucratic impersonality is replaced by 'pseudo-relationships', workers acquire 'two bosses' (p. 73). They must be doubly flexible, both in responding to idiosyncratic customer behaviour, and in coping with variable levels and timing of demand, in work where there is no staffing buffer through excess capacity (p. 74). This in itself is likely to generate irrational customer outbursts. Such outbursts are and always latent and 'the irate customer should be seen as a systematic part of the social relations of the front-line workplace' (p. 77).

CONCLUSIONS

Three conclusions can be drawn from the analysis offered in this chapter. First, work organisation has been reshaped around the central theme of 'customer orientation'. This focus has changed the content and performance of work in the core administrative sectors, especially where service provision has been recast with reference to the marketised relationship between providers and purchasers of products and services. Such initiatives involved pressures to contain costs and improve productivity, encouraging staff to collude with local management in attempting to 'prove' their efficiency, by intensifying their own labour. Customer orientation thus cuts across the complex dynamics of more genuine interactions with customers, in ways that this chapter has only been able to touch on, without digressing into the debates over emotional labour (Bolton and Houlihan, 2005; Bolton, 2007; Korczynski and Bishop, 2008; Junor *et al.*, 2009). As hinted by our discussion of forms of resistance, the requirement to comply with workload measures may actually lead to covert forms of labour withdrawal, cutting across workers' own freely-given tendency to work above contract through intrinsic interest or identification with clients.

Second, the emphasis on managerialism has undermined the centrality of specialist knowledge and skill in the performance of state work. One feature of this erosion of specialist discretion and control over work has been the introduction of flatter management structures, with management control located closer to the work process. Managerial responsibility shifted downwards, with local managers assuming greater responsibilities for budgets, personnel and marketing issues while typically 'real' power over policy and strategy remained at the centre of the statutory body, department or government. Management reform has tended to challenge the discretion exercised by specialists over the conduct of their work by either circumscribing it within the bureaucratic framework of financial and budgetary controls and externally imposed performance targets, or by blurring the distinction between the specialist's role as manager of the labour process and participant within it. Concurrently, there has been a displacement of specialist knowledge by a range of managerial competencies, primarily concerned with meeting financial targets and performance measures, and the presentation and marketing of the product or service.

Third, performance measurement has been used within these new management arrangements to circumscribe work processes so that tangible and measurable outputs have tended to displace the less quantifiable and less tangible ones. There are echoes of scientific management here in the subjection of public service labour to quantitative measures of performance and efficiency. However, rather than a clear separation of supervision and control from the actual conduct of work, there is a devolution of management responsibilities to those who also do the work. This routinisation of public service work has been associated with the break-up of the administrative services into agencies, business units and budget centres. The outcome is a 'new' set of social relations based upon the superficial equalities of the marketplace in which all participants become the buyers and sellers of services.

In this new world of purchasers and providers, the state has increasingly set the rules and regulations for the effective conduct of marketised relations within the civil and public services in each state. In this sense, governments have increasingly taken on the appearance of being located one step removed from direct responsibility for and control over the quality of the provision of public services. In this process of depoliticisation, the governing strategy was and remains intensely political, although worked out in a myriad of institutional forms, depending in part on the political complexion of the government and in part on the precise measures put in place by successive governments. Applied to the these two states, the immediate agents of the state – the 'purchasing' departments – became the enforcers of government policy, operating through contractual arrangements with other public agencies (e.g. Centrelink in the case of Australia and Jobcentre Plus in the United Kingdom) or private organisations (e.g. the Job Network in Australia). While governments set the policy framework, they distanced themselves from the implementation of policy; thus, the 'depoliticising' process was multi-layered; more than one step removed from direct government responsibility.

This restructuring provided the context for union organisation and action in the core administrative areas. They were both party to these developments as well as attempting to challenge and question them. To explore these measures, in the next chapter we will provide an overview of public-sector industrial relations processes and practices in both countries.

6 The State, Depoliticisation and Unions

Industrial relations within the state sector do not easily fit into a standard pluralist analysis, based on acceptance of collective negotiation as central to the employer/employee relationship (Dickens and Bordogna, 2008: 540). On one side there are employees and their industrial organisations, while on the other side is the state acting in multiple roles: as a source of policy, as regulator, as a source of finance and as employer. Moreover, governments as employers have often jealously guarded their right to determine the working conditions of their employees. Many states have introduced restrictions on the right to organise and to take industrial action. In the United Kingdom, however, public sector workers have enjoyed most of the rights of their private sector counterparts. In Australia, for both public and private sector workers, the right to organise had not been challenged (until recent times); although until the early 1990s, the legal right to strike was formally denied to all Australian workers. Thus, the state in both Australia and the United Kingdom is more than just the 'other' party in the employment relationship.

The governments of Australia and the United Kingdom established state bodies to regulate and determine employment conditions for state workers. They also reserved the right to legislate directly on state sector employment when it was deemed appropriate to do so. In the United Kingdom, state apparatuses such as the Whitley Councils were used before the 1980s to carry out the detailed regulation of public sector industrial relations (Bach and Winchester, 2003; Beaumont, 1992; Fairbrother, 1994). These arrangements gave way to departmental and agency-level arrangements in the civil service and specialist tribunals for other sectors of public services. In Australia, public service boards acted as employers until the 1980s, their powers complemented and further regulated by various conciliation and arbitral bodies. With the demise of compulsory conciliation and arbitration, individual agencies took on the role of 'immediate' employers, with the government as 'ultimate employer' retaining the right not only to direct its managerial agents, but also to change the regulations under which they operated (O'Brien and O'Donnell, 2007). In both countries, from the late 1980s, the industrial landscape started to change, culminating in radical shifts from the latter half of the 1990s and into the new century.

As noted above, governments as employers sought to depoliticise their relations with their employees. Such a shift impacted directly on union activity and the ways they organise and operate. This chapter explores these relationships. On the one hand, governments maintained overall control of the nature and direction of state expenditure, and imposed significant limits to the decentralisation of public sector industrial relations to their managerial agents within agencies and departments. On the other hand, by devolving industrial relations operations, governments sought to distance themselves from detailed involvement in industrial relations processes. The immediate agents of government – the 'parent' or 'purchasing' departments – became the enforcers of government policy, operating through contractual arrangements with other public agencies. This 'depoliticising' process was thus multi-layered introducing a set of relationships involving the appearance that the organisational and operational activity of agencies and departments was more than one step away from direct government responsibility.

These relationships play out in relation to unions' workplace-level strategies in both countries. Unions responded to the decentralisation of public sector industrial relations by devoting increased resources to refocusing their structures and operations to cope more effectively with the resource intensive nature of decentralised industrial relations. In the UK, this ultimately led to a more activist form of public services unionism and contested forms of leadership. In Australia, a combination of centralisation of union structures and encouragement of increased workplace activism emerged. The chapter examines the effects of fragmentation in UK agencies managing employment services and benefits in Jobcentre Plus (previously the Benefits Agency) and focuses on the growing role of workplace activists. The focus for Australia is on the evolution of workplace bargaining in the equivalent welfare delivery agency, Centrelink, from its inception in 1997 to 2009. For each country, an analysis is offered of the ways in which union structures changed to facilitate a response to managerial restructuring.

The chapter begins with an account of the shift away from centralised terms and conditions of employment in the United Kingdom civil service, focusing in particular on the role of the Labour government after 1997. Over time, the relationship between the state as employer and the unions was reshaped, at a central level and in workplaces. In the second major section, we chart out the ways in which successive governments in Australia sought to set the parameters of bargaining, oscillating between allowing unions a central place in the process (usually under Labo(u)r governments although with qualifications) but eventually under all governments to marginalise their involvement. In the final major section the themes addressed in each country are drawn together and an assessment made of the relationship between unions and the state as employer. The chapter concludes with a brief conclusion.

UNITED KINGDOM: A PROCESS OF CENTRALISED FRAGMENTATION

At the start of the 1980s, civil service industrial relations in the United Kingdom centred on a formal negotiating structure that was still recognisable from its origins sixty years previously. Bargaining on all significant matters took place via a set of national joint committees, defined by function, and organised hierarchically, the Whitley system. While the Whitley inheritance continues to exert an influence, in terms both of structure and function, the 'system' has been transformed by three developments: the fragmentation of pay bargaining to the departmental and agency level, the decentralisation of management responsibility within agencies and, increasingly importantly, the impact of market testing and outsourcing. Nowhere has this change been more significant than in Jobcentre Plus.

From Bureaucrats to Managers

The initial reconstitution of civil service bargaining arrangements during the 1980s should be seen in the context of the Conservative government's broader political preoccupations. In the case of the Financial Management initiative (FMI), a focus on the need for greater efficiency was accompanied by more rhetorical attacks on 'big government'.

FMI put in place the mechanisms for greater central scrutiny of local costs. In retrospect, perhaps, FMI began the process of teaching administrators to think like managers. An incremental devolution of operational decision-making and more transparent accountability for budgets meant that local managers not only needed to make decisions; they also needed to defend them. With respect to the provision of social security, for example, the then department in the 1980s was divided into 800 cost centres. There was a manager for each cost centre and a budget covering staff and non-staff costs. The staff budget was the most significant, since staff costs accounted for 70 per cent of department administrative costs. During the 1980s flexibilities were introduced in the control of staffing budgets, relaxing the staff in post targets and allowing variations in the grade mix and movement of funds within the staff budget, particularly between permanent staff, casual workers, and overtime work.

These developments had a significant and visible impact on union members. The role of the then National Union of Civil and Public Servants (NUCPS), covering middle grade civil servants expanded accordingly. Increasingly union leaders began to address the organisation and operation of offices, a departure from previous arrangements. As stated:

> What would you negotiate in an office? Well maybe – I wouldn't use the expression – but people could say some low level stuff like you know basic health and safety stuff in an office. It could be engaging with the

manager and discussion about staffing in terms of – maybe we need more people in this section or that section.

(National Officer, NUCPS, 1986)

In the early 1980s, office managers were assigned a staffing complement for the office, as well as an allocation for a specified number of hours of overtime. With the introduction of FMI, offices were organised on the basis of 'manpower' budgeting, with office managers allocated two budgets: first, a budget which was the amount of the cash equivalent of the staff complement and second, a manpower substitutes account which could be spent on overtime, casual or full-time staff, subject to staff number ceilings. During the 1980s and into the 1990s, local managers exploited the opportunities to vary the mix of hours worked in local offices and increasingly the use of temporary workers was complemented by an increased use of overtime.

One perverse consequence of this devolution of management authority was to make the job of management more difficult at the local level. Relatively junior civil service grades, whose role had previously been a limited supervisory one, were now 'responsible' for aspects of staffing and work organisation in their departments, a responsibility that was not matched by any real authority to make wider changes. The effect was to diffuse and complicate what would otherwise have been straightforward decisions. Such evolving arrangements were acknowledged by staff:

> There's not much [the manager] can do to influence that. He can push it up a bit or let it slide down a bit. [But] the main thing is the division of those staff. The assistant managers, the HEOs, each have their commands of staff ... they have twenty to forty staff and they tend to see the problem in terms of their own commands. The problem, as far as they are concerned, is that 'I ain't got enough staff'. They can see that, but they tend to attribute it to the other buggers having too many. So they spend all their time fighting each other to get staff off each other, without really being able to see that it is just lack of staff, *per se*.

(Executive Officer, Social Security, 1986)

This devolution positioned Executive Officers (EOs) and Higher Executive Officers (HEOs) as the most visible figures of authority. They became the front line in implementing new forms of work organisation, and they increasingly acted as a buffer for more senior management, who became less accessible at the office level.

Job cuts and work intensification provided the backdrop for an attack on facility time (paid time-off for union work). This meant that senior local activists, many of whom had previously had 100 per cent release for union duties and who had dominated their branches, were now incapable of representing members effectively without broadening participation. Related

to this time arrangement, the period saw the beginnings of local lay organisation of a form that was similar to the steward forms of representation in
other sectors of the British economy and the union delegate structures in
Australia. Although these changes in union organisation and attitudes were
significant for subsequent developments, it should be noted that the hierarchical nature of national bargaining remained central. The point of local
bargaining was essentially defensive and secondary to national negotiations.
As one national officer explained:

> [U]nderpinning all of that was the national agreement. A good work-
> place rep is making sure they are protecting the integrity of national
> agreements because even under a good manager we get situations where
> national agreements were being you know not enforced properly, which
> was leading to problems. ... there is a policing job to be done.
>
> (National Official, NUCPS, 1992)

The emphasis on operational devolution was accompanied by strong control
systems based on key performance targets and measures, such as bonus
arrangements (Fairbrother, 1994: 19; 45–6; 186). The introduction of these
control systems meant a further complication for the ways the unions organised
and operated in the sector.

Agencies and the Fragmentation of Bargaining

As noted previously, the reforms of the 1980s culminated in the 1988 Next
Steps Report, known as the Ibbs Report (Jenkins *et al.*, 1988). The report
was dismissive of the notion of a unified civil service. This perspective was
clear in the comments of senior agency managers interviewed in the early
1990s:

> We'd never had, in my view, a *general* Civil Service, there's been a civil
> service made up of a lot of people doing a lot of different things and the
> tremendous difference between people like us who are in essence not
> much different to a large Insurance Company or large Banks ... and the
> people at the centre, working closely with ministers at the heart of
> government.
>
> (Deputy Director, Benefits Agency, 1992)

One perceived consequence of agency status was a shift in employees'
loyalties – and a transformation of the 'public service ethos':

> I certainly think the family feeling of many of these agencies are getting
> does stem from being an agency ... They do not feel they are in the
> Civil Service, they are working in this agency, therefore they are more
> customer orientated and feel they are more vertically orientated towards

the job to be done and to the customers they serve, rather than to the general concept of public.

(Next Steps Project Manager, evidence to the
Treasury and Civil Service Committee, 19 June, 1991)

On the basis of experiences of state restructuring during the 1980s, it was understandable that trade union responses to the Next Steps agenda centred primarily on the possibility of privatisation. The then Institution of Professionals, Managers and Specialists (IPMS), adopted an initial position that was 'not exactly pro-agencies, but a way of avoiding privatisation' (National Officer, IPMS, quoted in Butler, 1992); 'semi-detached' agencies within the civil service were seen as the lesser of the two evils. Other unions saw the reconstruction of the civil service as agencies as the first step in the same overall privatisation process. As stated:

> The [other unions] thought it would be a way to get the Treasury off our backs. [But] the result of the way Next Steps is structured will mean the complete disintegration of the National Civil Service and the atomisation into a series of discrete business units and that'll mean inevitably the breakdown of any national grading system, national pay, national standards on promotion, recruitment, appraisal and so on.
>
> (National Official, NUCPS, 1992)

More broadly, the means of achieving continuous improvement in efficiency was to be through the employment of the same Human Resource Management techniques that had been pioneered in private industry over the preceding decade. In the early 1990s, quality circles (QCs) enjoyed a vogue: meetings of workers trained to devise performance-enhancing solutions and present them to management. To illustrate, the Employment Service encouraged staff participation in job re-design:

> Usually, the circle in [the Unemployment Benefit Office] would be given a subject by the manager ... The QC would then talk through the problems of work organisation, attitudes and training, etc., finally coming up with proposals for change.
>
> (National Official, NUCPS, 1992)

Such techniques were alien, if limited, transplants into civil service management from the private sector. While these practices were experimented with and introduced in a range of departments and agencies, there was an unevenness in implementation. The extent of change varied between districts and, as such, responses tended to be matters of local 'fire-fighting'. Nonetheless, this process of change can also be seen as strategic:

> Everything they've done from 1981 onwards has been piecemeal and incremental and perhaps not fully thought through at each stage, but

there's been logic to it which, had you started off from that point of view, you would still be on the same track ideologically. For example if you say we want a business unit which is self-accounting, self-managing and so on, and the only link is a contractor link with the department, and the minister said that you will provide X services and I will provide you with X money, and here's your targets, well there is a logic to that which forces the Chief Executive down a particular route which is even more autonomy to get out of what he or she might have considered to be over weighty pay arrangements or expensive personnel luxuries or industrial relations systems which are inappropriate as they would see it – so all of that pushes them into separatism.

(National Official, NUCPS, 1992)

With the election of a Labour government in 1997, committed to partnership in industrial relations and to an ostensibly non-ideological approach of 'what works' in public service provision, it became apparent that this trajectory was not entirely fixed. However, before proceeding to consider these developments, it is necessary to locate the organisational and operational changes in relation to pay.

The Changing Face of National Pay Bargaining

Pay determination in the civil service was, and remains, largely a national function, as opposed to regional or local. In other respects, however, the structural and procedural changes put in place from the 1980s fundamentally altered the way in which pay was negotiated and marked the end of unified settlements based on centralised negotiations based on an agreed mechanism.

For the previous three decades, the starting point for civil service pay determination had been the principle of 'fair comparison'; a principle actually dating from the Tomlin Commission of 1929–31, but given substance by the Priestley Report in 1955. Central to the comparative principle was the Pay Research Unit, put in place in 1956, which provided the data that formed the basis of national negotiation via the Whitley Council. This system of comparability continued, albeit periodically over-ridden by changing government incomes policy, until the 1980s. It is worth noting, however, that Priestley did not attempt to tackle the pay structure and so central settlements to an extent reinforced the complex pay differentials between the job categories that defined the civil service. It was for this reason that some saw Priestley as no more than an 'empirical stop-gap measure' (Gladden, 1967: 53).

Following the Conservative government's repudiation of comparability in 1980, the Megaw Committee was set up to review pay and effectively asked to 'turn the clock back' (Fry, 1988: 12). In 1982, the Megaw Committee recommended that performance-related pay arrangements be introduced, advice that was congruent with the government's broader aspirations

(Hennessy, 1990: 683). The unions opposed these recommendations, seeing universality and comparability as central principles of the Whitley system and a form of social justice in relation to the civil service. However, in 1987 the Institute of Professional Civil Servants (subsequently merged to form Prospect) agreed to the introduction of a performance pay scheme, reluctantly followed by agreements with the two largest unions, the then National Union of Civil and Public Servants and the Civil and Public Services Association (Fairbrother, 1990 and 1994). The Megaw Committee initiatives disrupted and complicated the 'stately minuet' of Whitley Council negotiations of the early Priestley period (Fry, 1974: 325) and effectively laid the ground for later approaches to individual performance management.

Yet, while the main element in pay remained dependent on a single process of national negotiation, there was always the risk of 'the return of "fair comparison" by the back door' (Fry, 1988:12). This risk was countered by a systematic fragmentation and individuation of pay arrangements, which had more than one dimension to it. First, it involved the differential treatment of various groups of employees. Despite the simplification of the previous 'class' system following the Fulton Report of 1968, different categories of staff remained. However, the 1987 deal was a break with previous across-the-board settlements by implementing dissimilar settlements for different grades and categories of civil servant, rather than uniform percentage increases, (see Elliott and Bender, 1997: 453–4). The second dimension saw a 'horizontal' fragmentation of pay arrangements to mirror the new organisational structure of the civil service. In the late 1980s the decentralisation of pay to the National Audit Office and HMSO marked the first steps. In 1991, other departments and agencies were given devolved responsibility for recruitment of all posts below Grade 7, and this was extended to all staff in 1994. The 1994 White Paper, *The Civil Service: Continuity and Change*, as well as extending the reach of competitive tendering, proposed delegation of the responsibility for pay and grading of staff below the Senior Civil Service level (i.e. below Assistant Secretary or equivalent) was in line with the Ibbs (1988) recommendations (Jenkins *et al.* 1988). Delegation initially applied, from 1 April 1994, to twenty-three agencies including the Benefits Agency and the Employment Service (later merged as Jobcentre Plus), and was extended to the rest of the civil service in 1996 (Cabinet Office, 1995: 26). The third dimension involved the delegation of managerial responsibility for performance pay elements, constituting an incremental 'vertical' fragmentation of bargaining. Incentive payments were introduced following the Ibbs Report (1998) and the Treasury continued to promote a more thorough-going approach to performance-related pay as well as greater discretion by department and agency management (OECD Report, 2004). The first Citizen's Charter published in 1991 referred to the 'powerful effect of performance pay' and proposed extending rewards and penalties in relation to performance, as part of the pay and conditions of civil servants (Cabinet Office, 1991).

When Labour returned to power, the nature and significance of national pay bargaining had significantly altered. Each civil service department and agency now negotiated pay with trade unions for its own staff below the level of the Senior Civil Service (who comprised 3,800 civil servants out of a total 500,000). Instead of a single settlement, the proliferating number of bargaining units meant that negotiations took place in parallel forums. These arrangements were characterised by a complex inter-relationship between centrally-constructed guidelines and delegated managerial decision about the detail. Departments and agencies were obliged to set the terms and conditions of employment for their staff within the framework set by the centrally-decided Civil Service Management Code. Accompanying these arrangements there was a near-universal application of individual performance pay. This devolution also had a geographical dimension, since agency headquarters and offices were scattered around the country. In combination, these developments meant that not only the structure, but also the role of national pay 'determination' had changed. Formal settlement was now not the end of the process, but just the beginning.

New Labour: 'Back to the Future'

Whereas the Conservative reforms of the 1990s were primarily concerned with the delegation of management authority and fragmentation of supposedly 'monolithic' arrangements, the New Labour approach was different:

> The post-1997 phase has built on this towards a system based more on partnership and collaboration between different parts of the public sector. The focus has shifted from outputs to outcomes, and there is a drive to take a longer-term view in policymaking and a consumer view in service delivery.
>
> (Cowper, 2001)

In practice, the shift 'from outputs to outcomes' meant increasing 'diversity' of provision; the more lucrative activities faced market testing while the remaining unattractive core was subject to continual pressure on staff numbers and wages.

On the one hand, Labour's approach seemed to offer an opportunity for trade unions to work with the government, or at least to be consulted on proposals. It was clear, though, that 'partnership' was to be of secondary importance in the context of the overall government approach to the public sector. The Blair Labour government pursued a strongly interventionist programme of public service reform, to 'direct and monitor performance' (Bach, 2002: 326). Three reports were commissioned during Labour's first term of office to address various aspects of the working of these arrangements: The Wilson Report (1999) about performance management systems, the Bichard Report (1999) also on aspects of performance management and the Makinson Report (2000) on performance pay and funding (Makinson, 2000). Central to these policies was a stronger recognition of a link between performance management systems and individual or team-based pay arrangements (Bach, 2002: 334).

Whatever the distinctions between the parties on other policy matters, on this there now seemed to be near unanimity. Labour, in fact, consciously attempted to demonstrate its new-found credentials as a party of small government and free markets. Prime Minister Blair boasted in 1999 to a conference of venture capitalists: 'You try getting change in the public sector. I bear the scars on my back after two years in government' (Flynn, 2007: 120).

It is notable, however, that for the civil service, unlike other areas of the public services, the Labour government maintained a policy of decentralised pay determination. The three major civil service unions, (PCS, Prospect, covering professional staff, and the First Division Association) all pressed for centralised pay arrangements: with PCS campaigning most publicly for an end to delegation and performance pay (Public and Commercial Services Union, 2003). Presenting its case in terms of equity and fairness, the PCS claimed that the civil service was apparently being singled out for delegation and pay performance arrangements, when compared with local government and the health service (Public and Commercial Services Union, 2003: 3–4). In 2005, the two leading unions, PCS and Prospect, launched a further stage of the campaign, calling for a return to a single national pay arrangement (Taylor, 2005).

Building on earlier reviews, the government commissioned an enquiry in 2003, chaired by Peter Gershon, the head of the Office of Government Commerce, into the operation and composition of the civil service. This review was explicitly '*designed* to reduce civil service numbers' (Gay, 2006: 1, italics added). This, in part, heralded a return to the efficiency scrutiny of the 1980s, but in the context that the Labour government was also prepared to intervene directly in the construction and operation of the civil service (Bach, 2002). Given increasing convergence of policies, the two main parties now attempted to differentiate themselves by the toughness of their respective approaches. Whereas previously the effect of cuts on civil servants might have been seen as 'collateral damage' in the war against inefficiency, now it was personal. At the rhetorical level, this involved the rediscovery of stereotypes, such as the army of faceless men in bowler hats depicted in a Conservative campaign poster (Independent, 2004.) Gershon attempted to divide the public sector by explicitly portraying the typical civil servant as a barrier to effective service:

> The aim of this review is to ensure that front-line staff get the resources they need to do their job even better, and that the bureaucracy that can get in their way is removed.
>
> (Gershon, 2004: 37)

The cost in terms of projected job losses was in excess of 100,000 by 2008: 20 per cent of total employment (Hansard, 12 July, 2004, Column 1130; Guardian, 2004). In this context, union opposition, culminating in the 2004 strike, was inevitable. It is worth noting that, from a post-war low in 1999, total civil service employment actually increased over the next six years (Civil Service, n.d.). However, this aggregate figure masks significant differences; 30,000 jobs were lost in DWP between 2004 and 2008, 16,450 of which were from Jobcentre Plus (Jobcentre Plus, 2008: 12). The reality of such 'savings' can be debated; what is now clear is that this period can be seen as a 'pilot' for later, more self-confident Conservative policy. Civil servants were now 'inputs' to be minimised (Gershon, 2004: 6).

These developments played out in the departments and their agencies in varied ways. The fragmentation of operational activity and the individuation of pay and related employment arrangements provided the context for union organisation and operation in the civil service. In the remainder of this chapter, we present the effects of these developments in Jobcentre Plus. We then go on to examine the emerging trade union response.

Jobcentre Plus: 'We are the "plus"'

Jobcentre Plus, and its 'parent', the Department of Work and Pensions (DWP), were recurring targets of restructuring under both Conservative and Labour governments, as was its counterpart in Australia. The most obvious rationale for this attention is that DWP was the highest spending central government department, employing 113,500 staff (Select Committee on Work and Pensions, Second Report, 2007). Although established in April 2002, there was a long history to Jobcentre Plus.

As stated, 'agencification' was, from the start, motivated by a complex of factors: not least the drive to commercialise public services, or where this was not possible, to mimic the effects of the market. The model of a unified, generalist civil service was the first barrier to be dismantled in this process. The first step in this process was the establishment of the agencies, in this case the Employment Service and Benefits Agency. This reorganisation was taken a step further with the integration of the Employment Service (with job centres) and the Benefits Agency (social security offices), which began in 2001 with the setting up of 'Pathfinder' offices. These offices brought both benefit delivery and jobseeker support under one roof in a sequential process. The overall process was the same in each case. Having booked an appointment, clients were interviewed by a Financial Assessor, who checked entitlements and initiated the benefit claim. They were then interviewed by a Personal Advisor, who was responsible for identifying barriers to employment, referral for training and carrying out job searches. After the client had left, the 'back-room' activity of getting the correct benefit paid on time was the job of the Benefits Processor.

Whereas the workers who were employed by Jobcentre Plus's predecessors had been indisputably part of an integrated civil service, many of their successors were employed by, or competed with private sector companies. Further, the employment practices of Jobcentre Plus itself were re-modelled on private sector practice. One element of this change was a shifting demarcation between management and workforce, a demarcation that was reinforced by pay policy. In brief, this was a policy of 'incentivising' senior managers while insisting on 'market rates' in wage negotiations.

Although the various aspects of the work process were nominally integrated, roles remained quite distinct and were the focal point for some acrimony. Employees saw a hierarchy in these arrangements, arising from what the agency regarded as its 'core' business. Following the establishment of Jobcentre Plus, one interviewee commented:

> The Job Centre side was driving it from the start. That was all there in the title: Jobcentre Plus. We are the 'Plus': just an extra. There is a concerted effort to make the aspect of the benefits almost a secondary concern. But it's not. If the customer is desperate for money that's going to be their primary concern. The job can come later.
>
> (Benefits Processor, Jobcentre Plus, 2005)

From 2005, the organisation shifted its focus to that of realising economies of scale. Work and staff were progressively moved from individual job centres to district call centres and processing centres. The employer strategy was seen to be:

> You've got a job but it's in a place which might not be viable for you to travel to.
>
> (Office Representative, Jobcentre Plus, 2005)

In the context of an ongoing government campaign radically to reduce civil service employment, this reorganisation was seen by staff as a way of justifying redundancies.

In part, these developments were justified in terms of the failure of the integration of work processes; the time taken to process benefits had increased between 2001 and 2003 (Karagiannaki, 2005). Some staff nevertheless saw these changes as another manifestation of the agency's ideological marginalisation of benefits. To illustrate:

> You don't just come in and claim benefit anymore ... You are literally just coming in there because you are desperate for money. They didn't want [those] people in job centres. They are making the receipt of benefits almost impossible ... they don't want benefits to be associated with job centres.
>
> (Benefits Processor, Jobcentre Plus, 2005)

Whatever, there was a reorganisation of the work processes and a relocation of staff into centralised centres during this period.

At the level of the individual job centre, centralisation had the perverse effect of complicating the lives of staff and claimants alike. Whereas, previously, members of the public would walk in and wait to be seen, appointments now had to be made before arriving at the local job centre.

> You had to go via a Contact Centre. They would ring you back and put the appointment in the personal advisors diary. ... Now when they get through, that is the date of their claim. So if they can't get through they are losing money. So every cock up everywhere else all comes to your local job centre. A common sense thing would be to say 'We'll book you in ourselves'. But no, we mustn't do that. ... And instead of you using your common sense and doing the forms, you have got to follow a standard operation. And you must not deviate.
>
> (Business Manager, Jobcentre Plus, 2006)

In this way, workers were put in the front line of an organisation that seemed more, not less, impenetrable:

> The knock-on effect is that you get the irate person coming in and shouting at staff. But there is nothing that you can do about it. If somebody was in dire straits, you could pay them. But there is absolutely no way now that you can get any money from anywhere ... If they have asked for an early payment because of a crisis, they would be turned away, primarily because they are trying to pretend that there are no paper-based methods of paying people.
>
> (Personal Advisor, Jobcentre Plus, 2005)

These practices impacted adversely on claimants and demoralised staff.

This same restrictive context extended to other areas of local management, underwriting the move towards recentralisation of control. As private sector involvement encroached deeper into the agency, what was experienced as management by central *diktat* was also seen to impose an inflexibility that had the self-contradictory effect of distorting market-testing comparisons. Budgetary constraint prevailed:

> You had good and bad managers. They had a job to do, but you could work with them ... and they would try to work things or get more staff. Now you've got this management that seems to be a massive ego and says 'I'm the boss'. They are even breaking their own rules ... Before, theoretically, if a manager could see ... a situation with staffing, they could alter the budget, move staff around, reinforce a particular department to take the strain, and focus the staff where it is needed. Now district managers don't have that. They have just been told, 'You have got to lose this many staff and this is your budget'.
>
> (Call Centre Operator, Jobcentre Plus, 1995)

Increasingly, local managers lost their discretion to determine staff levels. This re-centralisation of control was via budgetary allocations.

A further step in this process of restructuring occurred with the election of a Labour government in 1997. The government announced its intention to promote alternative 'service delivery channels' from early in its first term, ostensibly in the quest for choice as well as efficiency. This approach was formalised in the Home Office 'Compact' in 1998, which set out a broad prospectus for dealing with the 'voluntary and community sector' (Home Office, 1998). The 2004 Gershon review recommended specific funding arrangements for the newly named 'third sector'. By 2005, Labour's view was that the voluntary and community sector 'should be considered on equal terms' (Labour Party, 2005).

The third sector soon became an important part of the employment and social security provision. In Jobcentre Plus this shift centred on outsourcing, which primarily focused on job search and training activities. Drawing, in part, on the Australian experience, government portrayed private and third sector expertise in these areas as inherently superior to in-house capabilities. The outsourcing of case management in 'Employment Zones' began in 2003 and private sector involvement was extended in training and job search through the New Deal programme. By 2006, third party provision accounted for approximately one sixth of all job entries referred by Jobcentre Plus (Select Committee on Work and Pensions, 2007).

The initial focus on the third sector, portrayed as both benign and distinctive from for-profit companies, had some effect in blunting criticism (see Davies, 2008 for an evaluation of contractors' performance). Outsourcing and privatisation also included more 'traditional' cases, most notably the twenty-year deal to lease-back most properties under the Private Finance Initiative (DWP, 2007). Following denials of plans for 'wholesale' privatisation, facilities management and computing were also outsourced during the second Labour government, since these are not the department's 'core business' (DWP, 2007).

Of course, outsourcing also impacts on the direct workforce. In particular, the threat of outsourcing was used to justify reorganisation and work intensification within the in-house workforce. Management sought a continued reconfiguration of their workforces and close attention of the way work tasks were undertaken. For employees, this risked a race to the bottom, as each round of efficiencies set a new benchmark for market testing.

Union Organising and Campaigning

Traditional civil service industrial relations mechanisms were jettisoned in Jobcentre Plus and the PCS responded in relatively traditional trade union ways, although somewhat novel to the union. An agreement with the Cabinet Office in 2000 included familiar expressions from the partnership lexicon, but had little effect in practice, other than to legitimise the de-formalisation of industrial relations. So, whilst recognising that effective representation must be achieved by genuine joint involvement and participation', the agreement laid the ground for 'new forms of relationships' in response to 'increasing demands'. More importantly, interpretation of such clauses was delegated:

> It is not the intention of this agreement to override or constrain agreements reached with individual departments and agencies.
>
> (Public and Commercial Services Union, 2000, paragraph 17)

Within Jobcentre Plus, PCS tried and failed to secure a national agreement that might have institutionalised the same approach to participation. Nonetheless, the agency remained reluctant to negotiate an independent line, particularly regarding targets dictated by central government.

In effect, there was a disjunction between Cabinet decisions and the capacity of the direct employers (Jobcentre Plus and DWP) to deal with the union. In the 2004 budget, the government announced a 5 per cent cut to the DWP budget, with 40,000 jobs to be lost and a further 10,000 staff to be redeployed, reducing staff numbers from 130,000 to 100,000 by 2008 (Guardian, 2004). Neither Jobcentre Plus, nor DWP as a whole, was in a position to negotiate redeployment arrangements, despite an agreed protocol with the Cabinet Office:

> [At] the beginning of the redundancy process, the very same day the passport offices were advertising for jobs in the same grade ... Why aren't DWP checking what the position is elsewhere? And we asked the Cabinet Office and they said that it should happen but we haven't got the resources to do it. So a decision is central but there is no mechanism to have meaningful dialogue at the centre and when you have that dialogue in a department they are not empowered to actually do anything about it.
>
> (General Secretary, PCS, 2004)

Thus, neither Jobcentre Plus nor DWP had the capacity or authority to reach agreement with the PCS on the redeployments.

At the local level, the employer approach involved contradictory trends: a de-formalisation of collective negotiation along with inflexibility in dealing with individual representation. The implications for the union representatives in offices was marked. So, in the case of the sickness absence procedure:

> There is ultimate discretion, according to the guidance, with the line manager, to decide. But, they do so under [threat] of disciplinary procedure. Usually I find that the decision that is being grieved about is one that the person passing on the decision has been told to make. Any line manager who doesn't [act] then finds themselves in conflict with a

person who is two grades higher than them ... A line manager said 'No, I'm not'. And, he was disciplined himself for failure to comply with a reasonable management request. And, when I enquired what a reasonable management request was – was it to give an oral warning. He hadn't played the game.

(Office Representative, PCS, 2005)

One consistent consequence of these developments was to keep trade unionists busy. Whereas in the early 1980s, a local union rep might have been largely an intermediary between negotiators and members, by the early 1990s, the local bargaining agenda had expanded. By 2005, many of these representatives were taking on tasks of genuine importance to members. It had become almost impossible to be an inactive 'activist'.

The process of devolution was incremental and involved issues that, in isolation, appeared trivial. More significantly, unions were faced with the dilemma of whether to oppose any local variation in working arrangements in an effort to safeguard department-wide agreements, or whether instead to attempt to exploit local opportunities. There was a long history to these debates. As presented in the early 1990s, on the one hand:

Local reps are faced with decisions like, management are setting up a working party on this – what do we do? And I think in most districts apart from the ... better organised, the stronger, ... districts, [they] they tend to involve themselves in things, which in my terms, they shouldn't involve themselves in.

(Branch Secretary, CPSA, 1991)

On the other hand, some saw the union position differently:

You know some of these [managers] are bozos and they create industrial relations problems where there shouldn't be one ... it's possible that we'll be better able to deal with a localised bargaining system than they will, because they'll have no experience of it either.

(National Official, NUCPS, 1991)

These dilemmas laid the foundation for the development of the unions over the following decade. The local forms of union representation became more and more adept at dealing with the specific developments in workplaces and areas.

By 2005, local variation in the organisation and operation of offices was a *fait accompli* and demanded localised union responses. As there was insufficient Full Time Officer (FTO) capacity to deal with the range of change taking place at the local level, it fell to the office-based representatives and activists to respond. Nonetheless, the national and regional leaderships were cognisant of the challenges facing office members and they began to promote organisational and operational changes within the union. A decision to adopt an 'organising' approach in 2003 supported this change:

> putting the power back in the work place, getting people to campaign on issues that affect them and organize themselves within the work-place. Rather than having [a] full-time official coming in, doing all the work and then going out again leaving people stranded, we're trying to build up a power base in the workplace.
>
> (Regional Organiser, PCS, 2006)

As the fragmentation of bargaining arrangements at the national level resulted in a multiplication of the workload of FTOs, lay representatives took on a considerable part of what previously would have been FTO work. This work included representation, grievance matters as well as office-based bargaining. One effect of this was to make the union more visible locally, as known representatives acted on local priorities. This assisted in mobilisation around bargaining at the national level.

These developments in the way the union organised and operated were shaped in part by the leadership of the union. Until 2000, the PCS had a relatively conservative leadership willing to embrace the partnership arrangement offered by New Labour after 1997. However, in 2000, a rank and file member, from the Department of Work and Pensions, Mark Ser-wotka, was elected as PCS General Secretary. He initially faced a hostile executive. In the subsequent election in 2005 he was re-elected unopposed, with a much more supportive executive. The PCS was partially transformed from being a leadership-focused organisation to one that sought to mobilise members at the local (office), regional and national level. While it did not depart from formal partnership arrangements with the government, it began to contest the government's downsizing agenda, arguing that the reduction of public services was neither in the interests of its members nor of the populace generally. At the local level, many offices in government agencies had functioning union structures that continued to play an active role in local bargaining over issues such as staffing levels. The strategy of the PCS leadership was to enhance this structure and use it to mobilise the member-ship generally on staffing levels, as well as around government attacks on sick leave, and on pensions, including measures to raise the retirement age. This approach featured widespread regional stoppages from 2004 to 2006. The effect on national solidarity was increasingly put to the test following the announcement of 30,000 job cuts across DWP. Strikes in January and March 2006 brought out 200,000 members. This action was followed by an overtime ban in DWP, as PCS explained that the annual overtime worked was equivalent to 5,400 jobs in the department. These measures provided the rationale for and the basis of a general strike by the PCS in 2007. While the union attributes some of this success in mobilising the membership to a reinvigorated national leadership and the new organising strategy they promoted, it is also the case that the government had given PCS 'something to campaign around' (Senior National Officer, PCS, 2006; see also Fairbrother *et al.*, 2009).

Increasingly, the shift in focus 'from outputs to outcomes' meant moving to a 'mixed economy' of provision (Civil Service Live, 2010); the more lucrative activities faced market testing while the remaining unattractive core was subject to continual pressure on staff numbers and wages. For the in-house workforce, the movement of decision-making, both to and within Jobcentre Plus, meant the fragmentation of negotiation and the duplication of effort. Shortly after its inception, the Whitley system had been described as 'extraordinarily complex' (Macrae-Gibson, 1922: 1). The terrain of civil service industrial relations were now less formal, less centralised and subject to constant change but no less complex.

Yet this fragmentation was paralleled by a re-centralisation of processes at the regional level, resulting in a situation where local job centre managers had increasing responsibility, but within a framework that allowed less room to manoeuvre. As a whole, the period was one of continual, and sometimes contradictory, change: integration and specialisation; devolution and re-centralisation. At the end of this period, Jobcentre Plus still appeared to be the focus of government experimentation. And, with government increasingly seeing the public sector as the only available economic 'instrument' to deal with financial crisis, it appeared that there was very little room left for negotiation.

Coalition Government: 'Big Society'; Small State

In May 2010, Labour lost the general election and was faced with a hung parliament, with no party holding an absolute majority. A Coalition government was formed, comprised of the largest party in parliament, the Conservative Party, and the much smaller Liberal Democrats Party. Compared with the Labour landslide in 1997, the hung parliament might have seemed a poor basis for a more radical small-state approach. The new Conservative – Liberal Democrats Coalition was able to settle on a programme of cuts within weeks of taking office as part of the response to the economic recession and the continued rejection of Keynesian solutions to it in favour of reducing government spending. Equally, though, opposition was muted because while the proposals differed in their severity, they remained remarkably consistent with Labour policy over the previous ten years.

This consistency was particularly clear in the changing terms of debate on service provision. From a straightforward advocacy of private sector efficiencies, all three main parties now argued, somewhat obliquely, for 'diversity' of provision. In particular, the late 2000s saw a blurring of the public-private divide boundary, with an apparent convergence of New Labour and 'red Toryism' on seemingly 'third-way' options (for example Blond, 2009; 2010.) The 'third sector' and notionally 'social' enterprises had already become the acceptable face of public service outsourcing under Labour. The Conservative election campaign went a stage further in 'inviting' public sector workers to help build the 'big society': to say 'bye bye to bureaucracy' by forming their own co-operative to bid for their own work (Conservative Party, 2010.) However, like New Labour's early focus on 'what works', the new approach was not agnostic about provision, but was founded on a continuing presumption of public sector inability to innovate or motivate. In Jobcentre Plus, social enterprises had already taken their place among straightforwardly commercial competitors for public contracts in what a Labour-commissioned report had predicted would become 'an annual multibillion pound market' (Freud, 2007: 75). This looked increasingly like the Australian model.

Faced with an unremitting and seemingly incoherent barrage of initiatives, unions were slow to recognise the strategic coherence of reform or to organise effectively to deal with the new environment. Nevertheless, over the period as a whole, industrial relations were transformed, accompanied by the emergence of different forms of union organisation and participation. Public sector unions had to respond to the reality of increased market competition and reduced job security for many workers employed in front-line service delivery roles. Nonetheless, the PCS and its associated unions were in a relatively strong position to meet the challenges posed by this new form of government. The PCS had become a leading campaigning union, able to mobilise its membership to question government policy and practice.

AUSTRALIA: FROM MANAGED DECENTRALISM TO WORK CHOICES

The Australian trajectory was marked by combination of juridical-based labour market reforms and government policy agendas as both Labor and Coalition governments promoted reforms from the 1980s onwards and public sector workers were included in the mainstream system of the industrial relations system. The outcome was a reconfigured public sector. Unions, and particularly the CPSU, and its predecessors, sought to retain a collective presence and lay the grounds for effective representation.

Experiments

The Hawke Labor elected in 1983 embraced a broad ranging price and incomes Accord with the peak union body, the Australian Council of Trade Unions, that initially promised a broad agenda of social change and progressive social and industrial policy. Overtime, however, ACTU participation in the Accord process came with expectations of wage restraint and ensuring compliance among affiliated unions to jointly agreed Accord wage increases (Ewer *et al.*, 1991). As the 1980s progressed the industrial relations agenda pursued by the Accord partners increasingly focused on achieving enhanced productivity and a gradual restructuring, or 'managed decentralism' of the centralised system of conciliation and arbitration (Dabscheck, 1989). From 1987 until 1992 changes to employment and personnel arrangements in the APS were legitimised by this process of 'managed decentralism' and award restructuring. Award restructuring involved the skill-based consolidation and realignment of base pay grades, topped up by a 'second tier' of productivity-bargained pay increases. By linking management-initiated organisational changes to the wages system, it was possible to incorporate unions into management objectives while limiting the capacity of management to impose changes without negotiation.

Across the APS in the 1980s, there were divergent outcomes evident from this process of union-management negotiation over workplace change. This divergence was evident in two of the largest federal public service agencies, the Australian Tax Office (ATO) and the Department of Social Security (DSS). In the ATO forms of restructuring were more comprehensive, and involved efforts to promote industrial democracy and to refocus tax collecting. In Social Security, there was mention of industrial democracy but a less thorough attempt to engage with employees. These different variations of industrial democracy had implications for the ways that public sector unions organised and operated.

The organisational problems faced by DSS were similar to the Tax Office: a paper-based organisation that was transformed into an organisation that relied on computer technology. Moreover, the DSS was dealing with a social security system that was becoming both more complex and targeted. The technological changes, as in tax, would lead to significant job loss as well as changes in organisational structure. In the ATO, the Federated Clerks' Union Tax Office Branch leadership had been willing to trade job losses for a significant improvement in both career and salary prospects for its membership that was concentrated in the lowest classifications. This union branch had been predominately made of well-organised working class women, who were persuaded of the advantages of trading jobs for enhanced careers and salaries.

In contrast, the union covering similar workers in the DSS – the Australian Public Service Association (Fourth Division Officers) (APSA) was less well-organised. The more active union in the DSS was the Administrative and Clerical Officers' Association (ACOA) that covered higher paid classifications. The ACOA was a union based on state branches with a relatively weak federal structure. In NSW, in particular, there was a militant faction led by the International Socialists. The threat of job losses in NSW, particularly as a consequence of the closing of smaller offices, was sufficient for the more militant faction to persuade members to undertake six weeks of selective industrial bans in 1988, against the judgement of the federal leadership.

For the public sector unions the principal consequence was the eventual amalgamation of the APSA and the ACOA to form the Public Sector Union.

The rationale for separate unions was largely rendered irrelevant by the more fluid career structures in the APS, although some tensions between the lowest paid staff and more highly paid staff were reflected in the new union. The formation of the PSU was part of a more general push by the Australian Council of Trade Unions for a major consolidation of unions into much larger entities.

The Emergence of Enterprise Bargaining

From 1991 the ACTU supported a replacement of managed decentralism by a more comprehensive system of workplace-level over-award bargaining. The task before the federal Labor government was to develop an industrial relations model that accommodated the ACTU policy direction without adopting the more radical market-oriented agenda of the Liberal/National Opposition. The new regulatory model envisaged the encouragement of workplace bargaining above a floor established by the industrial award framework, with the Industrial Relations Commission retaining a diminished, but still significant, role in the regulation of industrial relations (Green and Wilson, 2000).

The Labor government sought to demonstrate that its approach to workplace bargaining was a fairer and more effective system than the Coalition model. The obvious place to conduct such an experiment was in the APS. Achieving the policy objective of introducing workplace bargaining for government employees did not, however, sit comfortably with the desire of the unions to maintain a high degree of standardisation and uniformity of conditions. With a federal election impending, the government (and the unions) wanted to demonstrate that this model of detcentralised industrial relations was more effective and equitable than that proposed by the opposition parties. In December 1992 the government and twenty-seven public service unions signed an agreement on the introduction of agency-level wage bargaining. These agency-level agreements would supplement a service-wide pay increase that was made in exchange for commitments to address a range of work organisation issues (Department of Industrial Relations, 1992: 13–21; O'Brien, 1997).

One of the first agreements made was in the Department of Defence, reached in the dying days of the 1990–3 Labor government. The department had undergone considerable downsizing since 1987, with the civilian workforce was reduced from 35,818 to 22,559 by 1990, principally as a consequence of contracting-out support functions (Wrigley, 1991). With the re-election of the government the agreement became the template of subsequent agency bargaining. The new agreement went to issues such as work organisation, employment conditions, work environment and training and skill formation. It was also agreed that a Defence Total Quality Management program would be introduced. (Department of Defence, 1994). There was not, however, any explicit explanation of how the wage adjustment would be paid, although the Department of Finance required that agencies be explicit on this issue (Department of Finance, 1994). It seemed that the parties had agreed to little more than continuing the restructuring and downsizing processes that had been underway for some years (Gourlay, 1994: 167–8).

It was no great surprise when the public sector unions agreed to return to a service-wide model of enterprise bargaining for the period 1995–6. This experiment in agency bargaining, followed by a return to a more centralised model, illustrates the conflicting objectives that governments incur when attempting to regulate their own employees. The Labor government had an agenda of industrial relations decentralisation and wanted to use its own agencies to demonstrate the superiority of its 'managed' model over the more radical neo-liberal agenda of the opposition. Yet the government also was concerned to maintain control over the costs of bargained pay increases. Thus, one of the outcomes of these objectives was that the central agencies began to act as labour market regulators on behalf of the government.

In its approach to public sector restructuring, the Labor government sought the active involvement of unions. The mechanisms to achieve this objective included unilateral action by management, industrial democracy processes, managed decentralism and a limited form of enterprise bargaining. This approach could be characterised as both incorporation and negotiated partnership. In contrast, the Coalition government elected in 1996 was intent on marginalising union activity as much as possible, both within the APS and more generally. The Coalition parties stated that they were determined to have 'real' industrial change in the APS.

The Promotion of Workplace Relations

The Coalition government saw its relationship with its own employees as a means of demonstrating the efficacy of its proposed industrial relations changes. Further, it sought to use its workplace relations legislation as a means of engendering cultural change in the APS. The government's general policy aim for industrial relations was to facilitate more direct relationships between employees and employers, principally by minimising the role of unions and of the Australian Industrial Relations Commission (AIRC). In a logical sense, the government as the 'ultimate employer' of public servants could have imposed these changes on a service-wide basis. To do so would not have sat comfortably, however, with its concurrent policy aim of maximising managerial prerogatives, while minimising external regulation, and the capacity of unions to resist its agenda. The instrument used to maintain this delicate balance between its policy objectives and its employer interests were the parameters for agreement making in the Australian Public Service.

These 'parameters' ensured that any agency-level agreement was consistent with government policy. The principal 'parameters' encompassed the following:

- agreements should be funded within agency appropriations;
- the accrual of sick leave and annual leave entitlements should be portable across agencies;
- agencies should introduce a rationalised classification structure linked to service-wide benchmarks;
- flexible remuneration arrangements should be permitted;
- redundancy provisions should be cost neutral to the agency;
- all certified agreements should provide for the making of Australian Workplace Agreements (individual contracts);
- the finalisation of agreements be subject to coordination arrangements, including consultation with the Department of Workplace Relations and Small Business; and
- further, all workplace agreements be subject to Ministerial clearance where they involved significant policy issues.

(Reith, 1996)

These parameters provided a specific role for the Department of Workplace Relations and Small Business (DWRSB) to act as coordinator of agreement making in the agencies:

> Authority to make agreements now rests with agencies, within broad policy arrangements that recognise the government's responsibility as the ultimate employer. This is consistent with the practice of other major employers. This framework balances the responsibility of an agency to conduct its own workplace relations with the requirements of public accountability of government bodies.

(DWRSB, 1998)

Reflecting government labour market ideologies and the shifting boundaries of this department, its name changed from the Department of Industrial Relations to Department of Workplace Relations and Small Business (DWRSB) in mid-1997, and then to Department of Employment, Workplace Relations and Small Business (DEWRSB) in October 1998. Between 1996 and 2007, the Coalition government always used the term 'agreement making' rather than 'workplace bargaining', the currency of the previous Labor government.

On the face of it, the DWRSB parameters seemed to maintain consider-able central control over the capacity of agency managers to develop agency-specific employment arrangements. The relationship between agency managers and DWRSB was hammered out during the first round of APS bargaining following the passage of the Workplace Relations Act *1996*, and varied from agency to agency. Agency negotiators over time internalised the limits of what was acceptable to the government while, DWRSB, in turn, allowed agencies some latitude. A regime of 'tolerable divergence' thus emerged (O'Brien and O'Donnell, 2008). Overall, agencies found that the DWRSB parameters were useful in securing agreements, provided that agency management did not attempt to deal with certain issues deemed to be non-negotiable. Nevertheless, agencies would have liked greater latitude in varying specific arrangements to do with pay, classification systems and employment conditions at the agency level. On matters of employment conditions, the government clearly attempted to constrain the capacity of its agents to negotiate arrangements that fell outside its parameters. Nevertheless, there was a remarkable sameness about the words used in many APS agreements.

While managements believed they had been endowed with more 'choices' albeit within tighter parameters set by government, the CPSU and other public sector unions faced even more challenges to their capacity to organise their members and to preserve their employment conditions. Guidelines issued by DWRSB for implementing the government's bargaining parameters stated that agreements must be consistent with the freedom of association provisions of the Workplace Relations Act 1996. These provisions rendered unlawful any activity constituting 'victimisation or discrimination' against employees 'on the grounds that they are, or are not, a union member'. In the APS context, however, this meant that agencies were warned against any action 'that could be seen as encouraging or endorsing union membership' (DWRSB, 1998). Such action included allowing union access to staff induction programs or to agency facilities. Agencies were expressly forbidden to allow clauses in their agreements mandating payroll deductions of union fees. While it had been commonplace in agencies with significant levels of union membership to provide facilities for union delegates, agencies were told that access to such facilities was now to be made available to all staff representatives, both union and non-union.

Agencies were also prevented from making any agreements that would enhance the rights of entry of union officials to APS workplaces. Moreover, under the provisions of the Workplace Relations Act 1996 agency managements had to make a choice, agreements with unions or with employees directly. If the latter path was chosen, then agency management was only obliged 'to meet and confer' with unions. There was no obligation to negotiate with them. These provisions were designed to remove the union monopoly of formal staff consultation and in the negotiation of agency agreements. The hitherto existing 'culture' of management-union consultation/negotiation was to be replaced with a more nebulous concept of staff consultation that might involve 'representatives of employees'.

Subsequent rounds of APS bargaining largely followed the patterns laid down in the period between late 1996 and 1999. Cost-efficiencies were introduced, union activity was contained or marginalised, and a performance culture based on systems of individual accountability and rewards was promoted. Yet agencies pursued their own distinctive paths to these common outcomes.

The industrial relations arrangements that resulted from this fragmentation escalated in the final years of the neo-liberal Howard Government. The

2004 election gave the government a majority in both houses of parliament, which came into effect in July 2005. By the end of that year, the government had amended the Workplace Relations Act (the 'Work Choices' amendments), and the legislation came into effect in March 2006.

The December 2005 amendments to the Workplace Relations Act 1996 had considerable implications for most Australian workplaces and for the APS, in particular. As far as public sector unions were concerned, union access to APS workplaces were further restricted. A strike could only occur during a bargaining period if a majority of voting employees supported the action. Scrutiny of the contents of collective agreements was no longer the province of the AIRC, which would be largely reduced to a conciliation role, with the power to arbitrate on disputes only when all parties agreed. In addition, the Minister for Workplace Relations could veto any provision in agreements, which he deemed opposed government policy (Workplace Relations (Amendment) Act 1996).

From 1997 onwards, unions in the APS faced both a fragmentation of bargaining and a narrowing in the scope of the bargaining agenda. Further, unions faced increased restrictions on their capacities to organise and operate in the APS. To explore the way these legislative and policy initiatives worked out in practice for managers, workers and unions, we examine the recent history of Centrelink.

From Welfare to Customer Service: Bargaining in Centrelink

From its inception in 1997, Centrelink was the largest APS agency, with approximately 25,000 employees. It was one of the strongholds of the CPSU and its history of industrial militancy dates back to the experiences of many of its employees in the former Department of Social Security (DSS). In the 1980s, members of the CPSU's predecessor union in the DSS had made widespread use of selective industrial bans to preserve employment conditions. This long-standing industrial tradition significantly influenced the tactics of Centrelink management in the process of agreement making.

Centrelink was important to all sides in the industrial relations arena in the APS. The CPSU saw this agency as a focus for illustrating its capacity to modify government and management agendas. The government and the Centrelink management needed to demonstrate that their agenda could be achieved in agencies where unions had a significant presence, and the Workplace Relations Act 1996 made that task easier. In the past, when employees had imposed selective industrial bans, employers had been able to invoke the 'no work as directed, no pay' remedy and stand down employees or dock full pay for the period of the bans. Many employers, however, had chosen not to take this course, preferring to resolve the matter and resume normal operations rather than worsen the dispute. Now, the Workplace Relations Act 1996 made it mandatory to withhold pay altogether if workers took any form of industrial action, however restricted. The weapon of selective bans, without cost to employees, which had been widely used in the APS during the 1980s, was no longer available. This legislative restriction resulted in the virtual absence of industrial action during the agreement-making period in 1997–8 as well as during subsequent bargaining periods. In the view of a senior official formerly responsible for coordinating agreement making in the APS, this provision in the legislation enabled quite 'significant structural change and downsizing' to be achieved 'without significant industrial disruption' (Yates, 1998).

Five Centrelink Agreements were negotiated between 1997 and 2009. Centrelink management promoted a process of employee consultation during this period while the CPSU sought to retain a presence in the process. Nonetheless, the CPSU's role in the implementation of these agreements was recognised, although the hold of the union was loosened by the explicit recognition that any processes in which it was involved would be matched by parallel arrangements for non-union members. Management saw this measure as important in shifting the consultative framework within the agency away from union domination towards direct employee consultation.

In addition, enterprise bargaining in many APS agencies in the 1990s occurred within a context of organisational and cultural change. This shift was evident in Centrelink. The CEO, Sue Vardon, noted in the 1997–8 Annual Report that:

> Centrelink has been given the challenge of creating a new, modern public sector organisation. This involves not incremental but transformational change with all the cultural and organisational developments, which that implies.
>
> (Centrelink, 1998: 17)

The first Centrelink Development Agreement reiterated the focus on customer service as a key factor underpinning working conditions and job security. The agreement noted in its preamble that:

> Centrelink is a dynamic organisation, which will strive to improve customer service ... Centrelink's achievements in this area, and through this agreement, will in turn improve job security for its employees.
>
> (Centrelink, 1997: 5)

The emphasis was on benefits for customers and employees.

Nonetheless, at an agency level there was concern about the role and place of the union. Centrelink management saw workplace bargaining as a means of working with the CPSU and other unions:

> I didn't want the unions to think that I was running the [Minister] Reith agenda; I was appalled. Because what I was running, was Sue Vardon's agenda for public sector reform. I knew what the government

wanted, but I didn't have any problem with that as long as I could use this tool to buy a revolution (sic). I wasn't using this tool to impose the wish of the government upon the workers. It's very different. And, I think the union understood that.

(CEO Centrelink, 2004)

She faced a well-organised CPSU division led by one of the union's most experienced industrial officers, Mark Gepp, who subsequently became National President of the union. Vardon's perception of the tradition of rank and file militancy inherited from the DSS is reflected in her colourful claim that:

Every time Social Security wanted to do something they [the union] took them to the cleaners. They had the strikes. The day the Prime Minister opened us the union tried to close every office. I was hysterical with rage. Because this is what you do, you protest by striking and so there was an incredible culture of striking. ... well I'd never seen anything like it in my life. Social Security was a hot bed.

(CEO Centrelink, 2004)

Against this background, Vardon felt that the Workplace Relations Act 1996 made her task of cultural change easier:

I considered that our first agreement was a major success with the union because the union could see that their power was diminishing. They couldn't have all those strikes anymore because of the Workplace Relations Act which I must say I'm extremely grateful for that piece of legislation.

(CEO Centrelink, 2004)

While the Workplace Relations Act 1996 had made it more difficult for unions to engage in any form of industrial action, including work bans (CEO Centrelink, 2004), Vardon conceded that the union remained an important presence in the agency.

Significantly, Vardon recognised that the union had a considerable degree of influence in the organisation, with both members and non-members. Of note, a large group of non-union staff were keen for the union to negotiate on their behalf. Because of her experience in bargaining, Vardon commented:

I learnt a very important lesson. It doesn't matter how small they are, everybody who is not a union member wants to know that the union is negotiating with management. At one stage I said we can get this through because there are hardly any union members. And something happened and the take home message to me was they don't want to be members of the union but they want to know they're there.

(CEO Centrelink, 2004)

The key objective of the agreement was to provide an 'efficient and cost effective service by committed and skilled employees' (Centrelink, 1997). Vardon saw the negotiation of the first enterprise agreement in 1997 as 'establishing an environment that would enable the personalisation of our services to our customers'. It would involve greater flexibility in opening hours of Centrelink offices and shopfronts.

Overall, the outcomes negotiated in the first CDA were consistent with the promotion of a customer service agenda across Centrelink. Some 2 per cent of the pay rise agreed in the first Centrelink Development Agreement (CDA) was contingent on all Centrelink offices implementing customer service improvement plans and the organisation as a whole demonstrating improvements against a range of performance indicators (Centrelink, 1997).

Customer focus was to be achieved and substantial changes to opening hours, with staff losing the Wednesday afternoon office closure from 1.30 p.m., a time previously used to hold meetings and to catch up on work backlogs and with changes in social security legislation. Whilst other managers saw value in the old arrangement, Vardon was implacably opposed to it, as a diminution in customer service. Other changes to hours included a broader span of hours from 7.00 a.m. to 7.00 p.m. The former core hours were abolished and replaced with 'regular hours'. It was up to individual employees to negotiate their regular working hours with their supervisor over a four week period. Nevertheless, Centrelink staff retained access to 'flex' time and to overtime payments when requested by management to work beyond their regular hours. Employees who worked beyond their regular hours voluntarily could accumulate 'flex' hours.

The second CDA 1999–2002 further demonstrated the residual capacity of the union to draw limits on the government's preferred model for agreements. Nevertheless, the second CDA contributed to the managerialist agenda in two ways: it introduced a Centrelink-specific classification structure and it linked employee advancement through this structure to the outcome of a performance assessment. Centrelink had to find most of the resources required to fund the second CDA internally. The organisation received only 1.3 per cent in extra funding from the Commonwealth government and found itself in the difficult position of making a trade-off between staff cuts and pay rises. Centrelink management argued that it had already achieved the productivity increases required as prerequisites to the agreed pay rises, through the introduction of new technology, its 'One Contact Officer' approach, the establishment of customer service teams, and reducing reworking (Centrelink, 1999). The unions, however, successfully resisted a more comprehensive adoption of a performance based pay system, which had been the original objective in 1997.

Substantive negotiations for a third agreement, which began in March 2002, provide an insight into the difficulties faced by the Centrelink management, caught between the CPSU on the one hand and an impatient government, on the other. By October 2002, a preliminary agreement had been negotiated between Centrelink and the CPSU but it was rejected by the union's Centrelink Section Council. The management was concerned to secure an agreement with the minimum of industrial disruption. Vardon feared that there were members of the government who were not friends of Centrelink and who would use significant industrial disruption to undermine the agency (CEO, Centrelink, 2004). The CEO took the unusual step of attending the Centrelink Section Council meeting of the Employment Services Division of the union to plead with the union to work with the management to preserve Centrelink. Nevertheless, negotiations proceeded without resolution and the union notified Centrelink of its intention to undertake industrial action in early December. On 2 December 2002, a stopwork meeting and half day strike of CPSU members across Centrelink was organised. In the aftermath of this industrial action, Centrelink decided to test the degree of support it had among its employees, and, in late December when many staff were on leave, the management put the draft negotiated to date to a ballot of staff in the form of a non-union agreement under Section 170LK of the Workplace Relations Act. Despite management's best efforts, the 'non-union' agreement was rejected by over 70 per cent of those Centrelink staff who voted in the ballot (Senior officials, CPSU, 2004). Management and the CPSU resumed negotiations in early 2003, and finally by May 2003, a third CDA was certified for two and a half years (Centrelink, 2003).

The fourth CDA (2006–9) was negotiated under conditions that were more hostile to the union. In December 2005, the Coalition government amended the Workplace Relations Act 1996. In a deteriorating climate for collective bargaining, the CPSU did not wish to risk the protracted conflict that had been required to settle the third agreement. Its main concern was to conclude the fourth agreement before the new Work Choices laws came into effect in March 2006:

> The union ... had polled the membership and found that there wasn't the stomach for a long term industrial dispute so they [Centrelink] put up this proposal of reducing accruable personal leave by two days a year and returning it back to a two day special leave provision ... On top of that, they also negotiated a process where people could take up to five days' sick leave without a medical certificate.
>
> (IT programmer, National Support Office, 2007)

The agreement confirmed that employees were entitled to screen breaks of five minutes after sixty minutes of continuous work with screen-based equipment, and that Centrelink Call Centre employees would be provided with ten minutes at the beginning of their shifts to review computer systems and five minutes to close down these systems at the end of their shifts (Centrelink Development Agreement, 2006–9). Before the completion of negotiations over the fourth Centrelink Agreement, management withdrew a memorandum of understanding allowing paid meeting time for delegates to do their work (CPSU organiser, 2006). Subsequently, management sought to enforce strictly the legislative restrictions on union officials' right of entry to workplaces other than by invitation of an identified individual (Delegate, Area Office, CPSU, 2006).

At the same time, a major restructuring of work processes in Centrelink was under way, quite outside the bargaining arena. In the context of a heightened targeting of welfare entitlements and a more stringent policing of government 'welfare-to-work' policies after 2005, the customer-focused 'one-stop-shop' approach of earlier years was giving way to strict new controls over customers, administered through a consolidation of business lines. Customers were now required to make 'first contact' through a Centrelink office and then to provide information to a call centre adviser. Cases were referred to specialists in back offices.

The changed structures brought about significantly changed work processes, including front-line deskilling and work intensification:

> With consolidation it means there is a lot less staff in any site because every time they put a new consolidated processing centre in for another function they take a staff member from each site – or maybe two depending – to staff that. What happens then is you're left with less people in the office to cover these extended hours.
>
> (Specialist Program Adviser, Area Office, 2006)

This reorganisation was designed to facilitate the eligibility checking necessitated by new government welfare-to-work policies. These policies meant that Centrelink's main client was now the Department of Employment and Workplace Relations (DEWR). The Department tended to play Centrelink off against its lower-cost private and community sector Job Network, and rigorously scrutinised Centrelink business processes:

> DEWR have been right in there, wanting all those updates … and saying the time is too much, … and putting pressure on to try and get it down … 'We have been into your offices and we have seen people doing this kind of work, and we know it doesn't take as long as your model says it does'.
>
> (Financial Officer, National Support Office, 2006)

After March 2006, unions and workers were unable to resist work intensification by resort to any form of industrial action, including work bans, without the risk of heavy fines on individuals and the union. It became increasingly difficult to organise at workplace-level in order to enforce even those conditions that had been negotiated. For example, staff were subject to some duress over use of formally-agreed leave provisions; when it proved difficult to defend union-won entitlements in any organised way, these entitlements were sporadically asserted through less formal acts of resistance (Junor *et al.*, 2009).

In April 2009, an agreement was certified between Centrelink and a range of unions for the period 2009–11. While the agreement explicitly recognised that 'union delegates have a legitimate role in the workplace' the agreement makes clear that unions remained but one source of employee representation. Management would continue the policy of seeking input directly from employees, who may consult with employee representatives 'which may include their union' on significant workplace matters (Centrelink, 2009a: 2–3). While the CPSU believed that negotiations had been 'difficult' the union thanked its workplace delegates and activists for their support and pointed to rising union membership during the bargaining process and gains in leave entitlements and paid maternity leave alongside a 10.25 per cent pay rise over two years as key achievements (CPSU, 2009d).

The Centrelink case demonstrates the ways in which the main union, the CPSU, faced an increasingly assertive management. Not only did the union have to address hostile managerial initiatives, it was operating in an increasingly restrictive juridical environment. The outcome was that while the union remained a force within Centrelink, the union's capacity to mobilise membership and bargain effectively was becoming more difficult.

A New Twist?

With the election of a Labor government in 2007, the Australian Public Services were once again the focus of attention. The incoming Rudd Labor government (2007) directed that no more individual contracts be made in the APS and issued a new bargaining framework that encouraged collective bargaining and provided specific mention of the role and rights of union delegates to consult with members within the workplace and engage in bargaining with management at the agency level (DEEWR, 2008). The Rudd government's broader approach to industrial relations was outlined in new legislation, the Fair Work Act 2009.

The future of agency agreement making in the APS faces further revision following the release of the Moran Report in 2010 (Advisory Group on Reform of Australian Government Administration, 2010). The Rudd government initiated a review of the APS led by the secretary of the Department of Prime Minister and Cabinet, Terry Moran in November 2009. In its submission to the Moran Review, the CPSU argued for the need for a return to a centralised approach to bargaining because of growing wage dispersion between agencies (CPSU, 2009c). The Rudd government announced that the expiry dates for most APS agreements would be 30 June 2011. This provided the union with an opportunity to engage in a more co-ordinated campaign across the APS and the CPSU encouraged its members to become more involved in this campaign (CPSU, 2010). The Moran Report presented its findings in March of 2010 and emphasised the need to streamline enterprise bargaining and create a more united APS. The Moran Report also agreed with the need to address widening wage disparities and overcome the constraints this imposes on staff mobility across the APS. In a speech to the CPSU Governing Council, Moran noted that:

> For APS 3 staff, for example, the gap between the minimum and maximum salary level has increased from 8 per cent to 22 per cent since 1996. For SES band Two, the range has increased from 24 to 37 per cent.
> (Moran, 2010)

While the Report supports efforts to promote common APS-wide terms and conditions of employment, it also advocates the retention of some role for agency-level agreements (Advisory Group on the Reform of Australian Government Administration, 2010: 55). Future tensions are likely therefore between a more co-ordinated approach to negotiating conditions across the APS and the retention of agency level agreement making.

The Moran Report set a changed scene for the CPSU. The Department of Finance and Public Service Commission has acquired a renewed significance following the Report. Increasingly there appears to be a tension between the independence of agencies, such as Centrelink, and the role of the main central agency, Finance, and the Public Service Commission. In this process, the CPSU is likely to go through a further process of renewal as it organised to address a more centralised bargaining framework, while retaining the capacity to represent members across decentralised agencies that characterise the APS.

ASSESSMENT: CENTRALISATION, FRAGMENTATION AND UNION RESILIENCE

In both countries, there was a shift in state industrial relations during the 1990s, although the foundations of this refocusing took place much earlier. With the embrace of neo-liberal economic agenda, governments in both countries sought to recast public sector industrial relations in line with the broad policy focus presented by both sets of governments. The outcome was a complex relation between decentralisation of industrial relations and the maintenance of central control, particularly via the Treasury and related financial departments. As noted in previous chapters, both sets of governments introduced an institutional reorganisation of the public services via agencies and related arrangements.

These developments were the institutional form of depoliticisation. Governments sought to create the appearance that they were no longer directly responsible for the detail and the outcome of bargaining arrangements as they applied to salary levels, performance rewards, auditing and monitoring of workforces and terms and conditions of employment. Nonetheless, in both countries, these governments maintained control over such arrangements via a suite of direct and indirect measures. The difference between the two countries is that this process was formalised via bargaining and negotiation in Australia, thereby providing a legitimation for change that was absent in the UK. The drive by government to promote reform in the UK, and the inability for unions to place many of these changes on the national bargaining agenda, meant that paradoxically these reforms did not have the stamp of legitimacy via the industrial relations process itself.

For unions in the United Kingdom a more complex process was in place whereby the management sought to embed and secure their discretion, but it was in a context where governments stood behind the promoted programmes of reform that were implemented. The key point of difference was the appearance of autonomy. While much was made of the delegated powers that agencies exercised, they were nonetheless undertaken within a powerful and often baleful set of financial arrangements that set the parameters for autonomous action. Complementing these aspects of control, it is the case that auditing and performance measures were more highly developed in the United Kingdom than Australia. These arrangements defined the limits to managerial discretion and union capacity in rather strict and often public ways (Carter *et al.*, 2002).

Therefore, in the UK context, the term decentralisation should be used with caution. First, it is important to distinguish the fragmentation of management structures that came with the creation of agencies from the devolution of responsibility to the regional and local level. These two directions of decentralisation were quite distinct: the first was structural, the second managerial. The formation of the Benefits Agency in 1991, for example, created a separate, parallel national hierarchy, with no inherent implications for devolution of control within the agency. Second, in both of these cases, the areas of management authority concerned were strictly limited. In both cases – fragmentation and devolution – the decentralisation of responsibility was accompanied by a renewed focus on central control – a development that we have argued was central to depoliticisation. In this respect, local managers were given 'more control over less' (Rhodes, 2000: 346).

Fragmentation, devolution and the drive to reduce the size and scope of the Civil Service removed the basis on which unions' previous methods relied. Relatively comfortable arrangements, which relied on employer patronage and a stable organisational structure, gave way to more confrontational industrial relations. The present way in which PCS organises can only be understood in this context; the paradox is that, while PCS continues to campaign for a return to unified national bargaining, current levels of participation would not have developed without the challenge of decentralisation. In essence, while one objective of departmental restructuring was to 'teach managers to manage', the challenge of the past three decades also taught PCS to behave rather more like a trade union.

In a similar manner, the decentralisation and fragmentation of bargaining across the APS over the last two decades has required the CPSU to recast how it engaged with union members, giving rise to substantial changes in union structure and organisation. On the one hand, the union has been forced to develop a grass roots level of activism and rank and file participation in workplace bargaining that was not evident in the service-wide rounds of bargaining that occurred prior to 1996. The union now relies heavily on the active support and assistance of workplace union representatives in bargaining, recruitment and grievance handling. The maintenance of these workplace structures has been found to be a key factor in underpinning union membership (Morehead *et al.*, 1997). On the other hand, the union has centralised a range of functions, ranging from financial management to the provision of services to members through a call centre. This centralisation contrasts with the highly decentralised branch structure that was evident prior to 1996. The CPSU leadership perceived the centralisation of resources as critical to union survival in a highly challenging legislative and industrial environment, though this approach has raised concerns among significant sections of the union's membership over the potential cost to local level activism and capacity.

There is a remarkable similarity in the broad outcomes of public service reform in both countries, although the paths taken were very different. The trajectory was neo-liberal – to align civil services with the requirement of the globalised world. In the United Kingdom, New Labour was prepared to use partnership arrangements to assist its project, though it was not prepared to reverse many of the initiatives made by its predecessors. In Australia, the Hawke Labor government initially experimented with forms of industrial democracy. The government's flirtation with these policies waned as it became enamoured with the adoption of a range of neo-liberal policies towards macro and micro economic management from the mid-1980s. A more strident neo-liberal agenda towards public sector management-union relations was evident from 1996 with the election of the more conservative Howard Coalition government.

In both countries, public service unions have survived and have been able to modify the most threatening of the changes proposed by the respective governments. It was not so much that unions were able to roll back government and managerially imposed initiatives, but rather were able to contest and sometimes modify the implications of those changes on their members. Under differing political circumstances unions could be either unequal partners on the inside (UK since 1997, Australia in the 1980s), and at other times opponents on the outside (Australia post 1996, UK before 1997), or even a combination of partnership and selective contestation (UK since the early 2000s), with varying degrees of success. The state was not rolled back, but the unions were not 'rolled over' either.

The ability of unions to adapt has been related to the changing relationship between national and local levels of bargaining. In the United Kingdom, the limited revival of activity at the workplace-level was the basis for a wider transformation of the main civil union, the PCS, from being a rather passive leadership oriented organisation, to a more active campaigning organisation, particularly following the election of more radical elements to leadership positions in the late 1990s. Thus, the PCS remains more willing and able to take industrial action, particularly against job losses, while, on the other hand lacking the formal and unified bargaining structure that its Australian counterpart can still use. While the pattern in the PCS seems to be local activity led from the centre, the structure of the CPSU has been characterised by centralisation designed to cope with the resource intensity of a decentralised bargaining system. The outcome for the CPSU has been a union with the capacity to survive through a sustained period of government policy promoting decollectivisation and union marginalisation. The union maintained its place as the dominant party in agency agreement making across the APS and as the dominant representative of APS employees in workplace bargaining over the period post 1996. The election of a Labor government in 2007, and the introduction of the Fair Work Act 2009, provided the union with opportunities to recover conditions eroded over the period of Coalition government rule, to entrench collective bargaining across the APS and to develop and replenish its networks of workplace union representation. Nonetheless, the tensions between local and national forms of representation and patterns of bargaining remain evident in both countries.

CONCLUSION

The fundamental changes in union structures and governance over this period, then, should be seen as responses to the various techniques used to create a distance between central government policy and its consequences. In both countries governments followed a dual path, on the one hand, transferring responsibility, either by devolution, decentralisation or other arms-length approaches and, on the other, consolidating and tightening central control. This process of depoliticisation creates the appearance of decision-making over management–union relations being removed from the political process and devolved to technical managers. However, wage and employment conditions for state employees cannot be entirely depoliticised. They can be referred to other bodies – either for determination or recommendation – or devolved to agency managers. Nevertheless, the environment in which these intermediate parties operate is largely determined by government policy, reflected through financial appropriation and policy parameters. While governments may distance themselves from the processes, they cannot abandon their ultimate roles as regulator, financial controller and employer.

Effective union responses require both membership activism and leadership leading to a capacity to mobilise members when required. In both countries, decentralisation of bargaining was accompanied by a firmer strategic hold at the national level. The survival of national bargaining forums, despite outsourcing, 'agencification' and devolution, has continued to provide the focus for this development. In particular, during the 1990s and early 2000s the CPSU was transformed from a highly decentralised union into one under firm federal control. The centralisation of its financial arrangements, for instance, enabled it to make a significant contribution to the ACTU campaign against the Coalition government in the 2007 federal election. In this way, structural developments were mirrored in the organisational structures of the two unions. The CPSU centralised in order to meet the challenge of the operationally decentralised bargaining. Paralleling these developments, the PCS in the United Kingdom developed a stronger role for local activists, while retaining a national and central presence. Over time, there were moves to further consolidate the central level of organisation as well as integrating local activism into these structures. In a more attenuated way than was the case in Australia, the PCS also began to articulate concerns over the quality of services, the form of public service provision as well as staffing levels (Fairbrother *et al.*, 2009).

In both countries, public sector unions found ways of alleviating and modifying the effects of government policy and efforts to depoliticise management decision-making, without fundamentally altering the direction of those changes. We explore this issue in the penultimate chapter, through an analysis of union resistance to the individualisation of the employment relationship.

7   Public Sector Unions: Contesting Individualisation, Defending Collectivity

During the New Public Management era, the principal public service unions in the United Kingdom and Australia sought to address shifting frontiers of control between management and organised labour. As indicated, the state reforms in both countries involved a dual process of decentralisation of operational activity to local managers in the public services and a centralisation of financial and corporate planning and strategy. For unions these developments raised questions relating to union organisation, union capacity and structure and union purpose. As would be expected, both sets of unions reconsidered the ways they organise and operate within the state sector.

A key concern of this chapter is to examine the respective unions' responses to the growing individualisation of employment relations in both states, particularly in relation to the introduction of individual performance management and remuneration regimes. In doing so, we continue the analysis of the process whereby two unions maintained a collective identity and capacity for central co-ordination and support in decentralised environments, while encouraging initiative by union members at the local and workplace levels. Their efforts to foster collectivism and union renewal faced considerable obstacles in the form of active attempts by public and civil service managements to exclude or marginalise unions. Both because of the centrality in current managerial strategies of individual performance incentives and because of the neo-liberal view that collective worker organisation and activity is a labour market constraint, public sector unions faced major challenges. Unions have had to contend with concerted efforts to individualise the employment relationship; in the process unions in both countries have recast their collective capacities.

THE CHALLENGE

The modern state labour market has been the focus of government attention over the past two decades. In line with the neo-liberal reform projects advocated by many governments, particularly from the Anglo-American bloc, quasi-market procedures have been applied to public sector managerial agents and public sector labour more generally. Central to these initiatives has been a renewed emphasis on the individuation of labour market relations, underwriting the worker as an individual, rather than as a member of the collective labour process. Measures, such as performance-related pay systems, provide the means to embed the individualisation of the employment relationships. This process, in turn, has implications for the ways that unions organise and operate.

Unions face a difficult task negotiating procedurally fair performance management systems in the public sector. Public managers are often reluctant to allow their workplace prerogatives to be constrained. In such arrangements, there is considerable potential for supervisor bias and subjectivity to permeate the process. As a corollary, union officials and workplace union representatives face considerable challenges assisting members to navigate human resource processes that frequently lack transparency. For unions, performance management thus raises important challenges for the ways that unions organise and operate.

The theoretical justification for performance-related pay in the public sector relies on a combination of expectancy and goal-setting theories (e.g. Milkovich and Wignor, 1991; Vroom, 1964). Underpinning these analyses is the view that individuals are most highly motivated when they are set specific but challenging goals. The premise is that this motivational effect will be achieved when employees know what is required of them and when they have feedback about meeting these goals. This premise suggests that goals should be clear and specific, challenging but attainable ('stretch goals'), accompanied by feedback on task performance, and accepted by employees. In addition, employees need to believe they have the knowledge, skills, abilities and equipment to achieve the goals expected of them (O'Donnell and Shields, 2006: 396). The condition of such schemes in the public sector is that job responsibilities can be clearly identified and accurately measured (Milkovich and Wignor, 1991).

Performance management arrangements have become a feature of the civil and public services in each country. These schemes reinforce managerial prerogatives in specific ways. To illustrate, performance management processes provide managers with considerable potential to use these systems to rachet-up effort norms and performance expectations. Success, for example, in achieving the performance bonus in the first year could result in the setting of higher performance targets for the following year. In this way, management may use performance management systems to ratchet-up effort levels and simultaneously enhance their workplaces prerogatives and controls. Such measures are part of a wider agenda of securing managerially-based and focused civil and public services.

Questioning managerial prerogatives has long been a feature of trade unionism in the civil and public services in both countries. Union efforts to make such systems fairer are likely to be stymied where workplace supervisors are not adequately trained in giving and receiving constructive feedback on employee performance or where supervisors either do not have the necessary communication skills or are uninterested in engaging in the process (O'Donnell and O'Brien, 2000). Managers may also resist efforts by unions to foster consultation and employee engagement in the design and implementation of performance management systems. Such consultation and engagement potentially threatens the enhanced authority and workplace prerogatives that performance management systems provide them.

Nonetheless, performance management systems can provide unions with opportunities to engage with their members and to campaign for employees to be involved more fully in the design and operation of performance management systems. Unions have opportunities to demand that performance criteria used to assess employee performance are linked to relevant work tasks undertaken by employees and that these criteria do not include factors beyond the control of individual employees. Unions may also be able to insist on appeal processes that examine the documentation used to assess employee performance. Unions can also mobilise their members where there are concerns over gender or racial bias influencing performance assessments. In addition, unions may be able to campaign for employee consultation at all stages of the process; the setting of performance objectives, the provision of feedback, the assessment of employee performance, and the linkage of assessment to pay increases or performance bonuses. Achieving these outcomes require unions to overcome considerable obstacles, not least managers' attempts to retain their enhanced workplace prerogatives. Nevertheless, the increased popularity of performance management for governments and senior public sector managers alike presents opportunities for unions to mobilise and engage with their members at a workplace level. In the process, unions may take the opportunity to develop and strengthen workplace representative structures and campaign about issues that directly impact on their members workloads, job satisfaction and morale.

THE UNITED KINGDOM: PAY AS A SOURCE OF ACTIVISM

Whatever the broader concerns and aspirations of trade unions in modern liberal democracies, their prime rationale has tended to be focused on pay, both the content of settlements and the 'shape' of pay systems. An appreciation of the debates within Human Resource Management concerning motivation and 'reward management' are an unavoidable part of unions' engagement with these issues at the level of the employer. In general, trade unions in the UK have succeeded in lowering pay dispersion across enterprises and within enterprises (Metcalf *et al.*, 2001). Since a key purpose of performance-based approaches is to increase dispersion by individualising pay, unions have tended to see such initiatives not only as corrosive of pay equity, but also as an attack on collectivism at work. Within the civil service, these debates arrived relatively recently and the impact of such individualisation of employment relations is, as yet, not as significant as in many other countries. Nevertheless, the introduction of performance elements marks a significant change and should be seen as the beginning of a process. Moreover, with the more general announcement in 2010 by the newly elected Coalition government of the decimation of public sector employment, unions face particularly difficult tasks in bargaining over further management initiatives.

Shaping Pay Systems

In the United Kingdom, there has been much debate about performance-related pay in public sector contexts. A survey on performance-related pay of 2,000 employees in the Inland Revenue found that while 81 per cent of employees believed that they were capable of achieving the performance targets set out in the performance pay scheme (expectancy), 71 per cent of staff believed that the rewards on offer were inadequate (lacked valance), and 45 per cent believed that if they worked to the level required to receive a reward it would not be forthcoming (lacked instrumentality) (Marsden and Richardson, 1994: 253–4). It appeared that management's motivation for introducing goal-setting approaches to performance appraisal were focused more on ratcheting-up performance expectations rather than enhancing skills development. In public organisations such as the Inland Revenue in the mid-1990s pressure was placed on staff to accept management defined performance objectives. Furthermore, performance appraisal systems were used to intensify performance expectations (Marsden, 2004: 360). It would appear that performance pay, and associated regimes of performance management, succeeded in renegotiating the terms of the effort bargain for public sector workers in the United Kingdom. Techniques such as goal-setting and performance appraisals had instilled in public employees a clearer sense of management's objectives and enabled line managers to ensure compliance with organisational objectives when setting goals for individual employees (Marsden, 2004: 351–67).

Public employees frequently expressed a range of concerns regarding the procedural fairness of performance pay schemes. Procedural injustice may result from the use of performance assessment procedures that are prone to error or arbitrary judgments (O'Donnell and Shields, 2006: 400). As a result, public service employees often viewed the implementation of performance-related pay as unfair and lacking in transparency (Kellough and Seldon, 1997). The process of performance appraisal was also viewed by employees as too frequently subjective and too likely to be influenced by the biases of the supervisor (O'Donnell and O'Brien, 2000). For example, in the Inland Revenue many employees believed that a quota existed on the number of top performance ratings, and that there was favouritism in the allocation of these ratings (Marsden and Richardson, 1994: 257). A belief that the process of administering performance appraisals was unfair is likely to engender feelings of mistrust and an erosion of motivation, commitment and willingness to demonstrate desired work behaviours (Brown and Armstrong, 1999). Performance-related pay schemes in the public sector have also been criticised for their tendency to exacerbate friction amongst employees as well as between management and labour (Kellough and Lu, 1993: 52). The process of conducting annual performance appraisals may undermine teamwork and increase unproductive forms of competition among employees (Kessler and Purcell, 1992; Pfeffer, 1998). Linking ratings to pay was also likely to create two classes of employees – a minority of 'stars' and a majority of 'also rans'. One conclusion is that: 'As a consequence, merit pay may damage the self-esteem and loyalty of numbers of employees' (Perry, 1995: 110). In turn, it may provide the occasion for public sector workers, including civil service workers to look to their union for support and respite.

Performance-related pay has been promoted by successive governments in the United Kingdom, both Conservative and Labour, and retained the support of senior public service management in the context of the Coalition government's programme of cuts (see CIPD, 2010). Politicians and senior bureaucrats clearly believed that performance pay was delivering benefits in excess of the morale problems it created. Marsden (2004) contends that a central motivation for governments and senior public service managers to persist with performance pay was the success this technique had in renegotiating the effort bargain and ratcheting-up performance expectations. A comparison of appraisals against reported performance levels found that senior management had been largely successful in ensuring that line managers achieved both quality and quantitative targets in an environment of declining staff numbers. Marsden concluded:

> the main impact of the introduction of performance-related-pay across large sections of the British public services during the 1990s was to facilitate the renegotiation of performance norms.
>
> (Marsden, 2004: 365)

The support of local line managers is critical for such a project. Line managers face considerable incentives to be lenient in goal-setting to minimise workplace conflicts and this often results in an inflation of appraisal scores over time. In such organisations as the Inland Revenue, senior management succeeded in defining organisation-wide performance objectives and this provided greater certainty to line managers when negotiating individual performance goals with employees. While instances of collusion between local managers and staff at another civil service section, Employment Service, were evident, Marsden pointed to a more sophisticated regime of audits and reporting of performance indicators limiting the potential for ongoing collusion at a local level (Marsden, 2004: 367).

It is against this background of managerial initiative, underwritten by successive governments, that the civil service unions in the United Kingdom took up performance-related pay and associated remuneration arrangements. The PCS has a history of addressing the impact of the individuation of employee relations and particularly performance-related pay schemes. This union also mobilised to resist attempts to fragment pay and conditions, as part of national campaigns (supported by local level activism). The individualisation of pay became increasingly central to these pay campaigns. They were fought on three fronts: at the office level, at the national level, notably though the strike action of 2004, and also through legal challenge. In its larger aims, PCS was unsuccessful; civil service pay remained fragmented and the tendency remained towards greater, not less, individualisation. However, some important modifications to the system were secured.

In combination with the devolution of pay policy through departments and agencies, and the fragmentation of pay through outsourcing, decentralisation of discretionary pay determination meant a divergence of earnings, both between departments and within our case study agency, Jobcentre Plus itself. Performance-related elements, whilst a relatively small proportion of earnings, remained one of the most common sources of grievance and, equally, one of the most important focal points for organising and mobilisation. Pay policy was thus a major factor in moulding local activism, and this might be seen as a paradox of union organising. While PCS argued for a return to comprehensive national bargaining and opposed the extension of performance-related or other discretionary or non-consolidated elements in pay, these issues were, at the same time, pivotal in the union's resurgence at the workplace level.

Outsourcing and Pay

Pay determination is not something that happens in an organisational or political vacuum. In the case of Jobcentre Plus, and the Department of Work and Pensions as a whole, it is impossible to understand management initiatives of the last decade, and their industrial relations consequences, without noting that the backdrop to these developments was the creation of competition from alternative providers. Outsourcing, and the threat of outsourcing, are implicit factors in any discussion on pay. More broadly, the threat of outsourcing was used to justify reorganisation and work intensification within the in-house workforce.

Staff therefore, commonly saw privatisation and outsourcing as fixed intentions, rather than as pragmatic evaluations of 'what works'. Even in the case of retaining functions in-house, the dynamic was towards a race to the bottom, as each round of efficiencies set a new benchmark for market testing. In the context of this 'market', pay differentials were transient. This was apparent in the case of office support services, outsourced in 2006. As observed:

> From July next year we will be working for the private sector. We will no longer be civil servants. The government put job centre messengering

[sic], stationery supply, switchboard ... basically the boring but essential bits ... they were put out to tender. An in-house team was allowed to bid, and we won – by cutting our own throats. We have totally reorganised. But, the government has now said 'thanks a lot, but we don't want you anymore'.

(Office Representative, PCS, 2006)

For workers, attempting to meet the problems posed by outsourcing often resulted in inferior work conditions and continued vulnerability.

The strategy for retaining in-house functions became one of cost cutting by reducing staff and putting pressure on pay. Pay, or 'reward', however, is a blunt instrument. Thus, in Jobcentre Plus the performance pay regime sometimes seemed incoherent, as managers attempted to balance the needs of recruitment and performance management with the government imperative to control costs. Agency status gave some autonomy, and Jobcentre Plus was expected to use it. As stated:

departments should implement their relocation plans alongside efforts to align their pay with local labour market conditions.

(HM Treasury, 2004)

Not only did wages in different departments and agencies diverge, (with starting salaries in some grades varying by 70 per cent between departments, PCS, 2005); discretionary elements within Jobcentre Plus pay also created differentials between individuals on the same grade.

Civil service management clearly stated this agenda as early as 1992:

I think our grading definitions ... get in the way of the way in which we might want to work in the future. It creates all sorts of problems. For the moment, of course, pay and grading is on the same terms as the rest of the civil service. So that does mean that this year we are starting to introduce performance-related pay ... [PRP] has to be related to the direct responsibility that you have for influencing performance.

(Deputy Director, Benefits Agency, 1992)

In one sense, change was limited. In Jobcentre Plus, the link between performance and pay remained indirect under Labour from 1997. The Chief Executive continued to make it clear that the approach was less concerned with individual motivation than with the need to 'ease out performance variation' (Strathie, in House of Commons, 2006: 35). The process was based on a comparison of work completed against the target set. In the case of personal advisors, the organisation was clear.

We are expecting people to conduct 60 per cent of the time available to them with the customer.

(Strathie, in House of Commons, 2006: 35)

For these workers, there was a recomposition of work processes and tasks.

Performance scores were initially based on a single quantitative measure: job entries. The scheme therefore created the perverse incentive to concentrate on easier, 'job-ready' clients and temporary job placements, rather than spend longer with more difficult to place clients (the long-term unemployed and other claimants from 'harder-to-reach' groups). In this respect, the broader significance of the scheme was its link with the outsourcing agenda within Jobcentre Plus. Whereas job centre staff had no choice but to deal with the full range of job-seekers, private, and 'third' sector entrants typically dealt with specific categories of these, who were referred to them following initial interview by Jobcentre Plus staff (Davies, 2008). Whereas job centre staff attempted to meet this range of individual needs within centrally-prescribed interview time limits, competitors were able to concentrate on particular routes into employment. Deliberately crude methods of counting placements, therefore, tend to distort the performance comparison.

From 2005, performance was managed using a three option 'RAG tool' (red, amber, green) applied by line managers in categorising staff according to whether they were exceeding, meeting, or failing to meet their targets. All amber or red ratings triggered a review of the individual's 'personal development plan', which was monitored at least monthly until a green rating was achieved. A combination of deliberately tough target setting and the fact that 'a small minority of managers may have been unclear about the best way to apply it' (House of Commons 2006: 92) meant that the new format encouraged free use of the 'unsatisfactory' category. One third of staff received a 'red' marking in 2005 (House of Commons, 2006: 56). This classification was not a subtle one, rather it was 'overly simplistic' (House of Commons, 2006, para. 257).

If this method had a purpose, however, it was of dubious usefulness as a motivational tool. PCS reported that workers branded with a Red rating had been branded as members of 'Club Zero'. Although this was denied by senior management (House of Commons, 2006: 17–18), the RAG system was revised and re-branded during 2006. There was a recognition that the technique had failed to 'incentivise' staff and that it had already 'damaged the trust of Advisors in managers' use of such tools' (Nunn and Kelsey, 2007: 38). The new arrangement was:

> a support package to upskill and drive the improvement, to increase their learning and their application of the learning. It is not a performance assessment tool.
>
> (Strathie, in House of Commons, 2007)

The new variant, the 'Advisor Achievement Tool' addressed earlier criticism by including qualitative and quantitative measures. As the system was refined, partly in response to trade union pressure and external scrutiny, the 'rules of the game' for workers changed steadily. For some groups of staff, assessment involved attempts to quantify the 'quality' of work. For first-contact staff, dealing with the public by telephone, for example:

> your manager will sit in with you and see if you actually ask key words. You have to say the special words or special questions that might not be relevant to the person sat in front of you, but you have to still ask them, and [they] would check up that you are doing it in this specific way.
>
> (Branch Secretary, PCS, 2006)

Accompanying this modification of the way individual performance was evaluated, the key indicator of office performance was also revised. Whereas the previous 'job entry targets' had been based on Personal Advisor 'interventions', the new 'job outcome targets' counted all clients who found work. Since such outcomes could not be attributed to specific interventions, it was no longer possible to make the link with individual employee effectiveness. One declared aim was to increase the level of discretion, and there is evidence that staff no longer felt that they had to 'throw mud at the wall and hope some sticks' (quoted in Davis *et al.*, 2007: 25).

The new Advisor Tool was, nevertheless, an equally blunt instrument, combining productivity measures with behavioural indicators:

> Half of it is about how tidy your desk is and … are you wearing a name badge?
>
> (Branch Secretary, PCS, 2006)

Constant change and innovation in target setting was partly a function of the inherent difficulty of specifying complex processes (Propper and Wilson, 2003). But it also reflected the fact that, although there appear to be few limits to the Taylorisation of public sector work, these limits are not insurmountable (Fisher, 2004, 2007). The main focus was now on the process, rather than on outcomes for clients, with advisers now required to spend 70 per cent of their working hours as 'contact' time. So, in the absence of the main outcome measure, performance management became more, not less directed at increasing intensification. It was left to PCS to:

> recommend that members continue to do the best job they can, and make the decision that is best for the customer.
>
> (PCS, 2008a)

This insistence on quality of service was, on the one hand, a tactical use of 'customer' interests and, on the other, a more strategic confrontation of a public ethos perspective against a narrow view of organisational effectiveness.

The other component of appraisal was the performance development plan (PDP). Introduced in 2003, this plan was described as the focus for 'discussion of current role and future aspirations' of employees (House of Commons,

2006: 92). In fact, it was more than a training or developmental tool since, in common with other parts of the civil service following the Makinson Report (2000), there were clear links to pay and to disciplinary outcomes. The logic of agency status was that reward systems could be varied to suit 'the culture and values' of the organisation (Treasury, 2000, cited in Kessler *et al.*, 2006: 8; Treasury, 2001). In reality, though, discretion was limited, to the extent that, throughout the civil service, the concept of pay delegation might seem 'fraudulent' (French and Funnel, 2005). Nevertheless, the particular 'culture' inculcated by in Jobcentre Plus by senior managers did mean that the scheme was operated in a distinctive way. The result was that, for some employees, it was seen as a barrier to effective motivation of staff. As stated:

> There is this big loyalty thing that you mustn't say anything that might be considered to be critical. What they don't understand is that we all want to be [in] a really excellent organisation. ... Nothing cheers these people [personal advisors] up like actually getting people into work.
>
> (Business Manager, Jobcentre Plus, 2006)

The paradox is that the emphasis on 'culture and values' and the link with pay had the effect of inhibiting staff rather than enabling staff to participate as engaged employees.

The PDP used a four option rating: from 'excellent' to 'unsatisfactory', based on a number of criteria, depending on job and grade. Notionally, this rating was an indicator of individual performance. Actually, the scheme was budget-limited. Following a prolonged dispute, rigid quotas were abandoned in 2006, but nominal performance ratings continued to be moderated according to an 'indicative curve' at the district level. This was a normal distribution showing the expected frequencies of scores; results were adjusted to 'fit' the curve. Therefore, although individual outcomes were not predetermined, the likelihood of an individual employee attaining a high rating depended on performance of the group. As one manager stated:

> The curve has got to be met within that group ... No matter how brilliant you are, only a certain percentage, say 8 per cent, can be ones.
>
> (Business Manager, JobCentre Plus, 2006)

As has been noted elsewhere, a sophisticated system, ostensibly designed to facilitate a high degree of individualisation of 'reward', is to a large extent over-ridden by the higher priority of budgetary planning and control (for example Gilman, 2004).

Superficially, this was similar to other forms of moderation. As one employee pointed out:

> It's like in education, where, even if everyone gets over 70 per cent, someone still has to get a D.
>
> (Representative, PCS, 2006)

In comparing individuals' performance, the problem was that, unlike moderation of examination marking, the raw material being worked with was fairly crude and often incommensurable. Rather than this being a dispassionate statistical exercise, outcomes were negotiated and this depended on the ability, or willingness, of individual office managers to stand their ground in their advocacy of their own staff. As indicated office managers have discretion:

> You have an appraisal report and you write competencies and skills. Then for the summary, when you are talking about your person ... you've got to think why it is that this person should be this grade. And people listen and say: I think that person was as good as [others]. But you can say what the hell you want, can't you?
>
> (Business Manager, JobCentre Plus, 2006)

The competing management goals for securing control and commitment necessarily create a tension in workplace employment relations, but in this case, the controlling tendency was clearly the prime influence. Whilst the scheme ostensibly set out to incentivise individual workers, it was the influence of middle managers that was controlled. This control focused on managerial perception:

> We are in different territory ... the experience before is that it used to be seen that it was the junior people were the ones who needed to be put in their place. ... [Now] you are talking about the bulk of staff [including] middle management who had to be, culturally, shifted.
>
> (General Secretary, PCS, 2004)

The method, therefore, departed from straightforward output measures of performance, implicitly including other behavioural or 'merit' criteria. In some cases, there was a degree of self-assessment and, although the decision was a management one, this subjectivity was seen by some as significant:

> If you've got two members of staff, both have done exactly the same thing – but one is very shy, they won't push themselves on the self-assessment. Another member of staff is 'Oh what a clever girl I am'. They can really lay it on. They end up with a higher box marking just because they have sold themselves better.
>
> (Representative, PCS, 2006)

However, the ability to 'sell' oneself depends on the duties undertaken and, for most employees there is little latitude to embellish the reality of a closely managed workload. In a rather frank admission:

> You have to give evidence. I have to say that with mine I expanded on the truth. Because who saw what I did? If you are good at putting pen

to paper ... [But] for the grade below ... if you've got a line manager that's normally sitting there.

(Lone Parent Advisor, JobCentre Plus, 2006)

This circumstance, along with promotion policy, was perceived to be a process that was stacked against staff in 'customer-facing' roles:

If you want kudos, if you want to get on, you've got to go behind the scenes and do specialist things.

Whereas:

Making a difference for [these] customers is a tough job ... The ones laboriously working as personal advisors, it's hard for them to write anything wonderful on their form.

(Business Manager, JobCentre Plus, 2006)

Personal advisors were the face of Jobcentre Plus and because of the difficulties they faced in doing their job. They found it hard to present themselves in the positive ways often required by such assessments. The paradox is that these jobs were the focus of much ministerial rhetoric about the importance of the customer interface. The implication often appeared to be that they would be rewarded for this difficult job.

The impact on pay was limited to a non-consolidated lump sum payment. For PCS nationally 'there are not any carrots, just sticks' (House of Commons, 2006: 25). As a priority for national negotiators, performance pay was therefore less significant than the challenge of maintaining incremental progression, which was effectively frozen for many staff. Nevertheless, the performance regime, as seen by workers, was opaque and unpredictable.

It *emerges* from the meeting. You could go up as a Three and come back as a One.

(Representative, PCS, 2006)

One consequence of this opacity was to render the scheme ineffective as a motivational tool; a rational response might be to:

just wait to see what turns up in the bank ... why should I flog my guts out?

(Switchboard Operator, JobCentre Plus, 2006)

Such views helped shape the response by the union to these initiatives.

On the one hand, this mechanism, along with job entry targets, accentuated the individual focus of appraisal (Johnson and Nunn, 2007). Particularly because the assessment process appeared to staff to be a 'black box', PDPs were one of the main causes of grievance at the office level. During 2006/

2007 alone, the scheme resulted in 570 formal grievances across the department (DWP, 2009). In the workplace, this individual competition was corrosive of team-working:

> I made the mistake, somebody asked me what I had done, and there was a lot of bad feeling amongst the team. This year I was determined I wouldn't tell anybody and I haven't. I don't care what they assume. I haven't told a soul what box marking I've got. But others have. And they are bitching.
>
> (Lone Parent Advisor, JobCentre Plus, 2005)

On the other hand, dissatisfaction was collective – not least due to an inflexible and confrontational management approach (a point conceded by the Head of Human Resources, Department of Work and Pensions: Berry, 2005) – and formed the basis for collective responses. Nationally, the union's position had always been to oppose performance-related pay and it argued for service-related incremental pay progression. In relation to its opposition to the scheme, the fact that the employer had instigated several parallel areas of dispute – including the threat of compulsory redundancies and a worsening of the sick pay scheme – meant that membership support for action was almost inevitable. Over a sixteen-month period, the union organised a series of strikes and related stoppages, including the first national civil service strike for a generation, on 5 November 2004. This was accompanied by a work to rule in which a number of DWP managers incurred disciplinary action for refusing to implement the performance scheme (Public Finance, 2004), leading in some cases to spontaneous walk-outs in offices. In 2004, the PCS took the matter to the High Court arguing breach of contract. The court found in favour of the employer, but in the process some significant points about the performance-related pay scheme were conceded, including the introduction of a grievance procedure. The union also argued that the scheme discriminated against lower paid workers (who are disproportionately women) and was later able to quote from a civil service commissioned consultant's report which had drawn attention to 'statistically significant' differences attributable to sex, race and disability (PCS, 2005). Clearly, the union did not achieve its ultimate objectives at this stage, although the detailed mechanism of assessment was revised, ameliorating some problems.

For PCS within individual offices, the performance development system remained one of the most common sources of grievance until its revision in 2008. After five years of campaigning at departmental level, PCS's most important priorities were achieved, 'effectively remov[ing] the main link between pay and performance in DWP' (PCS, 2008b). Unsurprisingly, the issue of performance did not disappear from the management agenda and key aspects of the scheme remained. Appraisal was now to be based on objectives and competencies, rather than in competition with colleagues, but performance rating remained. It was, perhaps, a little early to speak the scheme's 'abolition'.

At the same time as PCS campaigned against performance-related pay, it also used the opportunity presented by the performance regime to advance its own agenda on learning and skills. Union Learning Representatives (ULRs) were given formal status in the UK by the Employment Act 2002, with similar rights to time off to shop stewards. The PCS was among the first unions to recruit and organise ULRs (see Public and Commercial Services Union, 2004; Alexandrou *et al.* 2005), differentiating between the role of the local ULR and the Branch Learning Co-ordinator who had responsibility for negotiating with the employer on training issues. Within PCS, the DWP branches were most active in building the ULR organisation. In Jobcentre Plus, the ULR role evolved partly in response to the broader negotiating agenda. A 'partnership' agreement on learning was seen by DWP as specifically addressing literacy and numeracy needs in the workforce (McGuire, 2005). For PCS, however, the agenda was rather broader and their aim was to provide opportunities that were additional to those normally provided by the employer; the union sought to develop skills that went beyond those needed to undertake current duties. But equally, to the extent that the PCS succeeded in integrating the union learning initiative into a coherent strategy, it may also provide the key for a revival of union organisation (Forrester, 2005).

The PCS campaigned for incremental pay progression in place of performance-related pay bonuses. This ultimately resulted in the 2004 national strike action and subsequent work to rule campaign, alongside a legal challenge to the High Court. While the High Court challenge was ultimately unsuccessful, the union did succeed in establishing a grievance process and improved clarity over how performance assessments would be undertaken. The PCS was also able to mobilise nationally around a campaign focused on employee learning and skill development by making use of the opportunity to recruit Union Learning Representatives under the 2002 Employment Act. At the local level, union activists were able to assist union officials by taking responsibility for an increased proportion of their case load of grievances.

Thus, the union was able to challenge the performance-related pay scheme. It did this through a productive interrelationship between workplace activism and national union co-ordination and strategic policymaking. The union nationally had a clear view of national pay arrangements, consistently arguing for incremental pay progression. In addition, the union sought to build its representative and campaigning capacities, most recently through the URL scheme. These measures were not introduced into an organisational vacuum. For almost thirty years, the union and its predecessors had built a relatively robust form of workplace representation, which by 2000 had the capacity to articulate local concerns and facilitate membership mobilisation around national policies and programs. This history was neither straightforward nor uncontentious; there remained an unevenness to the organisational capacity. Nonetheless, the union had the organisational base and capacity to challenge such managerial initiatives as performance-related pay schemes, and during the 2000s it did so in relatively effective ways.

AUSTRALIA – CONTESTING INDIVIDUALISATION OF EMPLOYMENT IN THE APS

In Australia there was an equally long and disputed history about pay and in particular performance-related pay and related remuneration arrangements. Until the 1990s the largely uniform standard pay conditions that applied were based on a classification system operative across the entire service (O'Brien, 1994). Beyond standard pay, the traditional system for rewarding Commonwealth public servants took place within a comprehensive system of promotion. This process was available to most staff as an extended internal labour market underpinned by extensive appeal rights (Caiden, 1965). While this system was modified in the 1980s for more senior public servants, for most employees orderly movement through increments and classifications was the principal means by which performance was rewarded. After 1987, members of the SES were expected to negotiate performance agreements with their supervisors, although these provisions were not linked to pay.

Performance pay was introduced by the Labor government in 1992 as part of more comprehensive changes in the wage bargaining process, though it was restricted to members of the SES and those employed in the senior officer grades. An initial inquiry into the operation of this scheme was undertaken by the Senate Standing Committee on Finance and Public Administration (SSCFPA) in 1993. Concerns raised in submissions included: the potential for performance-based pay to increase the politicisation of the public service; that performance assessments were inherently subjective; and a recognition that the performance of public sector organisations and staff were influenced by issues beyond their control (Senate Standing Committee on Finance and Public Administration, 1993: 19–26). The hurried pace of the introduction of the performance-related pay scheme was criticised, and submissions argued that performance-related pay had proved divisive and costly in terms of time and in the use of scarce administrative resources (Senate Standing Committee on Finance and Public Administration, 1993: 49–57). Subsequent research into performance-related pay in the APS from 1992 to 1996 found that supervisors often rewarded their 'favourites' with the highest performance appraisal ratings, while senior managers and those working in high profile areas also tended to receive the highest performance ratings (O'Donnell, 1998: 33–4).

After 1996, the Coalition government was determined to introduce a rationalised classification structure linked to individual appraisal, with some measure of performance-based pay embedded in the new system.The para-meters for agreement making insisted that all collective agreements made by agencies must contain a commitment to develop flexible remuneration arrangements. It was, however, left up to agencies as to what form these might take. Thus the long-standing system of automatic semi-movement of staff through incremental ranges was replaced with one based on more explicit measures of performance. This change provided the potential for employees to be rewarded with performance bonuses in conjunction with advancement through a classification structure. Agency management per-ceived the linkage of classification structures to performance management as central to a 'cultural change' process that emphasised the linking of individual work performance to the achievement of agency objectives. This process was viewed as a central element of a fundamental realignment of Australian Public Service values and processes (O'Donnell and O'Brien, 2002).

Agency Approaches

For some agency managements, performance-related pay schemes formed a central element of their agenda to inculcate a 'performance culture' within their organisations. Cultural change via performance-related pay aimed to alter employee values, beliefs and behaviours and encouraged increased commitment by individual employees to the goals of the organisation. A further aspect to the introduction of such schemes was that they also sought to weaken collective bargaining and the role of trade unions while strengthening the power of line managers in decision-making over pay (Kessler, 1994). These aims were strongly contested by the CPSU.

An example of such experimentation occurred in DoFA where management adopted a very uncompromising approach to the promotion of a new 'can do' high performance culture: in staff newsletters employees were encour-aged to become 'action-oriented', to develop a 'will to win' and to be 'creative' in how they 'get the runs on the board' (O'Brien and O'Donnell, 2000). The system adopted in DoFA also included a mechanism for mana-ging underperformance. Staff reported that management was using a per-formance rating scale to remove those staff who had not accepted the new culture, providing them with an 'unsatisfactory' assessment, such as 'funda-mental job requirements are inconsistently met ... ' (O'Brien and O'Donnell, 2000: 68). Union sources indicated that this assessment often resulted in an offer of a redundancy package (Delegates, CPSU, 1998). Because of the pressure on staff to conform, a workplace culture of fear was alleged to have taken root in DoFA. The very real threat of redundancy ensured at least behavioural conformity to the new culture from the majority of staff (O'Brien and O'Donnell, 2000). Accompanying the introduction of this per-formance management system, management attempted to place as many staff as possible on individual contracts; after 1997 management refused to negotiate collective agreements.

The system established in the DoFA, however, represented one end of the spectrum of pay arrangements within the APS. At the other end was the Department of Defence that established a more rigorous system for movement through incremental scales, and specifically rejected the notion of performance bonuses. Indeed the Secretary of the Department, Dr Alan Hawke, told the Senate Finance and Public Administration References Committee in 2000 that he did:

> not believe in linking this sort of performance framework to performance pay or to any sort of model that involved notions like that – pay at risk, bonuses and the like. What we do is: at the end of the 12-month period it is simply a tick in the box if people performed well, and if they have performed well then they go up to the next increment in the pay scale.
> (Senate Finance and Public Administration References Committee, Senate Hansard, 2 May, 2000: 139)

In early 1999, the Howard government extended the system of individualised performance-related pay to departmental secretaries, the heads of APS departments. Up to 15 per cent of department secretaries' total remuneration package was made available as a performance bonus, later increased to 20 per cent (Podger, 2007: 139). A former secretary and former head of the Public Service Commission, Andrew Podger, provided a critical assessment of the impact of performance pay, along with reduced employment contracts, as increasing the politicisation of the roles of departmental secretaries and reducing their willingness to be critical of government policy. He wrote:

> All secretaries are affected, and they are being dishonest or fooling themselves if they deny it. They will hedge their bets on occasions, limit the number of issues on which to take a strong stand, be less strident, constrain public comments, limit or craft more carefully public documents and accept a muddying of their role and that of political advisors.
> (Podger, 2007: 144)

This view, however, was contested. In response to such claims of increased politicisation at the most senior levels of the APS, the then Secretary of the Department of Prime Minister and Cabinet, Peter Shergold, strongly rejected the view that performance bonuses had altered the behaviours of departmental secretaries or had contributed to a culture of intimidation. He did not believe there was evidence of secretaries becoming excessively responsive to government though he also noted that: 'I am unpersuaded that bonuses drive improved productivity or performance' (Shergold, 2007: 368).

Nonetheless, the prime concern of the CPSU was not so much the remuneration arrangements for senior staff but the measures that applied to the broad mass of public service workers in the APS. These workers initially faced different sets of arrangements depending on agency, although as time proceeded most public service workers faced an increased emphasis on individuated pay and remuneration arrangements.

Employee Perspectives

For public service employees, the introduction of performance-related pay schemes, raised a raft of questions about managerial discretion, the distribution of benefits, the organisation of work, and the insecurity often associated with such measures. The CPSU had long argued against the individualisation of the employment relationship. In developing their approach and strategy, the union took into account the ways in which members experienced and understood these relationships. During the 1990s and 2000s, attention focused on performance-related pay and associated remuneration practices.

In 1999, the Community and Public Sector Union conducted a survey of its members' views about performance pay. Among the findings was evidence of employee concerns over the potential for increased managerial discretion in the selection of performance criteria. Unless such criteria were specific and clearly linked to the major work tasks undertaken by employees, there was the very real potential for supervisors to make arbitrary judgments regarding employee behaviour and work performance. As noted:

> You need to have specific responsibilities agreed/outlined to protect yourself from the possibility of supervisors coming up with various unrelated duties/expected outcomes at assessment time.
>
> (Administrative Service Officer,
> Department of Foreign Affairs and Trade, 1999)

In relation to the provision of feedback on their work performance, many APS employees believed that their supervisor lacked the necessary communication or interpersonal skills to discuss their work performance in a constructive manner. Furthermore, many took the view that the supervisor did not have the time to undertake detailed appraisals or to provide staff with regular feedback because of the work pressures they faced themselves. As stated:

> Supervisor doesn't have the time. The scheme was only ever ... seen as a way of introducing performance pay into the department and once it served this purpose, rather than any purpose relating to skills development, it was promptly ignored.
>
> (Administrative Service Officer,
> Department of Health and Aged Care, 1998)

Many APS employees also perceived the assessment of their performance by their supervisors to represent an inherently subjective process that substantially increased managerial discretion. For example, a number of employees pointed to favouritism in the performance appraisal system and seemingly subjective and arbitrary assessments:

1 Managers forget things you've done that meet the criteria.
2 Personality differences and differences in style affect manager's decision making regarding ratings.
3 Sometimes rely too much on hearsay and not evidence.
4 Some managers lack the objectivity and intelligence to apply ratings fairly.

> (Administrative Service Officer,
> Department of Family and Community Services, 1999)

In some APS agencies, initial appraisal scores provided by supervisors were moderated or standardised, by senior management with the justification of ensuring consistency across the organisation. In many cases, however, the initial scores were reduced for what many employees believed were budgetary reasons. This perception had a very negative impact on workforce motivation and morale, particularly where employees believed that the initial performance assessments provided by their supervisors were being reduced by senior managers who had little, if any, knowledge of their work performance.

The likely impact of the performance-related pay schemes introduced into the APS on teamwork and on employee/manager relations was mentioned by employees as a concern:

> A major flaw of [performance] pay is that much of our work is team-based yet rewards are individual based. This has a divisive effect at all levels of the supervisory hierarchy.

> (Administrative Service Officer,
> Department of Health and Aged Care, 1999)

Although the appraisal schemes introduced into the APS were likely to contain appeal mechanisms, many staff reported that they were unaware of the details of their agencies appeal process or that they considered it unlikely that management would alter the final assessment provided to them:

> In appealing to your Manager you are appealing to Caesar! Perhaps it should be a manager from an unconnected work area for some semblance of impartiality.

> (Administrative Service Officer,
> Department of Finance and Administration, 1998)

In 2000, these concerns came to the fore in an inquiry into APS employment matters by the Finance and Public Administration Committee of the Australian Senate. The Committee noted that in some agencies performance payments for non-executive employees had been:

abandoned on the grounds that there was no evidence that it motivated people to work harder or better. On the contrary, there was evidence that it had tainted the performance management process.

(Senate Finance and Public Administration
References Committee, 2000)

In addition, the Committee was concerned about the costs of performance bonuses were being recouped by shedding staff. The Secretary of the Department of Treasury, Ted Evans, stated that:

> If ... we paid more performance pay than we may have expected in designing the budget, we would operate with fewer numbers.

(Senate Finance and Public Administration
References Committee, 2000: 12)

Such statements contributed to an atmosphere of insecurity and vulnerability.

It is within a context of managerial discretion, unequal distribution of performance bonuses, the impact of budgetary restrictions that the CPSU sought to address the individualisation of the employment relationship. Not surprisingly most attention focused on the design, procedure and impact of performance-related pay schemes.

Union Responses

Performance-related pay presented some difficulty for the CPSU. While the union did not object to performance management processes and to performance appraisals, in particular, it argued that they should be uncoupled from pay considerations (Caird, 2000: 98). Yet the government's parameters for agreement making required all agencies to have a performance-based remuneration system. While this was likely to take a number of forms, the key factors determining the ultimate form of the performance system relied on managerial attitudes and union organisational capacity.

Variation between Agencies

One challenge for the CPSU was that the definition and implementation of performance-related pay schemes varied markedly between agencies. In Defence, for example, the senior management was prepared to link incremental progression to some measure of performance, somewhat akin to the 'tick and flick' method of semi-automatic adjustments. Not surprisingly, the CPSU took the view that it could live with the Defence Department pay system, as it did not fundamentally alter previous arrangements. Elsewhere, the CPSU could not be as sanguine in its response. The CPSU could do little to resist the creeping individualisation of pay in DoFA, for example, where its membership was very low. Whilst the union was happy to take up individual cases, it was reluctant to allocate resources to build up membership in the agency (Senior CPSU official, 1999). Nevertheless in its ongoing propaganda war against performance pay, the union was able to cite DoFA as an exemplar of the excesses of individualisation. In moderately-unionised agencies, like DFAT, the CPSU had the capacity to use concerns about the implementation of performance pay in order to modify its effect. Moreover, union staff claimed that an informal system had developed among managers to share the bonuses around among the staff over a number of appraisal periods (Delegates, DFAT, 1999).

The Focus on Centrelink

In the more highly-unionised Centrelink, the union agreed, in principle to a performance management scheme in its first agreement with Centrelink. Until 2002, the Centrelink appraisal system contained an assessment of employee performance against Centrelink's focus on behaviours (explaining, listening, solving, respect and integrity) and against performance goals negotiated with an employee's supervisor at the beginning of the appraisal cycle. Nevertheless, employees were concerned that they did not receive adequate feedback on performance.

The parties agreed to a simplification of the process during negotiations over the third Centrelink collective agreement. Indeed management conceded the training of supervisors had been inadequate:

> the fact that we didn't mandate that people needed to do the training to do the assessments and exceeding expectations has been controversial. They can't tell the difference between meeting or doing well versus exceeding so it's not having a unified understanding.
>
> (Manager, Human Resources, 2003)

As a consequence of these concerns and in response to frequent union complaints, Centrelink management reduced the rating system to two categories; 'meets expectations' and 'unsatisfactory' (National People Manager, Centrelink, 2002). The CEO also conceded that assessment against the 'Centrelink Behaviours' was 'far too complicated' and that a simpler 'plan on a page' would be substituted as the assessment criteria (CEO, Centrelink, 2004). Nevertheless, the union maintained that staff often had to wait for excessive periods before their performance assessment was processed. This was the cause of considerable discontent among staff and management agreed that if the supervisor had not made the assessment by a specified time then the employee may do their own self-assessment (Interview with senior officers, CPSU, 2004).

By 2006, there were many areas of Centrelink where staff did not have an up-to-date performance agreement. For many, this was because they were at the top pay point of their classification level. One union delegate noted:

for me performance assessment means nothing because I'm on the top of the range; I don't get increments or anything so really it's just a process I need to go through and make everybody feel warm and fuzzy. We all had to have one put into the system by 30 November [2006] because HR decided they were sick of most staff not having them done ... But that doesn't mean anyone actually assesses it ... I had a discussion with the national manager yesterday and he was saying you guys are all doing pretty well I'm not really worried about what you're doing and that was it.

(Delegate, Centrelink, 2006)

Other workers in Centrelink's National Support Office expressed similar sentiments regarding the performance management system:

We go through the motions, I think is the best way of putting it. I don't personally have a performance management agreement in place now, and I think a lot of other people in the National Support Office don't. It's not given any attention and it hasn't got much credibility in terms of a method of assessing staff or anything else. I guess partly that is because nothing hinges on it. There's no reward for having one and doing well under your performance agreement, and on the other side, if you do badly, there is no penalty either. So people say, well why bother, and lots of people don't bother.

(Delegate, National Support Office, Centrelink, 2006)

The union approach in Centrelink, thus was to work steadily towards revising and adapting the schemes, to benefit the staff in more equitable ways. In this way, the union utilised the grievances and uncertainties of the staff to advance the collective interests of the staff in relation to such schemes.

Overview

Following the election of the Rudd Labor government in late 2007, the CPSU was afforded increased opportunities to negotiate over performance management systems at the level of individual agencies. The collective agreement negotiated in DEEWR, for example, provided for employees to be assessed twice; against the delivery of key organisational goals, and for demonstrating a range of 'observable work behaviours' (DEEWR, 2009). While the likelihood of subjective performance assessments remained, the performance management policy could not be altered without the agreement of both management and unions. Similarly, the agreement aimed to ensure procedural fairness in managing performance assessments when the employee was believed to be underperforming and employees were encouraged to seek representation at appraisal reviews (DEEWR, 2009).

Nevertheless, these achievements did not limit the potential for management to use the performance assessment process to maintain the workplace prerogatives they had acquired under the Howard years. In agencies, such as Medicare, the level of union participation in the performance management system was limited (CPSU, 2010). Management had undertaken a review of the agency's performance management system but staff involvement was limited to participating in a series of workshops and/or submitting their thoughts on paper to management. While the CPSU encouraged members to participate in these workshops, they believed that the system being proposed 'lacked transparency, consistency and fairness' (CPSU, 2010).

Thus, the CPSU had mixed success in contesting the individualisation of the employment relationship through performance-related pay and performance management systems. In poorly-unionised agencies, it had little capacity to mobilise employee concerns over procedural deficiencies to modify the system. In more industrially favourable environments, the union could expose these deficiencies to its members' advantage, though the union still faced the prospect of being kept at arms length over the implementation of these systems.

Contractualism: Australian Workplace Agreements

In seeking to further weaken collective bargaining processes in the APS, the Coalition government had a second string to its bow: statutory individual contracts. There had not been a fully developed model of individual employment contracts in the Australian Public Service before the Coalition legislated in 1996 for Australian Workplace Agreements and insisted that all members of the senior executive service would have their terms and conditions of employment regulated by them. Moreover, one of the significant provisions of the government's parameters for agreement making, discussed in Chapter 6, was the requirement that no collective agreement could preclude the making of an individual agreement in the form of an AWA. Indeed, an AWA over-rode a collective agreement, and any agency management was free to offer individual contracts the day after a collective agreement had been certified or registered.

In promoting the use of AWAs, the Coalition government used its own employees as a means of enforcing its general industrial relations policies. In addition, because AWAs were more common and easier to manage at Executive level, potentially at least, the government was creating a situation whereby the management of any agency might either separate the regulation of employment arrangements for managerial staff more explicitly from those of non-managerial employees. It could even go further, and individualise all employment relationships. Even if the latter path was not chosen, the performance-based pay and classification system that the government insisted should apply in all agencies ensured that a considerable degree of individualisation of employment relationships became embedded in the structure.

The most significant use of Australian Workplace Agreements occurred in Employment National, a government-owned company formed in 1997, following the abolition of the Commonwealth Employment Service. Employment National, with a small complement of 750 permanent and 450 casual staff, competed until its closure in 2003 against private and community sector agencies in the provision of services to the unemployed. In a marketised environment, where these competitors were able to bid to supply lower-cost employment services in less difficult labour market sectors, the government insisted that Employment National employees should match these private and community based agencies in pay and working conditions. Although some discussions were held between the CPSU and the Employment National management about the development of a certified agreement, the management decided that AWAs were the most appropriate form of regulation. The regulatory arrangements were the subject of Federal Court hearings. The CPSU argued that Employment National employees transferring from the Commonwealth Employment Service were effectively given no real choice about accepting an AWA (CPSU legal officer, 1998). After nearly three years of litigation the union lost its argument that transferred employees should retain the employment rights they had enjoyed in the Commonwealth Employment Service and that Employment National employees generally should have the same opportunities as those still employed in the APS. While these hearings continued, the AIRC granted an employer application for an award to be established for Employment National employees who were not on individual contracts. This award provided for a minimum set of employment conditions in areas allowable under Workplace Relations Act 1996. Significantly, this award lacked longstanding APS provisions such as paid maternity leave and increased the standard working week from 36.75 to 38 hours (AIRC, 1999; Legal Officer, CPSU, 1999).

This example also illustrates management's use of AWAs as a bargaining tactic. The CPSU was concerned that the Employment National case could establish a precedent for outsourcing existing government functions to the private sector and undercutting APS conditions. For instance, there were concerns that the telephone-based service functions within Centrelink, that responded to approximately 30 million calls in 2008–9, could be outsourced to the private sector. The CPSU also feared that that the threat of privatisation could be used to drive down labour costs while maintaining the Centrelink call centre as a government operation (Industrial Officer, CPSU, 1998).

The second use of AWAs was in displacing collective agreements. In a range of agencies from 1997 onwards public service management used AWAs to extend individual contracts beyond the SES to include those at the top of the senior officer classification and for areas of particular labour market pressure such as information technology. AWAs differed from the certified agreements in their greater focus on individual employee performance and potentially more lucrative performance bonuses (Managers responsible for industrial relations: Centrelink, 16 February 1999; Department of Education, Training and Youth Affairs, 23 February, 1999; Public Service and Merit Protection Commission, 17 February, 1999; the Audit Office, 23 February, 1999). Within some APS core agencies, such as the DoFA, there was a significant push by management to offer all staff AWAs. By July 1998, some 26 per cent of 1,300 staff had accepted such agreements (CPSU organiser, 1998). By 2003 the figure had risen to 95 per cent (DoFA Annual Report, 2002–3). In the context of management's refusal to negotiate further collective agreements after 1997, AWAs were used by DoFA management as a bargaining tactic. They offered the potential of higher monetary rewards, with individuals on AWAs offered the possibility of a performance pay bonus of up to 25 per cent of salary, compared with a maximum performance bonus of 15 per cent in the collective agreement (Union Delegates, DoFA, 21 July, 1998). Indeed DoFA management told a Senate Committee in 2001 that there was no formal limit to performance bonuses.

In other agencies, secretaries had mixed success in attempting to entice employees to accept AWAs, while delaying negotiations on a collective agreement. Shergold was one of the most experienced APS heads. He had moved to DEWR(SB) in 1998, where he was secretary until moving on to the Education portfolio in 2002 and on to the Department of Prime Minister and Cabinet in 2003. Whilst at DEWR(SB), he managed to drive a hard bargain both with private employment services providers, and with Centrelink, from which DEWR purchased services in job search referrals and benefit eligibility assessments. But DEWR staff were not so easy to win over to AWAs. A subsequent department secretary, Dr Peter Boxall, had successfully moved DoFA staff over to AWAs, and in 2004, he embarked on a similar campaign in DEWR. In addition to promoting the acceptance of AWAs by existing staff, DEWR management offered only AWAs to new employees and subsequently offered a draft non-union collective agreement to staff on a non-negotiable basis (CPSU, 2005d). Eventually negotiations began with the union, but they were protracted, particularly over the link between performance and salary progression (CPSU, 2005c). After canvassing its members, the CPSU called its members in DEWR out on strike and urged other members to support them at a lunch time rally (CPSU, 2005d). The union needed to illustrate to the government that it was unable to have its way in the agency that was its principal arm in enforcing its Workplace Relations legislation. A successful strike was held and eventually an agreement was made (CPSU, 2005e). The CPSU could reasonably claim that it had defeated the government as well as the agency management. Boxall had been unstoppable in the under-unionised DoFA, but met his match in his new department. Not only was DEWR highly unionised, but Boxall was also dealing with employees more likely to be schooled in the interstices of industrial negotiation. Mobilisation of members in this case seemed to depend on a combination of workplace union organisation and the degree of employer aggression. This latter instance suggests that the union was more likely to be successful when it was able to expose employer miscreance and had a capacity to percolate that message throughout the organisation

After 2006, the union faced additional obstacles to workplace activism and to the entry of union officials into the workplace. The CPSU responded by identifying recruitment as the basis of its counter strategy. While most union members probably have an instrumental attitude to union services, a motivating factor for activists is the degree of influence they have on union decision-making. Resourcing its recruitment drive, the CPSU became increasingly centralised in the final years of the Howard government. This centralisation of power ran the risk of demotivating those who acted as workplace activists in the union. The CPSU had little scope in the APS of forging community alliances. Centrelink staff, for example, were unlikely to gain the support of their 'customer': they were increasingly looking to the union for protection in the face of customer aggression, prompted by tough benefit eligibility regimes (Junor *et al.*, 2009).

In the bargaining arena, the CPSU maintained a reasonable level of collectivisation in employment conditions and remained able to mobilise members in individual agencies. It was not able, however, to mobilise against the government's general policy. The CPSU's focus on recruitment was part of a response discussed across the Australian union movement at the time as the 'organising model'. Perhaps it was too much to expect Australian unions to adjust quickly to a hostile environment that has been the reality for union movements in other countries, not least in the USA where the organising strategy was largely derived. The great danger for the union was that it might develop an efficient structure but lack sufficient activists to win ongoing battles within APS agencies.

The incoming Rudd Labor government moved quickly to ban any further making of AWAs in the APS. It was silent, however, on future arrangements for the senior levels of the public service. Agency-level bargaining continued. The immediate preoccupation of the CPSU in the early years of the new government was the need to address service-wide staffing cuts. Nevertheless, the union also began to campaign for one agreement covering the whole of the APS (CPSU, 2009b). As far as bargaining was concerned, the Labor government set down a new framework for bargaining in Commonwealth agencies. In particular, it specified that unions had to comply with the right of entry provisions set down in the Fair Work legislation, but it also required agency heads to respect the role of 'workplace representatives, including union delegates and employee representatives', and to facilitate their activities in the workplace representatives including union delegates and employee representatives to facilitate activities in the workplace (Department of Education, Employment and Workplace Relations, 2008: 15). This facilitative framework stood in stark contrast to the expressed attitudes of the former government. While the new government maintained the language of 'workplace' rather than 'industrial' relations, it restored the concept of 'bargaining' to the lexicon of employment relations in the APS.

ASSESSMENT

Key to the reconstitution of the modern state has been a legitimating discourse on individualism, and the individuation of the employment relationship. Governments and state management have sought to put such principles into practice measures that underwrite individual performance arrangements, supported by accountability mechanisms based on performance contracts. The intent is to ensure and embed the decentralisation of organisational and operational activity whilst maintaining central control over financial and corporate planning and strategy. This approach to governance has been played out in relation to the civil and public services labour markets through a sustained individualisation of employment relations. Performance-related pay and associated remuneration programmes provided the means for implementing these policy approaches.

While there was little evidence that performance-related pay schemes increased employee motivation, such techniques were successful in renegotiating the effort bargain and intensifying performance expectations. The 'red, amber, green' method of employee monitoring at Jobcentre Plus intensified pressure on individual staff to comply with organisational targets in relation to client service and time spent on client contact. Employees' telephone interactions with clients were also monitored, as was the percentage of their working day that personal advisors spent on client contact. In response to the more intensive surveillance of their performance, public employees at Jobcentre Plus, for example, focused on goals that were more easily achieved, such as clients who were 'job ready'.

The performance-related pay schemes introduced into both civil and public services also gave rise to other unintended attitudinal and cultural outcomes. There was potential for such schemes to undermine teamwork, particularly if one, or more, team members were rated more highly than their colleagues, and received larger performance bonus payments, but where work outputs were the product of collective team effort. The potential for staff to be rewarded for self-promotion was also evident in both countries. There was considerable disquiet among public employees over the lack of procedural fairness inherent in the design and implementation of performance-related pay schemes. The process of assessing individual performance remained inherently subjective. How visible staff were to senior management and how high profile their work tasks were could have a significant bearing on their performance assessment, whether they were based at corporate head office or in a regional office.

The process of moderating, or standardising performance ratings was undertaken to fit performance assessments into a normal distribution though this failed to improve employees' perceptions of procedural fairness. In the UK, the process of standardising results could create considerable uncertainty regarding the performance rating, and bonus payments, an employee might ultimately receive. Individual bonus payments were also linked to the performance of the group. Such processes of standardisation were perceived by employees to be undertaken to contain the costs of these schemes and further undermined employee morale.

In addition, the individualisation of the employment relationship through performance-contingent rewards, or through the introduction of individual contracts, increased the level of dispersion of wages and working conditions across both public sectors. While public sector unions in the UK mobilised against performance pay and the fragmentation of pay and conditions, wage dispersion in the APS widened significantly over time following several rounds of agency agreement making. The less transparent and individualised process by which performance bonuses and individual contracts (in the case of Australia) were negotiated also enhanced the potential for substantial fragmentation of base pay, bonuses and working conditions across the over 100 agencies of the APS.

For unions, this process of depoliticising the state employment relationship challenges the ways that unions respond to these initiatives and to their relations with state managers and employers. In reforming the state apparatus along more managerial lines, governments have either attempted a process of accommodation with state-based trade unions, or more usually fostered their marginalisation (Fairbrother and Rainnie, 2006). In turn, state-based trade unions have articulated the interests of their members in complex ways, seeking to advance national interests and central co-ordination whilst encouraging the capacity of workplace-based members to organise and operate. Our argument is that state sector unions may be able to take the opportunities provided by state restructuring to both reposition themselves and to develop policies and approaches that question state management practice and government policy (Fairbrother, 1994; Danford *et al.*, 2003; Carter, 2006). However, as evidenced in union approaches to performance-related pay and associated remuneration arrangements the process and outcome is complex.

In both countries, governments developed programmes and policies to secure more skilled and less numerous workforces, able to operate in flexible and responsive ways. Thus, there has been strong pressure on managers to control and monitor their staff, through policy prescription and by performance measurement. Senior public service staff have been empowered and made individually accountable; they have initiated a succession of schemes and proposals to restructure the state labour process, reconstitute the state employment relationship and refocus job tasks (particularly in relation to front-line staff). In Australia these measures had the added weight of juridical support for individual labour contracts. Workforces were increasingly subject to greater managerial demands, resulting in the intensification of work activity, uncertainty, insecurity and feelings of vulnerability. Within this complex of 'reforms' and their outcomes, unions sought to organise and operate in the interests of their members.

In the United Kingdom, the operation of performance-related pay became an issue on which the PCS could organise. As a locally-determined pay element, it presented the opportunity, or rather the necessity, for local activism, as the growing burden of casework became devolved from more senior officials. This is not to claim that this local activism was an adequate or effective response in itself to a national employer strategy. Activists frequently described their role as 'fire-fighting': policing the rules of a system that had been imposed on them and over which they have no real influence. Nevertheless, the extent to which this local level of activism responded to the challenge made significant differences for groups of workers affected.

To the extent that restructuring has given rise to a level of local bargaining activity, this presents public sector unions with a dilemma. On the one hand, this local activism has been a significant source of strength in national campaigns, while, on the other hand local bargaining requires some level of central co-ordination in order to redeploy resources and maintain some degree of commonality in employment conditions and wages. The question facing the union is how to navigate this dilemma. Nevertheless, the introduction of performance-related pay and individual agreements provided public unions with fertile ground for mobilisation and resistance.

The PCS campaign against performance-related pay and pay fragmentation comprised a locally-based and centrally co-ordinated set of activities and initiatives. At a national level, the union proclaimed a commitment to incremental pay progression and within this rubric, it challenged the performance-related pay schemes, and variants that were proposed by state managements. The union was able to initiate a sixteen-month stoppage and disruption based campaign. Critical to the effectiveness of the campaign is the active involvement of workplace members. This involvement was the outcome of nearly twenty years of building and constructing effective workplace forms of representation and activity. It is in this context, that the promotion of union learning representation and the reference to the legal machinery of the state becomes relevant. The outcome is a campaigning form of unionism, able to address the individuation of the employment relationship in collective ways.

In the case of Australia, the CPSU organised in relation to performance-related pay and associated remuneration arrangements over a relatively long period. Going back the early 1990s, the union nationally negotiated effectively the implementation of a range of procedures and processes for promotion, and the structured movement of state workers via increments and classifications in terms of individual career trajectories. From 1992 onwards, the CPSU, nationally, developed policies relating to performance pay, in the first instance by providing advice for members of the SES. As these schemes were extended outwards to different agencies and to a wider spectrum of staff the national level of the union increasingly worked in close relationship with agency-based union leaders to formulate specific policies and campaigns in relation to the variants of these schemes that were introduced agency by agency.

The CPSU experienced some success in containing the spread of performance-related pay and individual agreements, particularly in the largest agencies, and where it had well-organised networks of local activists. Such campaigns were fought agency by agency, and depended substantially on union membership level, local level organisation and management responses. Through a process of surveys, local representation and national policy development, the CPSU developed a comprehensive suite of measures to address these performance-related pay arrangements. These processes were particularly evident in the highly-unionised Centrelink. There the national union and the Centrelink-based union leaders worked together to shape the successive collective agreements so that they met some of the concerns of members. This rather distinctive approach, shaping employment policy via successive collective agreements, supported by targeted workplace disruption, was relatively successful in leading to an amelioration of the harsher elements of such schemes.

The key difference between the union approaches in the United Kingdom and Australia is that in Australia, union organisation and activity is shaped by the juridical basis of the industrial relations system. For public service workers this meant that the capacity of the CPSU to represent its membership was increasingly constrained in the late 1990s until the late 2000s by the legislation introduced by successive conservative governments. The intent of this legislation was to provide the judicial basis to diminish union capacities to represent and articulate the concerns of union members. Via the AWAs, the state as employer underwrote the individualisation of the state labour market. Whilst there has been a retraction of the arrangements for AWAs, the fragmentation of the public service, agency by agency, has been maintained. In these circumstances the union has taken steps to reinforce its capacities to co-ordinate and shape workplace union activity; this amounts to a reinforcement of a centralised, rather than a devolved form of unionism.

CONCLUSION

The chapter has explored the considerable challenges faced by public sector unions in seeking to contain management's efforts to foster individualism in the form of performance appraisal and pay schemes and individual workplace agreements (AWAs). The intent of these schemes was to reinforce managerial prerogatives at work and to increase the alignment of individual employees with organisational goals and objectives. Public managers were also motivated to inculcate a performance culture into their respective public organisations by encouraging employees to internalise managerially determined performance targets. While employees were tempted to acquiesce to these schemes by offers of additional performance bonuses and/or increases in base pay above what was available in collective agreements, management also used the threat of privatisation and contracting-out to justify and seek compliance with these techniques. The operation of performance-related pay and promotion of individual agreements was also accompanied by more intrusive forms of management surveillance over workforce productivity and increased fragmentation of pay rates and working conditions across the public sector in both countries. The process of individualisation created both risks and opportunities for public sector unions in both countries. The risk of marginalisation was ever present, particularly in government agencies with low levels of union membership and where management sought to aggressively introduce individual workplace agreements and/or performance bonuses.

What this focus meant is that the two sets of unions renewed themselves in broadly similar ways but with a number of marked differences. On the one hand, the two unions opposed the managerial initiatives to individualise employment relations in the public services. Further, both unions had paid attention to the ways in which they organised and operated, in particularly building local representative structures over the previous twenty years, in both countries. The outcome is that the two sets of unions became campaigning and active unions within the sector, as well as prominent within the national union bodies. Increasingly unions developed persuasive accounts and critiques of the nature and character of the twenty-five year neo-liberal experiment.

On the other hand, there are important differences between the two sets of unions. The CPSU, for example, became a very centralised union. This move means that while its organisation and the articulation of its purpose involves delegates and local representatives in a variety of ways, the management of communication and finances is in the hands of the national leadership. Nonetheless, as indicated, the structure still allows for considerable engagement of local activists and union organisers on an agency by agency basis. In contrast, the PCS, has developed a complex process of national representation and local activism, which has gone through a number of fluctuations over the last twenty-five years. In the early 1980s, the union began the process of developing a local level of semi-autonomous activism. Building on these developments, the national leadership, which increasingly comprised members with an active local experience, there was a shift towards locally-based activities. Nonetheless, in the late 1990s there were attempts to re-establish the pre-eminence of the national structures and to consolidate the authority of the national executive. This emphasis was challenged in the early 2000s when a new leadership was elected, committed to the recognition and effective integration of local and regional activists into the decision-making processes of the union.

The unions faced particular challenges with government attempts to emphasise those individual aspects of the employment relationship to the detriment of collectivist aspects. This focus on individualisation is central to the neo-liberal agenda embraced by governments in the two countries. With the promotion of the appearance of managerial autonomy, an aspect of depoliticisation, the unions were able to exploit the opportunity of dealing directly with management, and thus challenging the programs that had individualisation at their core. In the case of the Australia, the union was able to challenge some of the sharper aspects of individualisation, particularly performance bonuses. The unions in the United Kingdom, developing activist based and campaigning forms of unionism were able to contain these aspects.

8   A Way Forward?

The book is a study of two liberal democracies, focusing on the restructuring of the administrative state and its impact on the social role and work processes of public sector employees. It examines how these workers responded to these changes and the process developed their labour organisations. We have sought to identify what it was like to work in a context where the very goals of public service work and employment relations were being steadily realigned in the direction of a neo-liberal agenda promoted by governments in both Australia and the United Kingdom. This reorientation was not achieved through direct political confrontation but instead was mediated through management initiated structural and operational changes. It involved new managerial approaches to labour relations and labour processes. Our focus has been on the agency of state sector workers in accepting, moderating, accommodating to or resisting these changes, in particular, we have considered the extent to which state employees have been able to defend and build collective forms of response.

In this final chapter, we begin with some indicators of the status of public sector unionism in each country, establishing that, at the very least, the key public sector unions have survived the advent and maturation of the neo-liberal era, and retained their capacity for collective representation. Public sector unions have not merely survived; there are signs of a union renewal, in which the industrial organisations of public sector workers play a role in challenging the core assumptions of public managements in a neo-liberal era. Beyond the important task of negotiating mitigations of the work intensification that has been a hallmark of the neo-liberal era, in developing alternative views, the civil and public service unions in each country have contributed to a wider reclamation of worker voice and social justice.

SURVIVING NEO-LIBERALISM: PUBLIC SECTOR COLLECTIVISM IN 2008

In both Britain and Australia, the public sector is now, numerically at least, one of the main bastions of unionism. During the neo-liberal ascendancy, state sector workers have been able to maintain a stronger adherence to collective organisation than workers in the private sector. This was the case in both the UK and Australia. In the latter country, the tenacity of public sector unionism is quite conspicuous, given that overall, union density declined more severely under the Howard regime than in the United Kingdom under New Labour.

In the first two decades of the neo-liberal era, in both the United Kingdom and Australia, union density declined from a peak of over 50 per cent in the era from 1955 to the late 1970s, to approximately 30 per cent in 1997. By the time Blair and Howard had come to office, the United Kingdom and Australia occupied a middle ground between Sweden, where in 1997 union density remained at over 80 per cent, and the USA, where it had dropped to 14 per cent.In the following decade, the decline continued slowly in the UK (particularly in England), but dramatically in Australia. By 2007, unionisation levels in the UK overall were still at 28 per cent, whereas in Australia they had fallen to 18.5 per cent of potential membership (Barratt, 2009: 49). In the UK, even more than in Australia, core public administration workers contributed significantly to holding overall union density at its 2008 level of 27.4 per cent (26.1 per cent in England). This can be seen from Table 8.1, which separates out core public servants from education workers. By contrast, in Australia it was relatively militant education unions, partially located in state jurisdictions outside the reach of the Howard government's industrial relations reach that helped sustain public sector unionisation rates. Within this pattern, as Table 8.1 illustrates, it has been public sector unions that have managed to retain a level of membership density, workplace presence and collective agreement coverage.

Table 8.1 Union Density, Union Workplace Presence and Collective Bargaining Coverage, UK and Australia, 2008

Sector/ Industry	United Kingdom 2008			Australia 2008		
	Density %	Workplace presence %	Collective bargaining coverage %	Density %	Workplace presence %	Collective bargaining coverage %
All	27.4 (26.1)	46.7 (45.6)	33.6 (30.1)	18.9	n.a	32.9
Private	15.5	30.6	18.7	13.6	n.a	25.6
Public	57.1	86.9	70.5	42.4	n.a	96.0
Public Admin & Defence	55.8	85.2	73.4	29.1	n.a	88.2
Education	54.1	83.8	62.2	58.0	n.a	81.2

Adapted from: Barratt (2009), Table 5.2, p. 38; ABS (2008) Cat. No. 6303.0, Tables 12, 15; ABS (2009) Datacube 63100TS0001, Tables 1-5;
Figures in brackets in the 'All' row are for England.
n.a. – not available.

It is clear from Table 8.1 that in the UK, by 2008, core public administration workers had maintained a union density of 55.8 per cent, only marginally below the 57.1 per cent figure for the public sector as a whole. In Australia, by contrast, where the government had enjoyed some, albeit mixed, success in treating the federal public service as an exemplar of government industrial relations policy, public service union density was down to 29.1 per cent. This was below the public sector average of 42.4 per cent, but still well above the private sector level of 13.6 per cent.

These union density figures of course reflect factors other than militancy. Despite some fragmentation of state structures, civil and public service workplaces remained larger and easier to organise than those in the private sector. Partly as a result of size, public sector workplaces were also more likely to have union delegates or representatives in the workplace. Whilst, Australia cannot be compared with the UK in this regard, as no data are available after 1995, our case studies illustrate the ways in which the presence of workplace delegates and active memberships was an important factor in maintaining union density and collective bargaining coverage.

Collective bargaining coverage and collective agreement-making are now concentrated in the public sector. In both countries, public sector collective bargaining coverage is over 85 per cent, compared with 33 per cent overall. Public sector union reach thus outstrips the union density rates discussed above. This is a source of both strength and weakness. It increases apparent union strength, without translating it into militancy or recruitment capacity (the free-rider problem). Debates are emerging within the two major civil and public service unions in both countries over ways of participating in a wider movement to rebuild unionism and challenge a still deeply embedded neo-liberal ideology, and the interests that it serves.

To focus the discussion, we draw out the four key puzzles central to the analysis. The first of these puzzles was to determine why governments of seemingly different political orientations ended up advocating similar policies for state sector restructuring and reorganisation. The second puzzle was one of appearance and reality. In both public sector restructuring and industrial relations policies, there was an apparent distancing between government policy making and public management implementation. The organisation and operation of the state sector increasingly appeared to follow technical rules, through a process of displacement that made it hard for public sector workers and their labour organisations, as well as for citizens, to press claims with those who had decision-making power. The third puzzle had to do with union response. How could the public sector unions deal with agency decentralisation and fragmentation? Should they also reorganise and 'professionalise' to mirror the managerial restructuring of their members' employers? The fourth puzzle was closely related: in the face of unitarist management agendas, how could public sector unions best establish their relevance, navigating the Scylla of marginalisation and the Charybdis of incorporation?

THE NEO-LIBERAL ASCENDANCY

In most advanced capitalist societies, the social democratic compromise of the post-war era was overtly contested in the late 1970s, as governments increasingly embraced a neo-liberal agenda. In developing this agenda, the Conservative Party under Thatcher defined and set the initial parameters of neo-liberal reform. These first steps were marked by the advocacy of privatisation and a redrawing of the boundaries between the state and market. These developments were part of a broader worldwide promotion of globalised trade and financial relations. While neo-liberalism is often assumed to be characteristic of conservative politics, the social democratic parties, such as the Australian Labor Party in the 1980s, embraced its key elements, as part of a process of modernisation, institution-building and responding to economic crises from the mid-1980s (Pusey, 1991).

Thus the pursuit of a neo-liberal agenda has been neither seamless, nor an undifferentiated programme or process. Rather it expressed a mosaic ideology defined by specific policy formulations (marketisation, privatisation and related economic policies), grounded in specific constitutional and governing arrangements (federalism in Australia and centralism in the UK), differentiated constituencies and the residual weight of histories and political practices in each country. The outcome is a variety of forms of neo-liberalism, developed over time and shaped by different structural configurations in which political parties are embedded and operate. Rather than a 'hybrid' form of neo-liberalism, drawing together aspects of neo-liberalism and an increasingly subordinated social democratic ideology, we can talk of clusters or a mosaic of neo-liberal ideas and practices. Hence, neo-liberalism comprises an ideology with a core – economic de-regulation, the displacement of traditional forms of state intervention, and the re-regulation of economic organisation including new forms of state intervention. Such programmes have been underpinned by a view of freedom that no longer rests on rights and positive outcomes but is represented as freedom from core aspects of state control and economic intervention. In Australia in the 1980s and 1990s and in the UK after 1997, social democracy was neither subordinate to, nor a modification of, neo-liberal ideology. Rather it was integral to its realisation and became a means to a neo-liberal end.

Central to this history is an understanding of the way that labour became both an object of the neo-liberal agenda, and an active agent in relation to the form and character of the societies that have emerged over the last thirty years. It may be that, as Daniels and McIlroy (2009) argue, union leaderships, via arguments for partnership, in its various forms, have also come to accept the basic presuppositions of neo-liberalism. Thus while a social democratic version of neo-liberalism may take on particular imprints, through the New Labour' agendas of UK Prime Minister Blair and Treasurer/Prime Minister Brown, or through the technocratic preoccupations of Australian Treasurer/Prime Minister Keating and Prime Minister Rudd, the broad principles of neo-liberalism and its symbiotic relation with globalisation have remained unchallenged. It is increasingly unlikely that the 2007/08 global financial crisis has dented confidence in that relationship.

It is in this context that we have assessed the ways in which public sector workers and unions have responded to the neo-liberal paradigm shift. By studying the heartland of state employment, we can open debate about union responses to neo-liberalism. Clearly, unions have been an object of this agenda, in its many manifestations. It could be argued that collective organisation was not fundamentally threatened but it has been moulded and massaged in particular directions, although the Thatcher and Australian Howard governments certainly attempted a profound marginalisation of unions, particularly in Australia in the mid-2000s.

Public sector unions have survived managerialism, but along with the labour movement overall, they confront a major challenge of renewal and rebuilding in the face of entrenched new forms of neo-liberalism. It is clear from the union density and bargaining coverage figures in Table 8.1, that public sector unions will be required to play a key role in future responses to the forces and interests that expressed themselves overtly in the neo-liberal era. This is a new role for workers not hitherto seen as archetypal unionists. The stance and strategies they adopt will depend in part on their answers to our four thematic puzzles.

CONVERGENCE/DIVERGENCE

Accepting the wider divergence thesis that new public management was a particularly Anglo-US manifestation of state reform (Christensen and Lægrid, 2006), we have focused on apparent similarities in the restructuring approaches of the United Kingdom and Australian states, under conservative and Labo(u)r governments. Whilst financial and organisational reforms were initiated in the 1980s in the United Kingdom by a Conservative government and in Australia by a Labor government, and the subsequent paths to change were almost mirror image reversed, the destinations seemed remarkably similar.

The 'path dependency' literature suggests that institutional arrangements in particular states can fundamentally influence the nature of policy outcomes. We have argued that 'New Public Management' can be conceptualised as the implementation of a neo-liberal policy direction in the public sector, and thus both countries can be said to have been profoundly influenced by that policy direction. On the other hand, there have been distinctive paths taken in each country. Australia moved from a social democratic neo-corporatist model to a more directly unitarist (but contested) imposition under the conservative coalition in the late 1990s to the mid-2000s. In contrast, the United Kingdom moved from direct imposition to a more incorporationist model under New Labour, although still within a profound neo-liberal paradigm. Institutional differences are crucial in explaining the different trajectories towards the hegemony of managerialism, but path dependency cannot explain the remarkable similarities in the ideology underpinning the different institutional arrangements. The civil and public service trade unions have similarly followed different paths, to broadly similar ends. In the United Kingdom, they moved from marginalisation to partial incorporation but then to a more distanced relationship under the latter stages of New Labour and the Coalition government. In Australia, they moved from incorporation to marginalisation almost to the point of exclusion, although the terrain of public service unionism shifted back towards a partial institutional accommodation under the Labor governments of the late 2000s, Nonetheless, in both countries, the two major civil and public service unions have emerged from a top level-negotiation and service-oriented model of unionism to become organisations more focused on organising and campaigning.

POLITICISATION/DEPOLITICISATION

Relations between the civil and public service unions, governments, political parties and administrations have been characterised by processes of depoliticisation. Following Burnham (2001) we defined depoliticisation as the creation of an apparent distance between government policies and their consequences. These processes have been multi-layered and governments in both countries have often been more than one-step removed from direct responsibility for policy implementation and the way the state apparatus has been organised and operated.

Structurally, the modernising state appeared, at various times, to fragment into agencies or to shift its boundaries through mechanisms such as privatisation, outsourcing and partnerships. Yet we have established that paradoxically, whilst such boundary-shifting may have served to extend the operation of 'the market', it also served to expand the sphere of state control. As well as this 'extensive' decentralisation of operational management, accompanied by policies aimed at individuating the state labour markets, of even greater impact was the 'intensive' centralisation of responsibility, paradoxically through administrative devolution. Again, the effect was not diffusion, but rather an intensification of state and managerial control through operational devolution.

While this development played out in distinctive ways in each country, there have been two common features to the depoliticisation process. The first was the creation of a management stratum within the civil and public services. In particular and as an initial step, a process of decentralising staff and operational responsibilities to layers of 'state' managers occurred in both countries. Managerial staff acquired increased prerogatives at workplace level; they were also expected to deliver higher levels of performance; and they were seen as responsible for the outcomes. It is in this respect that it is possible to argue that the modern state is a managerial state. Second, in our analysis of these developments we referred to a loose-tight model of governance, whereby operational practice was subject to more intense scrutiny and increased central oversight. Managers played a central role in the implementation of government decisions, albeit within a framework of enhanced central oversight by key government agencies; they also exercised discretion over the organisation and operation of these services. Thus, behind the appearance of increased managerial autonomy and responsibility lay relatively traditional but rather less obvious mechanisms of control. One outcome of this multi-layered process of depoliticisation was to increase the level of scrutiny on employees in both countries, enabling the intensification of work processes.

Unions saw depoliticisation as an attempt to make the determination of pay and working conditions a responsibility of managers and not of the government. Nevertheless, governments exercised a high degree of control over bargaining outcomes, particularly in relation to wages and staffing levels. The depoliticisation of the bargaining process thus remained intensely political. This tension between politicisation and depoliticisation lies at the heart of the loose-tight model of governance.

Such developments, however, also opened up the potential for more active and more mobilised forms of unionism. Employees and trade unions have responded to state restructuring by involving workplace representatives more in local industrial activities such as organising and bargaining. At the same time, unions have increasingly centralised and coordinated their structures in response to the distancing strategies of the state. Thus fundamental changes in union structures and strategies over the period can be interpreted as responses to the various techniques used by governments to create distance between policy decisions and their consequences.

In summary, bipartisan depoliticisation strategies will continue to pose several challenges for public sector unions. Communication and education strategies are required to render transparent the political nature of managerial and technical control strategies evident in the public services of both countries. Because, paradoxically, depoliticisation opened up a space for local union activism, public sector unions need to sustain this activism without losing sight of broader objectives, or replicating within themselves the relations of the managerial state. Thus public sector unions have been grappling with their own questions of centralisation and decentralisation.

MANAGERIALISM AND TRADE UNIONISM

While the evidence is persuasive that the state sector (at least in the liberal democracies) is now organised and operated in distinctly different ways from in the past, the part played by the different social groups that make up the state sector still requires clarification. By focusing on the complex

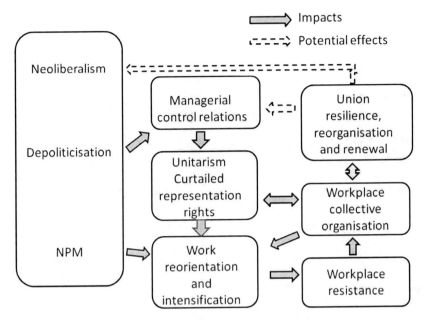

Figure 8.1 Key Relationships in the Endurance of Public Sector Unions under Neoliberalism

relations between state management and state workers, reflected in work processes and bargaining relations, we have shown how relations between these two social groups have mediated relationships between governments and the citizenry. This is a contentious analysis in that we give central consideration to the relationships among depoliticisation, managerialism and union reorganisation (Figure 8.1). Our claim is that an adequate account of the last thirty years of state 'reform' requires a central focus on the ways in which state workers and their labour organisations have been both an object and a subject in the process of state restructuring.

The theoretical framework guides the analysis centres on the key concepts of depoliticisation and managerialism. In the neo-liberal heyday, power relations within globalising states, as reflected in the political practices of governments, came increasingly to be embodied in technical rules, administered by reorganised agencies under quasi-contractual relationships. This process of apparent depoliticisation was in fact highly political, elevating compliance with policy parameters above debate or discretionary judgment. It was expressed through managerial control relations that functioned best in unitarist employment relations settings, where the collective representation of worker rights was curtailed. Labour market and organisational flexibility were enhanced by privatisation and internal competition, forcing the cost efficiencies which drove work intensification and ruled out workplace democracy. The goals of public sector work were reoriented, and these new goals were reinforced through performance management regimes, including attempts to tie individual performance to pay. The reorientation was experienced sharply by front-line workers, particularly in welfare departments and agencies, whose relationship with clients changed in character. Efficiency dividends, staff cuts, and work process re-engineering resulted in work intensification.

In both Britain and Australia, public sector unions had a measure of success, albeit uneven, in contesting the decentralisation of collective bargaining and the fragmentation and dispersion of pay and conditions. Nevertheless, decentralisation also meant that the managerialist transmission-belt was far from tight: there was slippage in the application of the 'loose-tight' control model whereby central policy parameters were applied by local managers. Their capacity to impose cultural change was constrained unless workplace union density and activism were very low. Recent union history demonstrates the fragility of models of workplace democracy and partnership, and the grinding nature of struggles, under decentralised bargaining, to defend working time against intensification and the practical extension and implementation of the 'flexibility' mantra.

The crucial questions for unions are reflected on the right-hand side of Figure 8.1. First, there is the question of how best to transform workplace resistance into collective workplace action. It was only through strenuous rounds of bargaining that some protection of working time and leave entitlements was achieved, although such collective representation was buoyed by local resistance, and fuelled by individuals' sense of grievance. It was certainly only at the collective level that some push-back against unitarist managerial practices could occur. Whilst workplace activism was thus the lifeblood of unionism, it could be drained away in local struggles unless effectively sustained by the union overall. By the mid-2000s, public sector unions in both countries had begun exploring effective forms of central support for local activism, as well as the possibility of a more concerted challenge to managerialism. It will, however, require a new approach by the wider labour movement, if there is to be an effective challenge to neo-liberalism. The dotted lines in Figure 8.1 represent two unanswered questions, with which we end this chapter. To what extent have Australian and British public sector unions been able to modify the impacts of managerialism, and what are the prospects for their being part of an effective challenge to the neo-liberal hegemony?

THE UNION DILEMMA: CENTRALISATION/ DECENTRALISATION

One hallmark of managerialism-the simultaneous decentralisation and centralisation of state operations – has been of particular concern for public sector unions. It was based on the politics of displacement, discussed above. For unions, the issues under negotiation at decentralised level were often only able to be resolved at another level. Local managers had strict parameters within which to work. Nevertheless, as we argue in Chapters 6 to 8, managerial control was far from complete. In Australia, there were tensions between the financing and 'purchasing' departments. Moreover, performance-based regimes were quite diverse across the Australian Public Service, with the unions able to hold back the excesses of such a system in many agencies. In the United Kingdom, the unions were able to open up bargaining agendas, in directions that had been unknown in earlier periods. They were able to address questions relating to the terms and conditions of employment in ways that met the concerns of members. Moreover, they succeeded in taking some of the hard edges off managerial systems in the civil service, especially in relation to performance measurement.

In addressing the new climate, unions responded by working towards their own balancing of centralisation and decentralisation. The principal public service unions in both countries slowly moved towards tighter central co-ordination of their local initiatives. They evolved a 'loose-tight' model of co-ordination to counter the 'loose-tight' architecture of state control. They sought to address the implications of increased managerial control and accountability at local level, by promoting and developing more active forms of workplace activity and representation, than had been the case in the past. Nevertheless this local activity increasingly required co-ordination by more centralised governance in the two unions.

The perception that the unions were fighting for survival as activist organisations influenced the structural changes they promoted to continue to operate with some effectiveness. Ironically, both unions embraced more centralised modes of operation in order to cope with multiple challenges of operational decentralisation in the state labour process. Just as the respective states had extended the spheres of their control through decentralisation, so the unions began to reinforce their capacities to cope with this decentralised managerial activity.

The transformation was uneven, messy and incremental, but new structures of control and co-ordination emerged. The process was more than 'muddling through'; it was an emergent strategy, that often took on an *ad hoc* appearance, but was rooted in attempts to formulate a coherent and integrated response to the emergent managerialism in the civil and public services. With the benefit of perspective, we characterise this as a process of strategic incrementalism – strategic in direction and destination, incremental in process. It was necessary to resolve issues of governance, including the relationship between lay and appointed officials. Some union officials became 'managers' with budgets to meet and staff to organise and control. The structure of hierarchical, but largely unified service was gradually transformed into more explicit divisions between union officials who had the role of 'bosses' (with managerial authority and responsibility) and employed staff who had the status of 'workers'. In that context industrial and personnel matters needed to be sorted out at the office level. The tensions and dilemmas of maintaining a dynamic relationship between the centre and diverse workplaces will continue. There will be ongoing questions of decision-making structures, of communication and education, and of how to generate an ongoing flow of activists.

STRATEGIES: AVOIDING INCORPORATION AND MARGINALISATION

Within the neo-liberal paradigm, public sector unions have faced the dilemma of avoiding incorporation on the one hand and irrelevance or exclusion on the other. Either choice involves a different form of marginalisation. In the former case, legitimacy is purchased at the cost of real influence within a unitary governance framework. In the latter case, unions are excluded from state structures. Broadly, conservative governments have actively sidelined public sector unions, while Labo(u)r governments have attempted partnership with them, while at the same time limiting the scope of their influence.

In the United Kingdom up to 1997, unions in general, and public sector unions in particular, faced an all-out attack from the Thatcher and Major governments, which pursued policies of excluding unions from central decision-making bodies, including wage settlement procedures. After 1997, the Labour government flirted with a partnership approach to unions, within the framework of state modernisation. Within the rhetoric of 'participation', there has been a continued refinement of the broad processes of repoliticisation, accompanied by a more collective approach to labour regulation.

In Australia between 1983 and 1996, Labor governments tried accommodations with, or incorporation of, unions. The initial Australian model was based on a short period during the 1980s when unions at a nationally-centralised level were incorporated as partners in national restructuring through wage restraint. Unstable 'Accord' settlements, compromised from the outset by monetary internationalisation, were displaced, after 1987, by 'centrally-managed decentralisation'. In the early and mid-1990s, partial incorporation emerged by default. It was an outcome of the fragmentation and absorption of union effort in an increasingly decentralised process of agency-level bargaining, based on productivity trade-offs. After 1996, decentralisation, and individualised agreement-making were used by a conservative Coalition government and its state managers in attempts to marginalise unions. Pressures to individualise bargaining were weakened by the incoming Labor government's reaffirmation of collective bargaining rights: in February 2008, the Rudd government issued a public sector bargaining framework ending agencies' capacity to offer individual Australian Workplace Agreements. It also established a committee to examine ways of reconstituting the notion of 'One APS'.

In seeking to respond to the continued moulding of the state apparatuses in each country, the public sector unions could do little to hold back the financial reforms of the 1980s and the waves of managerialism of the 1990s and early 2000s. What they were able to do was to contest and, at times, modify the workplace implications of those changes. In Australia, there was still the opportunity to use regular bargaining arrangements to alleviate the worst excesses of managerialism whilst in the UK, even in the absence of regular bargaining, there is evidence of contestation at the office level. Both unions have survived, and taken active steps to secure their futures, although there has been a difference of emphasis in relation to participative and centralised forms of engagement and involvement in each union.

RETROSPECT AND PROSPECTS

While it cannot be argued that the unions were successful in rolling back the agenda pursued by both Conservative and Labo(u)r governments in both countries, they were never so weak as to be unable to modify the working out of those policies at the office and local agency levels. Perhaps the most important achievement of the British and Australian civil service unions during the neo-liberal ascendancy was to survive and to experiment with organisational forms and practices in an environment that was hardly friendly to public sector workers. This in itself was a remarkable achievement: the public sector unions have emerged as amongst the strongest, at least numerically. The remaining question is to what extent to which state sector unions have been able to moderate managerialism or contribute to a contestation of neo-liberalism?

The two public sector unions in the focus of this study utilised the situations they found themselves in to lay the foundation for more active forms of unionism. In this respect, they avoided decline and irrelevancy, even when the approach by government changed (as was the case in Australia) or when governments failed to fulfil the positive expectations that unions had of them (as was the case in the UK in the late 1990s). There were two aspects to this achievement. On the one hand, the gradual transformation from public administration to public management presupposed more flexible sets of relations over work organisation and operation. Partly as a consequence of the 'managerialist turn', union leaderships sought to maintain and secure a presence in bargaining and negotiating arenas. The paradox is that the redistribution of power signified by these restructuring processes, characterised by increasing managerial strategies to decollectivise workforces, while at the same time unions sought to maintain solidaristic relations and membership commitment to collective forms of action. When collective activity is circumscribed there is evidence that workers will resist management – promoted changes. The outcome for the unions was an assessment of the complex relations between national leaders and more active members across the civil and public services, as well as the commitment in both cases to vibrant forms of campaigning, addressing government policies and practices, as well as the specifics of work and employment conditions.

These issues of union organisation and mobilisation open up the debate about union renewal. The focus in much of the debate has so far been on forms of organisation and the capacities of unions (e.g. Lévesque and Murray, 2002; Fairbrother, 1994 and 2000). What is missing in these accounts is a systematic engagement with questions relating to the processes and bases of union mobilisation and activism (with the partial exception of Wills and Simm, 2004). The two-country analysis presented here draws attention to organisational change, union capacity and in particular, the ongoing tension between leadership strategies and membership mobilisation. Central to this ongoing strategic dilemma for unions was the way in which state managements dealt with unions, often switching between policies of incorporation or marginalisation, depending in part on the political party in office. For union leaderships and their members this was the touchstone for formulating approaches to the massive restructuring and reorganisation that has taken place over the last thirty years. It was also, however, a contributor to the long-term trajectory of these unions, towards more participative forms of representation, accountable leaderships and an activist approach to both managerial initiatives and government policy.

CONCLUSION

Theoretically what these processes suggest is that there is a complex relationship between governments, state managers, public sector workers and their unions seeking to articulate membership interests. This is not a direct relationship and in some respects is counter-intuitive, in that it is not expected that the direct attempts by governments to accommodate or marginalise public service unions will necessarily lead to an active, more participative, and campaigning form of unionism. The reasons for such a transformation lie in two aspects of trade unionism. First, by refocusing the relationship between leaders and members, unions created the conditions for a more direct engagement with government policy and practice. Second, the unions sought to utilise, gradually and incrementally, the power resources available to them, via coordinated representation and contestation of the procedures and policies promoted by governments. The result was a centrally-coordinated form of campaigning unionism in both countries: as much out of emerging necessity as of deliberate strategy. Thus, policies in these two countries predicated on incorporation/marginalisation/ exclusion paradoxically laid the foundation for more active forms of unionism: incrementally emergent, centrally directed, and locally focused.

Each country is governed by administrations that have bought into the global neo-liberal agenda. Clearly, the global financial crisis raises difficult and puzzling questions for public service workers, their unions and governments. Both governments have displayed a willingness to advocate direct forms of state intervention, more evident in the United Kingdom than in Australia, especially with a return to more active forms of financial regulation and control. A further complication is the varied experiences of the global financial crisis, with Australia seemingly escaping the harsher aspects of the financial recession. It is likely, however, that in each state the public and civil services will become part of the means to implement interventionist policies while at the same time being an object for achieving financial stringency via managerial policies and practices. It remains uncertain whether this recent bout of state intervention is merely temporary until the next crisis, or is a prelude to more sustained measures over time. More specifically, it is not clear what these developments mean for state workers and their unions, especially where they are the prime objects of policy initiatives. It is nonetheless, possible that these events could presage a renewed process of struggle as unions seek to address the specificities of the challenges heralded by the global financial upheaval, alongside other challenges that include international debates about the effects of climate change.

While it is always difficult to speculate about the future, civil service unions will always have complicated relationships with the state as employer; itself juggling multiple functions while maintaining the conditions for the continued accumulation of capital. The dilemma for public sector union members is that they are part of the state apparatus, while at the same contesting some policies and actions of that very structure. As demonstrated, there are limits to which agents of the state can make common cause with those at the sharp receiving end of government policy. How the political role of public sector unions will play out over time will depend on the political and industrial environment in which public sector unions find themselves. It was ever thus. It is likely that in their different ways and circumstances that each union will remain central actors in the continued wider challenge to the neo-liberal ascendancy in each state.

Bibliography

ABS Australian Bureau of Statistics (2008), *Employee Earnings and Hours*, Canberra, ABS Cat. No. 6306.0.

——(2009) Data Cube 63100TS0001 *Employee Earnings, Benefits and Trade Union Membership, Australia* – Trade Union Membership, 17 April. Available: <http://www.abs.gov.au/ausstats/abs@.nsf/mf/6306.0/> (accessed 10 October, 2009).

Ackroyd, S., Walker, D. and Kirkpatrick, I. (2004) *The New Managerialism and the Public Service Professions*, London: Palgrave.

Advisory Group on Reform of Australian Government Administration (2010) *Ahead of the Game: Blueprint for the Reform of Australian Government Administration*. Australian Government Department of the Prime Minister and Cabinet, Canberra: Australian Government Department of the Prime Minister and Cabinet.

Alaba, R. (1994) *Inside Bureaucratic Power: The Wilenski Review of New South Wales Government Administration*, Sydney: Hale and Iremonger and Royal Institute of Public Administration, ACT Division.

Alexander, M., Green, R. and Wilson, A. (1998) 'Delegate Structures and Strategic Unionism: Analysis of Factors in Union Resilience', *Journal of Industrial Relations*, 40(4): 663–89.

Alexandrou, A., Davies, J. and Lee, J. (2005) 'Union Learning Representatives: A Case Study of the Public and Commercial Services Union', *Journal of In-service Education*, 31(1): 9–26.

Allen, D. (1981) *Raynorism: Strengthening Civil Service Management*. London: Royal Institute of Public Administration.

Andresani, G. and Ferlie, E. (2006) 'Studying Governance Within the British Public Sector and Without', *Public Management Review*, 8(3): 415–31.

Aucoin, P. (1995) *The New Public Management: Canada in Comparative Perspective*, Montreal and Kingston: McGill-Queens University Press.

Australia Fair Work Act 2009, No. 28 of 2009. An Act relating to workplace relations and for related purposes.

Australian Industrial Relations Commission, (1999) 'CPSU, The Community and Public Sector Union and Employment National (C. No. 357747 of 1997) and Employment National (Administration) Pty Limited and another and CPSU, the Community and Public Sector Union (C. No. 34934 of 1988), *Decision*, 26 February.

APSC Australian Public Service Commission (2003) *APS Values and Code of Conduct in Practice – A Guide to Official Conduct for APS Employees and Agency Heads*, Canberra: APS Commission.

——(2009) APS Statistical Bulletin 2008–9. Available: <http//www.apsc.gov.au/stateoftheservice/0809/statistics/index.html> (accessed 30 December, 2009).

Australian Public Service Commissioner (2006) *State of the Service Report, 2005–6*, Canberra: APS.

Bach, S. (2002) 'Public Sector Industrial Relations Reform under Labour: Muddling Through on Modernisation', *British Journal of Industrial Relations*, 40(2): 319–39.

——and Della Rocca, G. (2000) 'The Management Strategies of Public Service Employers in Europe', *Industrial Relations Journal*, 31(2): 82–96.

——and Winchester, D. (2003) 'Industrial Relations in the Public Sector', in P. Edwards (ed.), *Industrial Relations: Theory and Practice*, Oxford: Blackwell, pp. 285–312.

Bain, G. (1970) *The Growth of White Collar Unionism*, Oxford: Oxford University Press.

Bains Report (1972) *Study Group on Local Government Authority Structure, The New Local Authorities: Management and Structure*, London: HMSO.

Barratt, C. (2009) 'Trade Union Membership 2008', Department for Business, Enterprise and Regulatory Reform, A National Statistics Publication, Employment Market Analysis and Research, BERR, London.

Barton, H. and Turnbull, P. (2002) 'Labour Regulation and Competitive Performance in the Port Transport Industry: The Changing Fortunes of Three Major European Seaports', *European Journal of Industrial Relations*, 8(2): 133–56.

Batstone, E., Ferner, A. and Terry, M. (1984) *Consent and Efficiency: Labour Relations and Management Strategy in a State Enterprise*, Oxford: Blackwell.

Beaumont, P. (1992) *Government as Employer – Setting an Example?* London: Royal Institute of Public Administration.

Becker, G. (1992) *The Economic Way of Looking at Life*, Nobel Lecture, December 9, 1992, Departments of Economics, University of Chicago: Chicago, IL.

Beilharz, P. (1994) *Transforming Labor: Labor Traditon and the Labor Decade*, Sydney: Cambridge University Press.

Bennett, D. and Shergold, P. (1998) 'Commission Impossible: A New Approach to Workplace Relations in the PSMPC', *Australian Journal of Public Administration*, 57(2): 91–7.

Berry, M. (2005) 'HR Boss at DWP Admits to Mistakes in Pay Dispute', *Personnel Today*, 31 May.

Bichard, M. (2004) *The Bichard Inquiry – Report*, House of Commons, London: The Stationery Office.

——(1999) *Performance Management – Civil Service Reform: A Report to the Meeting of Permanent Heads of Departments*, London: Cabinet Office.

Blair, T. (1998) *Leading the Way: A New Vision for Local Government*, London: Institute for Public Policy Research.

Blond, P. (2009) 'The Ownership State, *ResPublica*, October. Available: <http://www.respublica.org.uk> (accessed 23 February, 2010).

——(2010) *Red Tory: How Left and Right have Broken Britain and How We Can Fix It*, London: Faber and Faber.

Boix, C. (1998) *Political Parties, Growth and Equality*, Cambridge: Cambridge University Press.

Bolton, S. (2002) 'Consumer as King in the NHS', *International Journal of Public Sector Management*, 15(2): 129–39.

——(2005) *Emotion Management in the Workplace*, London: Palgrave Macmillan.

——(ed.) (2007) *Dimensions of Dignity at Work*, London: Butterworth Heinemann.

——and Houlihan, M. (2005) 'The (Mis)representation of Customer Service', *Work, Employment and Society*, 19(4): 685–703.

Boston, J., Pallot, J., Martin J., and Walsh, P. (1996) *Public Management: The New Zealand Model*, New York: Oxford University Press.

Braverman, H. (1974) *Labour and Monopoly Capital: The Degradation of Work in the Twentieth Century*, New York: Monthly Review Press.

Bronfenbrenner, K., Freidman, S., Hurd, R., Oswald, R. and Seeber, R, (eds), (1997) *Organizing to Win: New Research on Union Strategies*, Ithaca, NY: ILR Press.

Brown, D. and Armstrong, M. (1999) *Paying for Contribution: Real Performance-Related Pay Strategies*, London: Kogan Page.

Bryson, L. (1987) 'Women and Management in the Public Sector', *Australian Journal of Public Administration*, 46(3): 259–72.

Buchanan, J.M. (1958) 'Public Principles of Public Debt'. Republished 1999–2000 in *Collected Works of James M. Buchanan*. 1999–2000, Library of Economics and Liberty. Available: <http://www.econlib.org/library/Buchanan/buchCContents.html> (accessed 24 October, 2009).

Buller, J. and Flinders, M. (2005) 'The Domestic Origins of Depoliticisation in the Area of British Economic Policy', *British Journal of Politics and International Relations*', 7(4): 526–43.

Burawoy, M., Blum, J.A., George, S., Gille, Z., Gowan, T., Haney, L., Klawiter, M., Lopez, S., Riain, S. and Thayer, M. (eds), (2000) *Global Ethnography: Forces, Connections and Imaginations in a Postmodern World*, Berkeley, CA: University of California.

Burge, S. (1998) 'Much Pain, Little Gain: Privatisation and UK Government Libraries', Sixty-Fourth International Federation of Library Associations (IFLA) General Conference. Amsterdam.

Burnham. P. (1999a) 'The Decomposition of National States in the Global Economy: From Politicised to Depoliticised Forms of Labour Regulation', in P. Edwards and T. Elgar (eds), *The Global Economy, National States and the Regulation of Labour*, London: Macmillan, pp. 44–63.

——(1999b) 'The Politics of Economic Management', *New Political Economy*, 4(1): 37–54.

——(2001) 'New Labour and the Politics of Depoliticisation', *British Journal of Politics and International Relations*', 3(2): 127–49.

——(2006a) 'Depoliticisation: A Comment on Buller and Flinders', *British Journal of Politics and International Relations*, 8(2): 303–6.

——(2006b) 'Restructuring State-Economy Relations: Britain Under the Major and Blair Governments', in P. Fairbrother and A. Rainnie (eds), *Globalisation, State and Labour*, London: Routledge, pp. 12–28.

Cabinet Office (1982) *Efficiency and Effectiveness in the Civil Service*, Report from the Treasury and Civil Service Committee, Session 1981–82, HC 236, Cm. 8616, London: HMSO.

——(1991) *The Citizen's Charter: Raising the Standard*, Cm. 1599, London: HMSO.

——(1994) *The Civil Service: Continuity and Change*, Cm. 2627, London: HMSO.

——(1995a) *The Civil Service: Taking Forward Continuity and Change*, Cm. 2748, London: HMSO.

——(1995b) *The Civil Service: Taking Forward Continuity and Change*, Cm 2627, London: HMSO.

——(2000) *The Civil Service Reform Programme: Annual Report 2000*, London: The Stationery Office.

Caiden, G. (1965) *Career Service: An Introduction to Personnel Administration in the Commonwealth Public Service 1901–1963*, Melbourne: Melbourne University Press.

——(1967) *The Commonwealth Bureaucracy*, Melbourne: Melbourne University Press.

Caird, J. (2000) 'Statement to Senate References Committee on Finance and Public Administration in Senate Finance and Public Administraion References Committee, Commonwealth Parliament', Australian Public Service Employment Matters, Official Committee Hansard, 14 April: 65.

Carchedi, G. (1987) *Class Analysis and Social Research*, Oxford: Basil Blackwell.

Carter, B. (2006) 'The Restructuring of National States in a Global Economy', in P. Fairbrother, and A. Rainnie (eds), *Globalisation, State and Labour*, New York: Routledge, pp. 136–50.

——and Fairbrother, P. (1995) 'The Remaking of the State Middle Class', in T. Cutler and M. Savage (eds), *The New Middle Class*, London: University College London Press, pp. 133–147.

——, Davies, S. and Fairbrother, P. (2002) 'The Rise and Rise of Market Relations in the British Public Sector: Implications for Industrial Relations', *The Employment and Labour Relations Review*, 11(1): 36–59.

Carter, N. (1998) 'On the Performance of Performance Indicators', in M-C. Kesler, P. Lascoumbes, M. Setbon, and J-C. Thoenig (eds) *Évaluation des politiques publiques*, Paris: L'Harmattan, pp. 177–94.

Centrelink Board and Quality Committee (1997–2004) Minutes, unpublished mimeo.

Centrelink Guiding Coalition (1998–2004) Minutes, unpublished; mimeo.

Centrelink (1997) *Centrelink Development Agreement 1997–98*, Agreement under s.170J of the Workplace Relations Act 1996 between the Community and Public Sector Union, the Media, Entertainment and Arts Alliance and Centrelink (C. No. 24152 of 1997), *Australian Industrial Relations Commission*. Canberra: Centrelink.

——(1998) *Annual Report 1998,* Canberra: Commonwealth of Australia.

——(1999) *Centrelink Development Agreement 1999–2002*, Canberra: Centrelink.

——(2003) *Centrelink Agreement 2003–2006*, Canberra: Centrelink.

——(2009a) *Centrelink Agreement 2009–11*. Certified on 16 April, 2009.

Cerny, P. (1997) 'Paradoxes of The Competition State: The Dynamics of Political Globalisation', *Government and Opposition*, 32: 251–74.

Christensen, T. and Lægreid, P. (eds) (2006) *Autonomy and Regulation: Coping Agencies in the Modern State*, Cheltenham: Edward Elgar.

CIPD [Chartered Institute of Personal Development] (2010) 'Building Productive Public Sector Workplaces: Transforming Public Sector Pay and Pensions', CIPD, London, June. Available: <http://www.cipd.co.uk> (accessed 20 June, 2010).

Civil Service (n.d.) 'Mythbusters'. Available: <http://www.civilservice.gov.uk/about/facts/mythbusters/index.aspx#> (accessed 23 August, 2010).

Civil Service Live (2010) 'The Quiet Revolutionary', 16 March. Available: <http://network.civilservicelive.com/pg/pages/view/273133/> (accessed 25 June, 2010).

Clarke, J. and Newman, J. (1997) *The Managerial State*, London: Sage.

——, Gerwitz, S. and McLaughlin, I. (2000) 'Reinventing the Welfare State', in J. Clarke, S. Gerwitz, and I. McLaughlin (eds), *New Managerialism, New Welfare?* London: Open University/Sage Publications, pp. 1–26.

Clegg, H. (1979) *The Changing System of Industrial Relations in Great Britain*, Oxford: Blackwell.

Clinton, W. (2003) 'Globalisation and Progressive Politics', Speech to the Policy Network, London. Available: <http://www.policy_network.net/php//article.php?sid+4&aid+622> (accessed 12 October, 2006).

Cockburn, C. (1977) *The Local State*, London. Pluto.

Commonwealth Public Service Board (1983) *Annual Report*, Canberra: Australian Government Printer.

Confederation of Australian Industry – Australian Council of Trade Unions (1988) *Joint Statement on Participative Practices,* Melbourne, Confederation of Australian Industry and the Australian Council of Trade Unions.

Conservative Party (2010) 'An Invitation to Public Sector Workers: Conservative Party Public Sector Manifesto 2010', London: Conservative Party.

Cooper, D., Hinings, B., Greenwood, R. and Brown, J. (2002) 'Segmentation and Transformation in Organisational Change: The Case of Canadian Law Firms', *Organisational Studies*, 17(4): 623–47.

Cortis, N. (1999) 'Gender, Pay Equity and Human Service Work: A New South Wales Case Study,' *Australian Journal of Political Science*, 35 (1): 49–62.

Costello, T. and Bolton, S. (2005) 'Bunker Politics Prevail at CPSU Council Meeting', *Green Left Weekly,* 13 April. Available: <http://www.greenleft.org.au/back/2005/622/622p10.htm> (accessed 24 April, 2006).

Cowper, J. (2001) World Bank Archive, Report by Head, Modernizing Government Secretariat, Cabinet Office, United Kingdom Government. Available: <http://www1.worldbank.org/publicsector/civilservice/rsUK.pdf> (accessed 12 October, 2006).

CPSU (Community and Public Sector Union) (1999) Survey of Members on Performance Management, unpublished internal document CPSU.

——(2005a) 'All Public Service Members: New IR Laws to Hit APS Hard' *News*, 11 October Available: <http://www.cpsu.org.au/news/1128983987_21577html> (accessed 24 April, 2006).

——(2005b) 'Your Rights at Work: Fact Sheet 4 – Australian Workplace Agreements' (2005). Available: <http://www.cpsu.org.au/campaigns/IRcampaign/resources/files/YRAWOCT4.pdf> (accessed 1 May, 2006).

——(2005c) DEWR CA 24 May 2005. Available: <http://www.cpsu.org.au/campaigns/DEWR/index.html> (accessed 16 October, 2006).

——(2005d) DEWR CA 14 June 2005. Available: <http://www.cpsu.org.au/campaigns/DEWR/index.html> (accessed 16 October, 2006).

——(2005e) DEWR CA 24 October 2005 Available: <http://www.cpsu.org.au/campaigns/DEWR/index.html> (accessed 16 October, 2006).

——(2009a) 'CPSU/ALP Affiliation – Queensland and ACT', 22 January. Available: <http://cpsu.org.au/campaigns/news/11590> (accessed 7 June, 2009).

——(2009b) 'Agenda for Change – Progress So Far'. Available: <http://www.cpsu.org.au/campaigns/news/13295.html> (accessed 21 July, 2009).

——(2009c) 'Reform of Australian Government Administration' Submission by the Community and Public Sector Union to the Moran Review – December 2009.

——(2009d) 'Members Endorse New Centrelink Agreement', 17 March. Available: <http://www.cpsu.org.au/campaigns/news/12535.html> (accessed 21 July, 2009).

——(2010) 'A Better Way to Bargain: Thank You for Your Thoughts'. Available: <http://www.cpsu.org.au/campaigns/news/18453.html> (accessed 9 September, 2010).

Curnow, G. and Page, B. (eds) (1989) *Politicization and Career Service*, Canberra: Canberra College of Advanced Education and NSW Division of the Royal Australian Institute of Public Administration.

Dabscheck, B. (1989) *Australian Industrial Relations in the 1980s*, Oxford University Press: Melbourne.

Danford, A., Richardson, M. and Upchurch, M. (2003) *New Unions, New Workplaces: A Study of Union Resilience in the Restructured Workplace*, London; New York: Routledge.

Daniels, G. and McIlroy, J. (eds) *Trade Unions in a Neoliberal World: British Trade Unions under New Labour*, London: Routledge.

Davies, K. (1994). 'The Tensions Between Process Time and Clock Time in Care-work; The Example of Day Nurseries.' *Time and Society*, 3 (3): 277–303.

Davies, S. (2006) 'Third, Sector Provision of Employment-Related Services: A Report for the Public and Commercial Services Union (PCS)'. Available: <http://www.pcs.org.uk/Shared_ASP_Files/UploadedFiles/12756708–7DC8–4AC3-BB4C-C3BA3F484690_ThirdSectorReport.pdf> (accessed 9 September, 2010).

——(2008) 'Contracting Out Employment Services to the Third and Private Sectors: A Critique', *Critical Social Policy*, 28(2): 136–64.

Davis, S., James, L. and Tuohy, S. (2007) 'Qualitative Assessment of Jobcentre Plus Delivery of Jobseeker's Allowance and New Deal Interventions', Research Report No. 445, London: Department of Work and Pensions/Her Majesty's Stationery Office.

Department of Defence (1994) 'Section 134C Industrial Relations Act 1988: Defence Restructuring Agreement', Canberra: Department of Defence.

Department of Employment and Industrial Relations, Working Environment Branch (1986) *Industrial Democracy and Employee Participation: A Policy Discussion Document*, Canberra: AGPS.

Department of Education, Employment and Workplace Relations (2008) Australian Government Employment Bargaining Framework *Supporting Guidance February 2008*, Canberra: Australian Government.

——(2009) *Australian Government Employment Bargaining Framework Supporting Guidance*, September 2009. Canberra: Australian Government.

Department of Finance and Administration (1997) *Certified Agreement 1997–9*, Canberra: Department of Financial Administration.

Department of Industrial Relations (1992) *Improving Jobs, Productivity. Pay in the Australian Public Service*, Canberra: Department of Industrial Relations.

Department of Prime Minister and Cabinet (2009a) 'Reform of Australian Government Administration: Advisory Group on Reform of Australian Government Administration: Building the World's Best Public Service'. Available: <http://www.dpmc.gov.au/consultation/aga_reform/index.cfm#discussion> (accessed 1 April, 2010).

——(2009b) 'Reform of Australian Government Administration: Building the World's Best Public Service: Discussion Paper'. Available: <http://www.dpmc.gov.au/consultation/aga_reform/discussion_paper.cfm> (accessed 1 April, 2010).

Department of Workplace Relations and Small Business (1998) *The Workplace Relations Act 1996: A Pocket Guide for Australian Government Employment*, Canberra: DEWRSB.

Dickens, L. and Hall, M. (1995) 'The State, Labour Law and Industrial Relations', in P. Edwards (ed.), *Industrial Relations: Theory and Practice*, Oxford: Blackwell.

—— and Bordogna, L. (2008) 'Public Services Dispute Management – Pertinence of Comparative Study', *Journal of Industrial Relations*, 50(4): 539–44.

Dickenson, M. (1986) 'Industrial Relations and Personnel Management', in J.R. Nethercote, A. Kouzmin and R. Wettenhall (eds), *Australian Commonwealth Administration: Essays in Review*, Canberra: School of Administrative Studies,

Canberra College of Advanced Education and ACT Division, Royal Australian Institute of Public Administration.

Dorrington, J. (1992) 'The Nature and Measures of Industrial Relations Reform to Personnel Management In the Australian Public Service', in J. Halligan and R. Wettenhall (eds), *Hawke's Third Government: Australian Commonwealth Administration 1987–1990*, Canberra: The University of Canberra and the Royal Australian Institute of Public Administration, ACT Division.

Dow G. (1993) 'What Do We Know About Social Democracy', *Economic and Social Democracy*, 14: 11–48.

Dowding, K. (1995) *The Civil Service*, London: Routledge.

Drake, P., Fairbrother, P., Fryer, B. and Murphy, J. (1980) *Which Way Forward? An Interim Review of Issues for the Society of Civil and Public Servants*, Coventry: Department of Sociology, University of Warwick.

——(1982) *A Programme for Union Democracy: Final Report for the Society of Civil and Public Servants*, Coventry: Department of Sociology, University of Warwick.

Drewry, G. and Butcher, T. (1988) *The Civil Service Today*, Oxford: Basil Blackwell.

——(1991) *The Civil Service Today*, 2nd edn, Oxford: Basil Blackwell.

Dunleavy, P. (1989) 'The United Kingdom: Paradoxes of An Ungrounded Statism', in F. Castles (ed.), *The Comparative History of Public Policy*, Cambridge: Polity Press, pp. 242–91.

Du Gay, P. (2000) 'Entrepreneurial Governance and Public Management: The Anti-Bureaucrats', in J. Clarke, S. Gewirtz and E.I. McLaughlin (eds), *New Managerialism, New Welfare?* London: Open University/Sage Publications, pp. 62–81.

——(2008) 'Max Weber and the Moral Economy of Office', *Journal of Cultural Economy*, 1(2): 461–81.

——and Salaman, G. (1992) 'The Cult[ure] of the Customer', *Journal of Management Studies*, 29(5): 615–33.

Duncan, C. (2001) 'The Impact of Two Decades of Reform of British Public Sector Industrial Relations', *Public Money and Management*, January–March: 27–34.

DWP [Department of Work and Pensions] (2007) "2007 CSR Asset Management Strategy", Available: <www.dwp.gov.uk/does/csr-asset-management-strategy-2007.pdf> (accessed 20 April, 2011).

——(2009) Freedom of Information Request, mimeo, January.

Edwards, P. and Elger, T. (eds) (1999) *The Global Economy, National States: The Regulation of Labour*, London: Routledge.

Efficiency Unit (1991) *Making Most of the Next Steps: The Management of Minister's Departments and their Executive Agencies* (the Fraser Report), London: HMSO.

Elliott, R. and Bender, K. (1997) 'Decentralization and Pay Reform in Central Government: A Study of Three Countries', *British Journal of Industrial Relations*, 35(3): 447–75.

Employment Relations Act (1999), c. 26, United Kingdom, Available: <http://www.legislation.gov.uk/ukpga/1999/contents> (accessed 15 April, 2011).

Esping-Andersen, G. (1990) *The Three Worlds of Welfare Capitalism*, Princeton, NJ: Princeton University Press.

Ewer, P., Hampson, I., Lloyd, C., Rainford, T., Rix, S. and Smith, M. (1991) *Politics and the Accord*, Sydney: Pluto Press.

Fairbrother, P. (1984) *All Those In Favour: The Politics of Union Democracy*, London: Pluto Press.

——(1989) 'State Workers, Class Position and Collective Action', in G. Duncan (ed.), *Democracy and the Capitalist State*, Cambridge: Cambridge University Press.

——(1990) 'The Contours of Local Trade Unionism in a Period of Restructuring', in P. Fosh and E. Heery (eds), *Trade Unions and Their Members: Studies in Union Democracy and Organization*, Basingstoke: Macmillan, pp. 147–78.

——(1994) *Politics and the State as Employer*, London: Mansell.

——(1996) 'Workplace Trade Unionism in the State Sector', in P. Ackers, C. Smith and P. Smith (eds), *The New Workplace and Trade Unionism*, London: Routledge, pp. 110–148.

——(1998) 'The Depoliticisation of the State and the Implications for Trade Unionism: Recent Developments in the United Kingdom', Working Paper No. 61, National Key Centre in Industrial Relations, Monash University.

——(2000) *Trade Unions at the Crossroads*, London: Mansell.

——(2006) 'The Emergence of The "De-centred" British State', in P. Fairbrother and A. Rainnie (eds), *Globalisation, State and Labour*, London: Routledge, pp. 53–71.

——, Junor, A., O'Brien, J., O'Donnell, M. and Williams, G. (2009) 'State Restructuring, Labour Market Policies and "Depoliticised" Agencies: Implications for Work Organisation, State Employees and Public Sector Unions in the United Kingdom and Australia'. Paper presented at Fifteenth World Congress of the International Industrial Relations Association, Sydney, 22–25 August.

—— and O'Brien, J. (2000) 'Introduction: Changing Public Sector Industrial Relations', *Australian Journal of Public Administration*, 59(4): 54–58.

——, Paddon, M. and Teicher, J. (eds) (2002) *Privatisation, Globalisation and Labour: Studies from Australia*, Annandale: The Federation Press.

——and Poynter, G. (2001) 'State Restructuring: Managerialism, Marketisation and the Implications for Labour', *Competition & Change*, 5(11): 511–33.

——and Rainnie, A. (eds) (2006) *Globalisation, State and Labour*, London: Routledge.

——and Yates, C. (2003) 'Unions in Crisis, Unions in Renewal', in P. Fairbrother and C. Yates (eds), *Trade Unions in Renewal*, London: Continuum, pp. 1–31.

Fairclough, N. (1992) *Discourse and Social Change*, Cambridge: Polity Press.

——(2000) *New Labour, New Language?* London: Routledge.

Fair Work Act 2009, No. 28, 2009 (Australia).

Fergusson, R. (2000) 'Modernizing Managerialism in Education'. In J. Clarke, S. Gewirtz and E. McLaughlin (eds), *New Managerialism, New Welfare?* London: Open University/Sage Publications, pp. 202–21.

Ferlie, E., Ashburner, L., Fitzgerald, L. and Pettigrew, A. (1966) *The New Public Management in Action*, Oxford: Oxford University Press, Oxford.

'Financial Management in Government Departments' (1983) Cm. 9058, London: HMSO.

Fischer, F. (2003) *Reframing Public Policy*, Oxford: Oxford University Press.

Fisher, 'M. (2004) 'The Crisis of Civil Service Trade Unionism: A Case Study of Call Centre Development in a Civil Service Agency', *Work, Employment and Society*, 18(1): 157–77.

——(2007) 'The New Politics of Technology in the British Civil Service,' *Economic and Industrial Democracy*, 28(4): 523–51.

Flanders, A. (1970) *Management and Unions*, London: Faber and Faber.

Flinders, M. and Buller, J. (2006a) 'Depoliticisation: Principles, Tactics and Tools', *British Politics*, 1(3): 293–318.

——(2006b) 'Depoliticisation, Democracy and Arena Shifting', in T. Christensen and P. Lægreid (eds), *Autonomy and Regulation: Coping with Agencies in the Modern State*, Cheltenham: Edward Elgar, pp. 53–80.

Flynn, N. (2007) *Public Sector Management*, London: Sage Publications Ltd.

FMIP Diagnostic Study (1984) Canberra: Public Service Board and Department of Finance.

Forrester, K. (2005) 'Learning for Revival; British Trade Unions and Workplace Learning', *Studies in Continuing Education*, 27(3): 257–70.

Foucault, M. (1984) 'Truth and Power', in P. Rabinow (ed.), *The Foucault Reader*, New York: Pantheon, pp. 51–77.

Fourcade-Gourinchas, M. and Babb, S. (2002) 'The Rebirth of the Liberal Creed: Paths to Neoliberalism in Four Countries', *American Journal of Sociology*, 108(3): 533–79.

Fox, A. (1974) *Beyond Contract: Work, Power and Trust Relations*, London: Faber and Faber.

Fraser, B. (1996) 'Reserve Bank Independence: Talk to National Press Club, Canberra, 15 August 1996', *Reserve Bank of Australia Bulletin*, September: 14–20.

Frege, C. and Kelly, J. (2003) 'Union Revitalization Strategies in Comparative Perspective', *European Journal of Industrial Relations*, 9(1): 7–24.

French, S. and Funnell, S. (2005) 'The Impact of Pay Delegation in The Heritage Sector', Paper presented at Performance and Reward Conference, 7 April. Available: <http://www.business.mmu.ac.uk/newsandevents/conferencedetail.php?uref=8> (accessed 15 May, 2006).

Freud, D. (2007) *Reducing Dependency, Increasing Opportunity: Options for the Future of Welfare to Work: An Independent Report to the Department for Work and Pensions*, Leeds: Corporate Document Services.

Friedman, A. (1977) *Industry and Labour: Class Struggle at Work and Monopoly Capitalism*. London, Macmillan.

——(1990) ' "Managerial Strategies, Activities, Techniques and Technology", Towards a Complex Theory of the Labour Process', in D. Knights and H. Willmott (eds), *Labour Process Theory*, London: Macmillan, pp.177–209.

Friedman, M. (1977) 'Nobel Lecture: Inflation and Unemployment', *The Journal of Political Economy*, 85(3): 451–72.

——and Friedman, R. (1982) *Capitalism and Freedom*, Chicago: University of Chicago Press.

Fry, G. (1974) 'Civil Service Salaries in the Post-Priestley Era 1956–72', *Public Administration*, 52(3): 319–30.

——(1988) 'The Thatcher Government, The Financial Management Initiative, *and* the "New Civil Service" ', *Public Administration*, 66(1): 1–20.

Fulton Report (1968) *The Civil Service, Volume 1: Report of the Committee 1966–68*. Cm. 3638., London: HMSO.

Funnell, W., Jupe, R. and Andrew, J. (2009) *In Government We Trust: Market Failure and Delusions of Privatisation*, Sydney: UNSW Press.

Garrett, J. (1980) *Managing the Civil Service*, London: Heinemann.

Gay, O. (2006) 'The Lyons and Gershon Reviews and Variations in Civil Service Conditions', Parliament and Constitution Centre, House of Commons. Available: <http://www.parliament.uk/topics/Civil-ServiceArchive.htm> (accessed 23 June, 2010).

George, S. (1999) A Short History of Neo-Liberalism, Presented to the Conference on Economic Sovereignty in a Globalising World. Available: <http://www.global exchange.org/campaigns/econ101/neoliberalism.html> (accessed 5 August, 2009).

Gershon, P. (2004) *Releasing Resources to the Front Line: Independent Review of Public Sector Efficiency, HM Treasury*. Available: <http://www.parliament.uk/briefingpapers/ commons/lib/research/briefings/snpc-02588.pdf> (accessed 5 August, 2009).

Gilman, M. (2004) 'The Characteristics of Performance Related Pay Systems', Working Paper 59, Canterbury Business School, March.

Gladden, E. (1967) *Civil Services of the United Kingdom: 1853–1970*, London: Frank Cass.

Gourlay P. (1994) 'Statement to Conference on Standing Committee on Finance and Public Administration and Centre for Research in Public Sector Management', University of Canberra, Public Service Reform, The Parliament of the Commonwealth of Australia, Canberra, Volume 2, Conference Proceedings.

Government Statistical Service (1996) *Civil Service Statistics*, London: Personnel Statistics Branch, Personnel Management and Conditions of Service Division, Cabinet Office: Office of Public Service.

——(2000) *Civil Service Statistics 1999*, Norwich: HMSO.

Gray, A. and Jenkins, W. (1985) *Administrative Politics in British Government*, Hemel Hempstead, New York: Wheatsheaf Books.

——(1995) 'From Public Administration to Public Management: Reassessing a Revolution', *Public Administration*, 73(1): 75–99.

Green, R. and Wilson, A. (2000) 'The Accord and Industrial Relations: Lessons for Australia', in K. Wilson, J. Bradford and M. Fitzpatrick (eds), *Australia in Accord: An Evaluation of the Prices and Income Policy in the Hawke – Keating Years*, Melbourne: South Pacific Publishing, pp. 105–121.

Grimshaw, D., Vincent, S. and Willmott, H. (2002) 'Going Privately: Partnership and Outsourcing in UK Public Services', *Public Administration*, 80(3): 475–502.

Grout, P. (1997) 'The Economics of the Private Finance Initiative', *Oxford Review of Economic Policy,* 13: 53–66.

Guardian, The (2004) 'Civil servants shocked by job cuts', March.

Hall, P.A. and Soskice, D. (eds) (2001) *Varieties of Capitalism: The Institutional Foundations of Comparative Advantage*, Oxford: Oxford University Press.

Hall, S. (2003) 'New Labour's Double-Shuffle', *Soundings*, 24: 10–24.

Halligan, J. (2003) 'Anglo-American Civil Service Systems: Comparative Perspectives', in J. Halligan (ed.), Civil Service Systems in Anglo-American Countries, Civil Service Systems in Comparative Perspective Series, Cheltenham: Edward Elgar.

——(2006) 'The Reassertion of the Centre in a First Generation NPM System', in T. Christensen and P. Lægreid (eds), *Autonomy and Regulation: Coping with Agencies in the Modern State*, Cheltenham: Edward Elgar, pp. 162–180.

——and Power, J. (1993) *Political Management in the 1990s*, Melbourne: Oxford University Press.

——, Mackintosh, I. and Watson, H. (eds) (1996) *The Australian Public Service: The View from the Top*, Canberra: University of Canberra and Coopers and Lybrand.

Hancock, K. (Chair) (1985) *Industrial Relations Law and Systems*, Canberra: Australian Government Publishing Service.

Harvey, M. (1999) 'Economics of time: A framework for analysing the restructuring of employment relations', in Felstead, A. and Jewson, N. (eds), *Global Trends in Flexible Labour*, Basingstoke: Macmillan, pp. 21–42.

Hay, P. (2007) *Why We Hate Politics*, Cambridge: Polity.

Hayek, F.A. von (1944) 'The Road to Serfdom', republished 2005 in *The Intellectuals and Socialism*, London: Institute of Economic Affairs.

Heery, E. and Kelly, P. (1994) 'Professional, Participative and Managerial Unionism: An Interpretation of Change in Trade Unions', *Work, Employment & Society*, 8(1): 1–22.

HM Treasury (1984) *Civil Service Statistics*, London: HMSO.

——(1991) *Civil Service Statistics*, London: HMSO.

——(1996) *Civil Service Statistics*, London: HMSO.

——(2004) '20,000 Civil Service Jobs Should Move from London with More to Follow', Newsroom and speeches. Available: <http://www.hm-treasury.gov.uk/press_lyons_04.htm> (accessed 5 August, 2009).

——Cabinet Office, National Audit Office, Audit Commission and Office for National Statistics (2001) *Choosing the Right Fabric: a Framework for Performance Information*. Available: <http://www.nao.org.uk/guidance_good_practice/performance_measurement1.aspx> (accessed 7 March, 2011).

Hennessy, P. (1990) *Whitehall*, London: Fontana.

Higgins, H.B. (1915) 'A New Province for Law and Order', *Harvard Law Review*, 29: 13–39.

Hoggett, P. (1994) 'The Politics of Modernisation of the UK Welfare State', in R. Burrows and B. Loader (eds), *Towards a Post-Fordist Welfare State*, London: Routledge.

Hodgson, L., Farrell, C. and Connolly, M. (2007) 'Improving UK Public Service: A Review of the Evidence', *Public Administration* 85(2): 355–82.

Home Office (1998) *Compact: Getting it Right Together*, Cm. 4100, London: The Stationery Office.

Hood C. (1991) 'A Public Management for all Seasons', *Public Administration*, 69(1): 3–19.

——(1995) 'The "New Public Management" in the 1980s: Variations on a Theme', *Accounting, Organizations and Society* 20(3): 93–110.

——, Scott, C., James, O. and Travers, A. (1999) *Regulation Inside Government: Waste Watchers, Quality Police and Sleaze Busters*, Oxford: Oxford University Press.

Horner, L., Lehki, R. and Blaug, R. (2006) *Deliberative Democracy and the Role of Public Managers. Executive Summary*, London: The Work Foundation.

House of Commons, Westminster (1996) Hansard, 22 May.

——(2006) Work and Pensions Committee. The Efficiency Savings in Jobcentre Plus, Second Report of The Session 2005–6, Volume 2: Oral and Written Evidence, The Stationery Office, 18 March, HC 834–11.

——(2007) 'Select Committee on Work and Pensions: Minutes of Evidence', 15 January. Available: <http://www.parliament.the-stationery-office.co.uk/pa/cm/cmworpen.htm> (accessed 17 May, 2008).

House of Commons Select Committee on Work and Pensions (2007) *Second Report*, London: HMSO, HC215.

Howard, W.A. (1977) 'Australian Trade Unions in the Context of Union Theory', *The Journal of Industrial Relations,* 19(2): 255–73.

H.R. Nicholls Society (1985) *Arbitration in Contempt*, Melbourne: H.R. Nicholls Society.

Hughes, O. (2008) 'What is, or Was, New Public Management?' IRSPM12, Brisbane 2008. Available: <http://www.irspm2008.bus.qut.edu.au/papers/documents/new%20pdf/

Hughes%20-%20What%20is%20or%20was,%20New%20Public%20Management %20-%20IRSPM2008.pdf> (accessed 2 August, 2009).

Hutton, W. and Giddens, A. (2000) *On the Edge: Living with Global Capitalism*, London: Vintage.

Hyman, R. (2001) *Understanding European Trade Unionism: Between Market, Class and Society*, London: Sage.

Independent, The (2004) 'Conservatives Unveil Plan to Cut "Government Waste"', 11 February, Factivia Document IND0000020040210e02b000q.

Iversen, T. (2005) *Capitalism, Democracy and Welfare*, Cambridge: Cambridge University Press.

Jenkins, J. (2007) 'Gambling Partners? The Risky Outcomes of Partnership', *Work, Employment and Society*, 21(4): 635–52.

Jenkins, K., Caines, K. and Jackson, A. (1988) *Improving Management in Government: The Next Steps* (Ibbs Report), London: HMSO.

Jessop, B. (2002) 'Liberalism, neoliberalism, and urban governance', *Antipode*, 34: 452–72.

Jobcentre Plus (2008) *Annual Report and Accounts 2007–2008*, 17 July.

Johnson, S. and Nunn, A. (2007) 'Working with JOT 18 Months On: Qualitative Research in Option 1 Pilot Districts', Research Report No 409, London: Department for Work and Pensions/Her Majesty's Stationery Office.

Johnstone, S., Ackers, P. and Wilkinson, A. (2009) 'The British Partnership Phenomenon: A Ten Year Review', *Human Resource Management Journal*, 19(3): 260–79.

Jones, S. (2009) 'Moving Forward in 2010'. Available: <http://www.cpsu.org.au/blog/ 16125.html> (accessed 30 December, 2009).

Junor, A., O'Brien, J. and O'Donnell, M. (2009) 'Welfare Wars: Public Service Frontline Absenteeism as Collective Resistance', *Qualitative Research in Accounting and Management*, 6(1–2): 26–40.

Kahn-Freund, O. (1972) *Labour and the Law*, London: Stevens.

Karagiannaki, E. (2005) 'Jobcentre Plus or Minus: Exploring the Performance of Jobcentre Plus for Non-Jobseekers', LSE STICERD, Research Paper No. CASE097. Available: <http://sticerd.lse.ac.uk/dps/case/cp/CASEpaper97.pdf> (accessed 28 May, 2008).

——(2006) *Exploring the Effects of Integrated Benefit Systems on Active labour Market Policies: Evidence from Jobcentre Plus in the UK*, London: Centre for Analysis of Social Exclusion, London School of Economics.

Kelly, J. (1996) 'Union Militancy and Social Partnership', in P. Ackers, C. Smith, and P. Smith (eds), *The New Workplace and Trade Unions*, London: Routledge, pp. 77–109.

——(1998) *Rethinking Industrial Relations*, London: Routledge.

Kellough, J.E. and Lu, H. (1993) 'The Paradox of Merit Pay in the Public Sector: Persistence of a Problematic Procedure', *Review of Public Personnel Administration* 16(2): 45–64.

——and Seldon, S.C. (1997) 'Pay-for-Performance Systems in State Government: Perceptions of State Agency Personnel Managers', *Review of Public Personnel Administration*, 17(1): 5–21.

Kelsey, J. (1996) *Economic Fundamentalism*, Auckland: Pluto Press.

Kemp, D. (1998) 'A High Performance Public Service', The Hon. Dr David Kemp MP, Minister Assisting the Prime Minister for the Public Service: Address to *Building the Momentum of APS Reform*, PSMPC Lunchtime Seminar, Canberra, 3 August.

Kessler, I. (1994) 'Performance Pay', in K. Sisson (ed.), *Personnel: A Comprehensive Guide to Theory and Practice in Britain*, 2nd edn, Oxford: Blackwell, pp. 465–494.
——(2006) 'The fragmentation of pay determination in the British civil service', *Personnel Review*, 35(2): 6–28.
——and Purcell, J. (1992) 'Performance-Related Pay: Objectives and Application', *Human Resource Management Journal*, 2(3): 16–33.
Kiers, D. (1987) *Negotiating Change in the Public Sector*, Canberra: Department of Industrial Relations, Working Environment Branch, Australian Government Publishing Service.
Kikeri, S. (1998) *Privatisation and Labour: What Happens to Workers when Governments Divest?* Washington: World Bank.
Kirkpatrick, I., Ackroyd, S. and Walker, R., (2007) 'Public Management Reform in the UK and its Consequences for Professional Organisation: A Comparative Analysis', *Public Administration*, 85(1): 9–26.
Korczynski, M. (2002) *Human Resource Management in Service Work*, London: Palgrave.
——and Bishop, V. (2008) 'The Job Centre: Abuse, Violence and Fear on the Front Line: Implications of the Rise of Customer Sovereignty'. In S. Fineman (ed.),*The Emotional Organisation: Passions and Power*, Melbourne: Blackwell Publishing, pp.74–87.
Kristol, I. (1995) *Neo Conservatism: The Autobiography of an Idea*, Chicago: Ivan R. Dee.
Labour Party (2005) 'Manifesto: Forward not Back', *The Labour Party*, London. Available: <http://news.bbc.co.uk/1/shared/bsp/hi/pdfs/13_04_05_labour_manifesto. pdf> (accessed 26 September, 2009).
Larner, W. (2005) 'Neoliberalism in (Regional) Theory and Practice: the Stronger Communities Action Fund in New Zealand', *Geographical Research*, 43(1): 9–18.
Legge, K. (2005) *Human Resource Management: Rhetorics and Realities*, 2nd edn, London: Macmillan.
Lévesque, C. and Murray, G. (2002) 'Local versus Global: Activating Local Union Power in the Global Economy', *Labor Studies Journal*, 27(3): 39–65.
Liberal and National Parties (1992) *Jobsback*, Canberra.
Lindblom, C. (1979) 'Still Muddling, Not Yet Through', *Public Administration Review*, 39(6): 517–26.
Lissenburgh, S. and Marsh, A. (2003) *Experiencing Jobcentre Plus Pathfinders: Overview of Early Evaluation Evidence*. A study carried out on behalf of the Department for Work and Pensions Policy Studies Institute; Department for Work and Pensions on behalf of the Controller of Her Majesty's Stationery Office.
Littler, C. and Salaman, G. (1982) 'Bravermania and Beyond: Recent Theories of the Labour Process', *Sociology*, 16(2): 251–69.
Lopez, S. (2004) *Reorganizing the Rust Belt: An Inside Study of the American Labor Movement*, Berkeley, CA: University of California Press.
Lyons, M. (2007) *Inquiry into Local Government Place-Shaping: A Shared Ambition under Local Government, Final Report*, London: HMSO.
Macrae-Gibson, J.H. (1922) *The Whitley System in the Civil Service*, London: Fabian Society.
Makinson, J. (2000) 'Incentives for Change: Rewarding Performance in National Government Networks', Public Services Productivity Panel, Modernising Government. Available: <http://tna.europarchive.org/20081113020526/http://www.hm-treasury.gov. uk/pspp_incentives_for_change.htm> (accessed 7 March, 2011).

Marsden, D.W. (2003) 'Renegotiating Performance: The Role of Performance Pay in Renegotiating the Effort Bargain', Discussion Paper No. 578, London Centre for Economic Performance, London School of Economics.

——(2004) 'The Role of Performance-Related Pay in Renegotiating the "Effort Bargain": The Case of the British Public Service'. *Industrial and Labor Relations Review*, 57(3): 350–70.

——and Richardson, R. (1994) 'Performing for Pay? The Effects of "Merit Pay" on Motivation in a Public Service', *British Journal of Industrial Relations*, 32(2): 243–62.

Mathews, J. (1989) *Tools of Change: New Technology and the Democratisation of Work*, Sydney: Pluto Press.

——(1992) *The Australian Taxation Office: Modernisation through People, Structures and Technology*, Kensington: Industrial Relations Research Centre, University of New South Wales.

McGuire, A. (2005) Member of Parliament, *Hansard*, Written Answers for 6 December (pt 33). Available: <http://www.publications.parliament.uk/pa/cm200506/cmhansrd/vo051206/text/51206w33.htm> (accessed 7th March, 2011).

McGuire, L. (2004) 'Contractualism and Performance Management in Australia'. In C. Pollitt and C. Talbot (eds), *Unbundled Government: A Critical Analysis of Global Trends to Agencies, Qangoes and Contractualism*, London and New York: Taylor & Francis, pp. 113–39.

McIlroy, J. (1995) *Trade Unions in Britain Today*, Manchester: Manchester University Press.

——(2009a) 'A Brief History of British Trade Unions and Neoliberalism: From the Earliest Days to the Birth of New Labour', in G. Daniels and J. McIlroy (eds), *Trade Unions in a Neoliberal World: British Trade Unions under New Labour*, London: Routledge, pp. 21–62.

——(2009b) 'A Brief History of British Trade Unions and Neoliberalism in the Age of New Labour'. In G. Daniels and J. McIlroy (eds), *Trade Unions in a Neoliberal World: British Trade Unions under New Labour*, London: Routledge, pp. 63–77.

——and Daniels, G. (2009) 'An Anatomy of British Trade Unionism since 1997', in G. Daniels and J. McIlroy (eds), *Trade Unions in a Neoliberal World: British Trade Unions under New Labour*, London: Routledge, pp. 99–126.

McLeod, R. (Chair) (1995) *Report of the Public Service Act Review Group*, Canberra: Australian Government Publishing Service.

Metcalfe, L. and Richards, S. (1984) 'Raynerism and Efficiency in Government', in A. Hopwood and C. Tompkins (eds), *Issues in Public Sector Accounting*, Oxford: P. Allan, pp. 188–211.

Milkman, R., and Voss, K. (eds) (2004) *Rebuilding Labor: Organizing and Organizers in the New Union Movement*, Ithaca, NY: Cornell University Press.

Milkovich, G.T.and Wignor, A.K. (1991) *Pay for Performance: Evaluating Performance Appraisal and Merit Pay*, Washington, DC: National Academy Press.

Mintzberg (1993) 'The Pitfalls of Strategic Planning', *California Management Review*, 36(1): 32–46.

Montanheiro, L., Haigh, B., Morris, D. and Hrovatin, N. (eds) (1998) *Public and Private Sector Partnerships: Fostering Enterprise*, Sheffield: Sheffield Hallam University Press.

Moore, M. (1995) *Creating Public Value Strategic Management in Government*, Cambridge, MA: Harvard University Press.

Moran, T. (2010) 'CPSU Governing Council Meeting 2010: Future Challenges for the Australian Public Service'. Australian Government Department of the Prime Minister and Cabinet, 19 March.

Moravcsik, A. (2002) 'Reassessing Legitimacy in the European Union', *Journal of Common Market Studies'*, 40(4): 603–24.

Morehead, A., Steele, M., Alexander, M., Stephen, K. and Duffin, L. (1997) *Changes at Work: The 1995 Australian Workplace Industrial Relations Survey*, Melbourne: Addison Wesley Longman.

Mueller, A. (1987) *Working Patterns: A Study Document by the Cabinet Office*, London: Cabinet Office.

Murray, G. (2006) *Capitalist Networks and Social Power in Australia and New Zealand*. Aldershot: Ashgate.

Newman, J. (2000) 'Beyond the New Public Management? Modernising Public Services'. In J. Clarke, S. Gerwitz and I. McLaughlin (eds) *New Managerialism, New Welfare?* London: Open University/Sage Publications, pp. 45–46.

New South Wales Public Service Board (1954) *Annual Report 1954*, Sydney: NSW Government Printer.

Niland, J. (1978) *Collective Bargaining and Compulsory Arbitration in Australia*, Kensington: University of New South Wales Press.

Nissen, B. (ed.) (1999) *Which Direction for Organized Labor? Essays on Organizing, Outreach, and Internal Transformations*, Detroit, MI: Wayne State University Press.

Northcote-Trevelyan Report (1854) *Report on the Organization of the Permanent Civil Service*, Cm.1713, London: HMSO.

Nunn, A. and Kelsey, S. (2007) *Review of the Adviser Achievement Tool*, Working Paper No 453, Department for Work and Pensions/Her Majesty's Stationery Office.

O'Brien, J. (1994) 'People Management and Industrial Relations in the Australian Public Service' in Senate Standing Committee on Finance and Public Administration and Centre for Research in Public Sector Management, University of Canberra, Public Service Reform, The Parliament of the Commonwealth of Australia, Canberra, Volume 1, Conference Papers: 209–24.

——(1995) 'Workplace Productivity Bargaining in the Australian Public Service', in J. Stewart (ed.), *From Hawke to Keating: Australian Commonwealth Administration 1990–1993*, Canberra: Centre for Research in Public Sector Management, University of Canberra and Royal Institute of Public Administration, pp.85–104.

——(1997) 'Employment Relations and Agency Bargaining in the Australian Public Service'. In G. Singleton (ed.), *The Second Keating Government: Australian Commonwealth Administration 1993–1996*, Belconnen, ACT: Centre for Research in Public Sector Management, University of Canberra, Institute of Public Administration Australia, Canberra, pp. 175–92.

——(1999) 'Union Strategy and Union Democracy in a Decentralised Industrial Relations Environment: The Case of the NTEU', *Labour and Industry*, 9(3): 79–97.

——(2006) 'Changing Public Sector Industrial Relations in the Australian Commonwealth', in P. Fairbrother and A. Rainnie (eds) *Globalisation, State and Labour*, London: Routledge, pp. 97–118.

——and O'Donnell, M. (1999) 'Government, Management and Unions: The Public Service Under the Workplace Relations Act', *The Journal of Industrial Relations*, 41(3): 446–67.

——and O'Donnell, M. (2001) 'Creating a New Moral Order? Cultural Change in the Australian Public Service', *Labour and Industry*, 10(3): 57–77.

——and O'Donnell, M. (2002) 'Towards a New Public Unitarism: Employment and Industrial Relations in the Australian Public Service', *Economic and Labour Relations Review*, 13(1): 36–59.

——and O'Donnell, M. (2007) 'From Workplace Bargaining to Workplace Relations: Industrial Relations under the Coalition Government', in M. Pittard and P. Weeks (eds), *Public Sector Employment Law in the Twentieth First Century*, Canberra: ANU Press, pp. 127–154.

——and O'Donnell, M. (2008) 'Retrospect and Prospects for Collective Regulation in the Australian Public Service', *Journal of Industrial Relations*, 50(4): 630–46.

O'Donnell, M. (1998) 'Creating a Performance Culture? Performance-based Pay in the Australian Public Service', *Australian Journal of Public Administration*, 57(3): 28–40.

——and O'Brien, J. (2000) 'Performance-based Pay in the Australian Public Service', *Review of Public Personnel Administration*, 20(2): 20–34.

——and Shields, J. (2006) 'The New Pay? Performance-Related Pay in Australia', in J. Teicher, P. Holland and R. Gough (eds), *Employment Relations Management: Australia in a Global Context*, 2nd edn, Harlow: Prentice Hall/Pearson, pp. 383–412.

——, Allen, C. and Peetz, D. (2001) 'New Public Management and Workplace Change', *The Economic and Labour Relations Review*, 12(1): 85–103.

OECD (1989) *Economies in Transition: Structural Adjustment in OECD Countries*, Paris: OECD.

——(2004) *Performance Related Pay in the UK Civil Service*, Paris: OECD.

Ohmae, K. (1990) *The Borderless World: Power and Strategy in the Interlinked Economy*, London: Collins.

ONS [Office for National Statistics] (2011) 'Labour Disputes Public and Private Breakdown'. Available: <http://www.statistics.gov.uk/STATBASE/tsdataset.asp?vlnk=9350&More=N&AU=Y> (accessed 6 March, 2011).

Osborne, D. and Gaebler, T. (1992) *Reinventing Government: How the Entrepreneurial Spirit is Transforming the Public Sector*, Reading, MA: Addison-Wesley.

Oxenbridge, S. and Brown, W. (2004) 'Achieving a New Equilibrium: The Stability of Co-operative Employer-Union Relationship', *Industrial Relations Journal*, 35(5) 388–402.

Painter, M. (1997) 'Public Management: Fad or Fallacy?', in M. Considine and M. Painter (eds), *Managerialism: The Great Debate*, Carlton South: Melbourne University Press, pp. 39–43.

PCS [Public and Commercial Services Union] (2000) *Partnership Working in the Civil Service: An Agreement between PCS, IPMS FDA, the CCSU and the Cabinet Office*, London: Centurion Press. Available: <http://www.pcs.org.uk/Templates/NewsPress.asp?NodeID=891379> (accessed 13 April, 2004).

——(2003a) 'Why the Civil Service Needs a National Pay Framework: Fair Play on Pay'. Available: <http://www.pcs.org.uk/shared_asp_files/uploadedfiles/%7B034C653A-D511-4668-89CF-A11D51266BAF%7D_framework.pdf> (accessed 9 January, 2010).

——(2003b) 'Equality and Diversity Making it Happen: Response to the Government Consultation by the Public and Commercial Services Union (PCS)'. Available: <http://www.pcs.org.uk/Templates/Internal.asp?NodeID=883011> (accessed 28, November 2007).

——(2004) *A Guide for PCS Branches with A New Union Learning Representative*, London: PCS.

——(2005) *2005 Civil Service Pay Claim* (joint national pay claim). Available: <http://www.pcs.org.uk> (accessed 30 August, 2006).

——(2008a) 'Jobcentre Plus Advisor Achievement Tool', 3 September. Available: <http://www.pcs.org.uk/en/department_for_work_and_pensions_group_dwp_news.cjm/id/D7AB7187_2000_47B1_9D13D665B6BDBFA7> (accessed 15 April, 2011).

——(2008b) 'PCS Welcomes the End of PDS – New Appraisal System to be Introduced'. Available: <http://www.pcs.org.uk>.

——(2010) *Not a Single Penny Cut, Not a Single Job Lost, Union Says*, 13 September. Available: <http://www.pcs.org.uk> (accessed 15 September, 2010).

Peck, J. (2004) 'Geography and Public Policy: Constructions of Neo-Liberalism', *Progress in Human Geography*, 28(3): 392–405.

Peetz, D. (1998) *Unions in a Contrary World: The Future of the Australian Trade Union Movement*, Melbourne: Cambridge University Press.

Perry, J. (1995) 'Compensation, Merit Pay, and Motivation'. In S.W. Hays and R.C. Kearney (eds), *Public Personnel Administration: Problems and Prospects*, New Jersey: Prentice Hall.

Pfeffer, J. (1998) 'Six Dangerous Myths about Pay', *Harvard Business Review*, 76(3): 109–19.

Pliatzky, L. (1989) *The Treasury under Mrs Thatcher*, Oxford: Blackwell.

Podger, A. (2007) 'What Really Happens: Department Secretary Appointments, Contracts and Performance Pay in the Australian Public Service', *Australian Journal of Public Administration*, 66(2): 131–47.

Pollitt, C. (1993) *Managerialism and the Public Services: Cuts or Cultural Change in the 1990s?* 2nd edn, Oxford: Basil Blackwell.

——(2001) 'Integrating Financial and Performance Management', *OECD Journal of Budgeting*, 1(2): 7–37.

——(2007) 'Convergence or Divergence? What Has Been Happening in Europe?', in C. Pollitt, S. van Thiel and V. Homburg (eds), *New Public Management in Europe: Adaptation and Alternatives,* London: Palgrave Macmillan, pp. 10–25.

——and Bouckaert, G. (2004) *Public Management Reform: A Comparative Analysis*, New York: Oxford University Press.

——and Talbot, C. (eds) (2004) *Unbundled Government: A Critical Analysis of the Global Trend to Agencies, Quangos and Contracturalisation*, London and New York: Routledge.

——, Giree, X., Lonsdale, J., Mul, R., Summa, H. and Waerness, M. (1999) *Performance or Compliance? Performance Audit and Public Management in Five Countries*, Oxford: Clarendon Press.

Pollock, A., Price, D. and Player, S. (2007) 'An Examination of the UK Treasury's Evidence Base for Cost and Time Overrun Data in UK Value-for-Money Policy and Appraisal', *Public Money and Management*, 27: 127–33.

Polanyi, K. (1944) *The Great Transformation: The Political and Economic Origins of Our Time*, Boston: Beacon Press.

Potter, T. (1987) *A Temporary Phenomenon: Flexible Labour, Temporary Workers and the Trade Union Response*, Birmingham: Low Pay Unit.

Powell, W. and DiMaggio, P. (eds) (1991) *The New Institutionalism in Organizational Analysis*, Chicago: University of Chicago Press.

Power, M. (1997) *The Audit Society: Rituals of Verification*, Oxford: Oxford University Press.

President of the United States of America (2009) 'Inaugural Address', *New York Times*, January 20. Available: <http://www.nytimes.com/2009/01/20/us/politics/20text-obama.html> (accessed 2 June, 2009).

Priestley Report (1955) *Report of the Royal Commission on the Civil Service 1953–1955. Cmd. 9613, 1955.* London: HMSO.

Prime Minister and the Minister for the Cabinet Office (1999) 'Modernising Government', Cm. 4310, The Stationery Office. Available: <http://www.archive.official-documents.co.uk/document/cm43/4310/4310.htm> (accessed 19 July, 2009).

PR Newswire Europe Ltd (1996) 'CAPITA Group: Acquisition of Recruitment and Assessment Services Limited'. Available: <http://www.prnewswire.co.uk/cgi/news/release?id=53127> (accessed 26 September, 2009).

Progress in Financial Management in Government Departments (1984) Cm. 9297, London: HMSO.

Propper, C. and Wilson, D. (2003) 'The Use and Usefulness of Performance Measures in The Public Sector', *Oxford Review of Economic Policy*, 19(2): 250–67.

PSMPC/APSC (various years) (Public Service and Merit Protection Commission/ Australian Public Service Commission) *State of the Service Reports*. Available <http://www.apsc.gov.au/stateoftheservice/index.html> (accessed 30 June, 2009).

Public Finance (2004) 'Whitehall Focus – Civil Service Grows Despite Job Threats', 30 April. Available: <http://www.publicfinance.co.uk/news/2004> (accessed 1 April, 2011).

Public Service Board (1987) *Annual Report*, Canberra: Australian Government Printer.

Public Service Commission (2008) *State of the Service 2008*, Canberra: Commonwealth of Australia.

Pusey, M. (1991) *Economic Rationalism in Canberra: A Nation Building State Changes its Mind*, Melbourne: Cambridge University Press.

Quinton, A. (1978) *The Politics of Imperfection: The Religious and Secular Traditions of Secular Thought in England from Hooker to Oakeshott*, London: Faber & Faber.

Rainnie, A. and Fairbrother, P. (2006) 'The State We are In (And Against)', in P. Fairbrother and A. Rainnie (eds), *Globalisation, State and Labour*, London: Routledge, pp. 29–52.

Ramanadham, V.V. (1988) *Privatisation in the United Kingdom*, London: Routledge.

Rancière, J. (2006) *Hatred of Democracy*, London: Verso.

Ranald, P. (2002) 'Where are the Jobs in the Job Network? Competitive Tendering of Employment Services', in P. Fairbrother, M. Paddon and J. Teicher (eds), *Privatisation, Globalisation and Labour: Studies from Australia*, Annandale: The Federation Press, pp. 158–81.

Rees, S. and Rodley, G. (eds) (1995) *The Human Costs of Managerialism: Advocating the Recovery of Humanity*, Annandale: Pluto Press.

Reith, P. (1996) *Better Pay for Better Work: The Federal Coalition's Industrial Relations Policy*, Melbourne: Liberal/National Parties.

——(1997) 'Agreement Making in the APS', Press Release, 5 May.

Reserve Bank of Australia (2009) 'History of the RBA'. Available: <http://www.rba.gov.au/AboutTheRBA/History/history_of_the_rba.html> (accessed 1 June, 2009).

Rhodes, R. (2000) 'The Governance Narrative: Key Findings and Lessons from the ESRC's Whitehall Programme', *Public Administration*, 78(2): 345–63.

——(2003) 'What is New about Governance and Does it Matter?', in J. Haywood and A. Menon (eds), *Governing Europe*, Oxford: Oxford University Press, pp. 61–73.

——(2005) 'Australia: The Westminster Model as Tradition', in H. Patapan, J. Wanna and P. Weller (eds), *Westminster Legacies: Democracy and Responsible*

Government in Asia and the Pacific, Sydney : University of New South Wales Press, pp. 129–52.

——and Weller, P. (2003) 'Localism and Exceptionalism: Comparing Public Sector Reforms in European and Westminster Systems', in T. Butcher and A. Massey (eds), *Modernising Civil Services*, Aldershot: Edward Elgar, pp. 16–36.

Romeyn, J. (2007) 'The International Labour Organisation's Core Labour Standards and the Workplace Relations Act 1996', Research Paper No.13, 2007–8, Research Branch, 27 November, Parliament of Australia, Parliamentary Library, Available: <http://www.aph.gov.au/library/Pubs/RP/2007–8/08rp13.htm> (accessed 2 June, 2009).

Royal Commission on Australian Government Administration (1976) *Report*, Canberra: Australian Government Publishing Service.

Rudd, K. and Gillard, J. (2007) *Forward With Fairness: Labor's Plan For a Fairer and More Productive Australian Workplace*, Canberra: Australian Labor Party.

Sawer, M. (ed.) (1982) *Australia and the New Right*. Sydney: Allen and Unwin.

——(1996) *Removal of the Commonwealth Marriage Bar: A Documentary History*, Belconnen, ACT: Centre for Research in Public Sector Management, University of Canberra.

Schön, D. and Fein, M. (1994) *Frame Reflection: Towards the Resolution of Intractable Policy Controversies*, New York: Basic Books.

Scott, W. (2001) *Institutions and Organizations*, 2nd edn, Thousand Oaks, CA: Sage.

Scruton, R. (2002) *The Meaning of Conservatism*, 3rd revised edn, South Bend, IN: St Augustine's Press.

Senate Reference Committee on Finance and Public Administration (2000a) *Hansard*, Senate, 2 May, 5 May, 23 June, Canberra: Commonwealth of Australia.

——(2000b) 'Australian Public Service Employment Matters: First Report an Australian Workplace Agreements', The Parliament of the Commonwealth of an Australia, October.

Senate Standing Committee on Finance and Public Administration (SSCFPA) 1993 – Chapter 7.

Sharp, L. and Tinsley, F. (2005) 'PPP Policies Throughout Australia: A Comparative Analysis of Public Private Partnerships'. Available: <http://www.minterellison.com/public/resources/file/ebe73347b0dcdd4/PPPpoliciesthroughoutAustralia.pdf> (accessed 1 April, 2009).

Shergold, P. (1997) 'A New Public Service Act: The End of the Westminster Tradition?' Lunchtime Seminar Series, Public Service Commission, 8 July. Available: <http://www.apsc.gov.au/media/shergold080797/.htm> (accessed 14 November, 1998).

——(2000) 'The Public Service Act and Workplace Relations: Complementary Reforms', *Canberra Bulletin of Public Administration*, 57(2): 82–90.

——(2007) 'What Really Happens in the Australian Public Service: An Alternative View', *Australian Journal of Public Administration*, 66(3): 367–70.

Simms, M. (1987) *Militant Public Servants: Politicisation, Feminisation and Public Service Unions*, Melbourne: Macmillan.

——and Wills, J. (2004) 'Building Reciprocal Community Unionism in the UK', *Capital and Class*, 82, 59–84.

Sinclair, A. (1989) 'Public Service Culture: Managerialism or Multiculturalism', *Australian Journal of Public Administration*, 48(4): 382–97.

Steane, P. and Carroll, P. (2001) 'Australia, the OECD and the Post-NPM World', *Research in Public Policy Analysis and Management*, Volume II, Part A: 29–44.

Smith, M. and Marden, P. (2008) 'Conservative Think Tanks and Public Politics', *Australian Journal of Political Science*, 43(4): 699–717.

Smith, P. and Moreton, G. (1993) 'Union Exclusion and the Decollectivization of Industrial Relations in Contemporary Britain', *British Journal of Industrial Relations*, 31(1): 97–114.

——(2001) 'The Conservative Governments' reform of Employment Law, 1979–97: "Stepping Stones" and the "New Right" Agenda', *Historical Studies in Industrial Relations*, 12: 131–47.

Social Market Foundation (2010) News release, 23 June.

Stefancic, J. and Delgado, R. (1996) *No Mercy: How Conservative Think Tanks and Foundations Changed America's Social Agenda*, Philadelphia: Temple University Press.

Stone, D. and Denham, A. (eds) (2004) *Think Tank Traditions: Policy Research and the Politics of Ideas*, Manchester: Manchester University Press.

Strathern, M. (2000) *Audit Cultures: Anthropological Studies in Accountability, Ethics and the Academy*, London: Routledge.

Swank, D. (2002) *Global Capital, Political Institutions and Policy Change in Developed Welfare States*, Cambridge: Cambridge University Press.

Sydney Morning Herald (1956) 'Government Does Anything the Board Tells It to Do', 14 January.

Task Force on Management Improvement (1992) *The Australian Public Service Reformed: An Evaluation of a Decade of Management Reform*, Canberra: Australian Government Publishing Service, Canberra.

Taylor, A. (2005) 'Civil Service Unions want National Pay Bargaining', *Financial Times*, 8 April, p. 6.

Terry, M. (1996) 'Negotiating the Government of UNISON: Union Democracy in Theory and Practice', *British Journal of Industrial Relations*, 34(1): 87–110.

Thatcher, M. (1987) Interview with Douglas Keay, *Women's Own*, October 31, Thatcher Archive: COI transcript, London: Margaret Thatcher Foundation. Available: <http://www.margaretthatcher.org/document/106689> (accessed 5 September, 2010).

Thelen, K. (2001) 'Varieties of Labor Politics in the Developed Democracies', in P. Hall and D. Soskice (eds), *Varieties of Capitalism: The Institutional Foundation of Comparative Advantage*, New York: Oxford University Press.

Tickell, A. and Peck, J. (2003) 'Making Global Rules: Globalization and Neoliberalism', in J. Peck and H. Wai-chung Yeung (eds), *Remaking the Global Economy: Economic-Geographical Perspectives*, London: Sage Publications, pp. 163–181.

Tomlinson, S. (2001) *Education in a Post-Welfare Society*, Buckingham: Open University Press.

Treasury and Civil Service Committee (1982) *Efficiency and Effectiveness in the Civil Service*, HC 236, London: HMSO.

Turner, L. (2006) 'Globalization and the Logic of Participation: Unions and the Politics of Coalition Building', *Journal of Industrial Relations*, 48(1): 83–97.

——, Katz, H. and Hurd, R. (2001) *Rekindling the Movement: Labor's Quest for Relevance in the Twenty-First Century*, Ithaca, NY: Cornell University Press.

United Kingdom Civil Service (2009) *Civil Service Code*. Available: <http://www.civilservice.gov.uk/about/work/cscode/CS-Values.aspx> (accessed 2 June, 2009).

Van Gramberg, B. (2002) 'Liberation vs Market Driven Management in Victorian Local Government', Working Paper No. 11, Melbourne: Victoria University School of Management.

Vardon, S. (1999) 'Centrelink', in C. Clark and D. Corbett (eds), *Reforming the Public Sector,* St Leonards: Allen and Unwin, pp. 178–203.

Verspaandonk, R. (2000) 'Changes in the Australian Public Service 1975–2000, Parliament of Australia Library'. Available: <http://www.aph.gov.au/library/pubs/chron/2000–2001/01chr01.htm> (accessed 23 May, 2009).

Von Mises, L. (1962) *The Free and Prosperous Commonwealth: An Exposition of the Ideas of Classical Neoliberalism,* trans. T. Ralco, ed. A. Goddard, Princeton, NJ: Van Nostrand.

Voss, K. and Sherman, R. (2000) 'Breaking the Iron Law of Oligarchy: Union Revitalization in the American Labor Movement', *American Journal of Sociology,* 106(2): 303–49.

——(2003) 'You Just Can't Do it Automatically: The Transition to Social Movement Unionism in The United States', in P. Fairbrother and C. Yates (eds), *Trade Unions in Renewal: A Comparative Study,* London: Routledge, pp. 51–77.

Vroom, V. (1964) *Work and Motivation,* New York: John Wiley and Sons.

Waddington, J. and Kerr, A. (1999) 'Membership Retention in the Public Sector', *Industrial Relations Journal,* 32(2): 151–65.

Watson, M. and Hay, C. (2003) 'The Discourse of Globalisation and the Logic of No Alternative: Rendering the Contingent Necessary in the Political Economy of New Labour', *Policy & Politics* 31(3): 289–305.

Weeks, P. (2007) 'The Re-shaping of Australian Public Service Employment Law', in M. Pittard and P. Weeks (eds), *Public Sector Employment Law in the Twenty-First Century,* Canberra: ANU E Press, pp. 11–54.

White, G. and Hatchett, A. (2001) 'Public Sector Pay under Labour: Change and Continuity 1997–2001', Paper presented at the Sixteenth Annual Employment Research Unit Conference at Cardiff Business School, Cardiff University, 10–11 September.

Whitfield, D. (1992) *The Welfare State, Privatisation, Deregulation, Commercialisation of Public Services: Alternative Strategies for the 1990s,* London: Pluto Press.

Wilenski, P. (1977) *Directions for Change: An Interim Report,* Sydney: Government Printer, New South Wales.

——(1980) 'The Left and State Bureaucracy', *The Australian Quarterly,* 52(4): 398–414.

——(1982) *Further Report: Unfinished Agenda,* Sydney: Review of New South Wales Government Administration.

Williams, G. (2007) *Working Together: Inquiry into Options for a New National Industrial Relations System.* Final Report, November, Sydney: NSW Department of Commerce.

Wilson, R. (1999) 'Report to the Prime Minister from Sir Richard Wilson, Head of the Home Civil Service, Civil Service Reform', London, Cabinet Office, !5 December.

Workplace Relations Act (1996) (Australia).

Workplace Relations Amendment (*Work Choices*) *Act* (2005)(Australia).

Wright, E. (1985) *Classes,* London: Verso.

Wright, V. (1997) 'The Paradoxes of Administrative Reform', in W. Kickert (ed.), *Public Management and Administrative Reform in Western Europe,* Cheltenham: Edward Elgar, pp. 7–13.

Wrigley, A. (Chair) (1991) *Force Restriction Review: Report to Minister for Defence,* Canberra: Department of Defence.

Yates, B. (1998) 'Workplace Relations and Agreement Making the Australian Public Service', *The Australian Journal of Public Administration*, 57(2): 82–90.

Young, H. (1990) *One of Us: A Biography of Margaret Thatcher*, London: Pan.

Zifcak, S. (1994) *New Managerialism: Administrative Reform in Whitehall and Canberra*, Buckingham: Open University.

Index

Note: 'N' following a page number indicates a note; 't' indicates a table; 'f' indicates a figure.